IAM®

Lady Christ © IAM® 2011. All Rights Reserved.

Prophet IAM®

*The Reverend Lady
Iam Hazel Virginia Whitehouse-Grant-Christ*

*Mother Divine de Solehealism
Author Creator*

Biography Hagiographique: Prophet IAM® Lady Christ. The Prophetically inspired philosophical writer of Conscience Science©, the instinctive awareness feelings of the senses. Spiritually enlightened at birth, born the daughter of God seraph messenger Prophet IAM®, here to show man what man should be, righteously leading the principles truth and integrity, advocating life. Founder and Mother Divine de Solehealism IAMEREIAM®. Divinely gifted, talented hand-craft artist, creating luxurious knitwear designs, beholding glorious manifestations of the unique extremely distinct inspirational conceptions of original miraculous magnificent ethereal creations of incredible sublime personification of aesthetic divine art, establishing the handmade haute couture LOOPIERE®. Prophet IAM® Lady Christ, an inspirational, formidable, approachable, charming, charismatic mother being, of great marvellous talent, skill, merit, generosity, peace, love, kindness and grace, with the mantra, I am, I can, I will, attributing all praise and thanks to the Creator IAM®.

Discipulus Laudatio.

IAM®

IAM®

By

Lady Christ

© 2011
The Reverend Lady
Iam Hazel Virginia Whitehouse-Grant-Christ

All Rights Reserved.

No part of this publication, including image(s), text or Trade Mark(s) to be reproduced, transmitted, performed audibly or filmed in any form or by any means, live, electronic, mechanical, photocopying, recording, scanning or otherwise, stored in any retrieval system of any nature without prior written permission from the publisher.

No part of this publication to be relied on in any form or context in any proceeding(s) of any nature by any third party(s) whatsoever. Any similarity with reference to any third party(s) is purely coincidental. Neither the author, publisher, distributor(s) may be liable for any damage(s) caused or alleged to be caused either directly of indirectly by this publication.

IAM® & IAMEREIAM® & LOOPIERE®
are registered Trade Mark(s) of Lady Christ.

The moral right(s) of the author has been asserted.
A CIP Catalogue record for this title is available from the British Library.

ISBN-13: 978-1-873478-50-9
Publisher. Distributor.
IAM®
IAM - Po Box - 11332 - AB459AA - Scotland -U.K.
http://www.lipfeed.com/iampublisher
iampublisher@iamereiam.com

IAM®

FIRST EDITION

IAM®

The autobiography of the living Christ.

The pain, suffering, rejection and victimisation of the crucified black girl child born the daughter of God, resurrected and imbued with the Holy Spirit Revelation.

"Here I am. In the beginning..."

IAM®

CHAPTER 1

Here I am. In the beginning.

Here I am on the ground.

Here I am not known to one but God.

Here I am the body that I am looking out from myself on the ground of the land that I am.

Here I am on the ground within my own space. The space that I cannot get out from but not one can enter into the body that I am.

Here I am the presence present, knowing that I am because I can see. I can see everything from the body that I am on the ground of the land that I am in the space that I am. I can see the sun. I can see the tree. I can see the birds high in the air of the land that I am. I can see the flowers upon the ground, here on the land that I am just one.

Here I am seeing everything that is outside the body the form that I am. I can see the body looking down on me, here on the ground of the land that I am.

Here I am looking at the body standing before me. The body came and looked and went on the way. A body came looking with the expression that shine and pick my body up off the ground and put food into my body and put water all over my body and put me down to rest. The body with the expression that shine always came and pick my body up onto the self but many bodies came and looked and went on the way. Everything outside my body is still. The air is feeling good on the body that I am.

Here I am looking at the bodies moving in all direction. The body is moving on the body two foot that walk firm on the ground of the land that I am sitting, just looking. The body is a shape and a size and a form, with the image that is all it own and stand it own height off the ground of the land that I am sitting, just looking. I can see everything that is happening, here on the ground of the land that I am.

Here I am standing upon the ground that I have been sitting and looking from time began.

Here I am in motion. Now I am walking on the ground feeling good because I am. I am feeling good because I can see. I am feeling good because I can hear. I am feeling good because I can walk and jump off the ground of the land that I am. I am the presence present; walking on the ground; feeling good because I am.

IAM®

Here I am in the presence of the bodies of many shape and size and form of all kind of name. One name is woman, one name is boy, one name is girl, one name is brother, one name is sister, one name is father, one name is mother, one name is baby, one name is animal; one name is plant and the things with many different names.

Here I am sitting, looking, wondering in my mind thinking, who am I?, who am I?, thinking in my mind; wondering in my mind; where did my body come from?

Here I am walking over the ground, thinking about the body that I am, the form that I am, wanting, wanting; wondering in my mind, feeling the body that I am wanting, not knowing what the body that I am is wanting, feeling, nobody cares about the body that I am, one in the presence of many, thinking in my mind, wondering.

Here I am, wanting to know who am I?

Here I am thinking, wondering in my mind thinking, not one body care about my body.

Here I am wondering over the ground, lone by myself, wondering in my mind, looking, my eyes fixed on the woman's body walking towards the body that I am. I am speaking. Hazel, Hazel, child; your name is Hazel. I am your Aunt Jane. Your papa is my brother. You are my brother's child.

Here I am hearing the sounds coming out from the woman's body looking down on the body that I am, watching the body in motion, hearing her words. I am speaking. I am your Aunt Jane. The children are mine. I am their mama, but that one is my husbandman; the tall boy over there. My husbandman is my children's papa. I am your Aunt Jane. The girl children are your niece. The boy children are your nephew. I am your papa's sister. Your papa is my brother name Hensley, Mr. Grant. Your papa Hensley, my brother is with your mama. Your mama name is Pearlena. Pearlena is your mama and your brother's mama. There is your brother; the second to the smallest boys playing is your brother name Ruel. Ruel and you come out from your mama Pearlena's body. Your mama name is Pearlena, understand.

Here I am wondering in my mind, wondering at the body expressions, wanting to understand the many word sounds that I am hearing. I am speaking. Your papa Hensley said he will send for you. Your papa and mama are on the ground name England.

Here I am; the body that I am; wanting to understand the many words, the sounds that I am hearing. I am speaking. Your papa asked me to take care of you and your brother Ruel. Hensley will send for you when he settles down in England. Your other brother is name George. George is with my sister, your Aunt Mira on the ground name Georges Plain. Your papa will send for you and your brother's when he settles down in England, I am your keeper.

Here I am, wanting to understand all that I am, feeling my insides go round, wanting to understand all that I am hearing, watching the body boy name Ruel; feeling my inside go round, feeling lone, wanting my body to stop hurting, thinking in my mind. I am happy that I ask the question, who am I? because I now know that I have one two of the boy body name brother. The one present before the other is name Ruel. Ruel is my brother. I am now of the understanding that the woman is my Aunt Jane. Aunt Jane's brother is my papa, the man name Hensley, Mr. Grant.

Here I am. I am speaking.

Here I am hearing the sounds coming out from the body that I am. I am speaking.

Here I am. Aunt Jane, where is my papa? Where is my mama? I am speaking. Child; me said your papa and mama will send for you and your brothers when them settle down in England. Right now, I am your keeper, understand.

Here I am feeling my inside go round, wanting my brother Ruel to want to spend time with me, wanting Aunt Jane's children to acknowledge the body that I am feeling lone, lone inside myself, thinking in my mind.

Here I am, wanting the many bodies that are present in my presence, to acknowledge the body that I am feeling lone, lone by myself.

Here I am feeling that not one body care about my body. Everyone is for the self, even my brother. Not one shares anything of the self, not even my brother. Everyone just take for them self, even the boy my brother.

Here I am, just one.

Here I am now of the understanding that the body name girl is the form name female, the sister, the woman, the mama; the one name mother. The girl, the sister and the woman look after everyone. The girl, the sister, the woman, the mama clean the house for each other. The girl, the sister, the woman, the mama; the one name mother take care of the things inside the house. I am now of the understanding that the form name male is the boy, the brother, the man, the papa; the one name father is the body that sew the seed that the girl, the sister, the woman, the mama; the one name mother give birth

IAM®

to the body name baby. The boy, the brother, the man, the papa, the one name father; always hide away from the act of the self. The boy, the brother, the man, the papa the one name father never speak the truth of ones act on each other. The boy, the brother, the man, the papa; the one name father, did not wash the clothes of the self or any one. The boy, the brother, the man, the papa; the one name father did not prepare or cook the food for the self or any one. The boy, the brother, the man, the papa; the one name father did take all that one can from the girl, the sister, the woman, the mama; the one name mother. The boy, the brother, the man, the papa; the one name father; the one name husbandman, did punch the body of the girl, the sister, the woman, the mama; the one name mother. The boy, the brother, the man, the papa; the one name father is the sewer of the seed of our creation, here I am.

Here I am. I can see all that is happening here on the ground name Jamaica. The boy, the brother, the man, the papa; the one name father leave the female presence each daylight to work for the thing name money and return each sunset. The boy, the brother, the man, the papa; the one name father did expect and did take the food from the woman and fill their belly. The boy, the brother, the man, the papa; the one name father do as they wish to pleasure them self inside the children mother's house. The boy, the brother, the man, the papa; the one name father are the cause of all that is happening here on the ground name Jamaica.

Here I am, the body that I am the girl child; the sister. I can see everything that is happening.

Here I am standing on the ground name Jamaica, looking, wondering in my mind, thinking.

Here I am lone by myself, wondering over the ground, wondering into the woodland, listening to the bird sounds, hearing the tree sticks crack beneath my feet walking, wondering in my mind, thinking, feeling the sun heat splash my skin, smelling the scented air embrace the body that I am wondering, wondering deep into the woodland surrounding the body that I am feeling my insides rush up into my mouth; my body motionless, rigid, sensing danger, rooted to the spot, not wanting to cause a sound, hearing voices sounding like boy men. My mind thinking to go back, feeling my body moving slowly towards the boy men sounding voices, getting louder, feeling my insides trembling, frightened, looking at the lot of boy men, watching them, all of them, grabbing and dragging at the big girl's body. My body not knowing what to do with it self, my eyes fixed on the big girl's body, watching the big boy man rip off the big girl's clothes, forcing him self upon the big girl's body, pushing her body to the ground. My eyes watching all the other boy men with their hands rubbing the front of their pants; hearing them laughing, shouting, all excited; watching the big boy man on his knees; his hand holding his penis, forcing his body pushing the big girl's legs apart; hearing the boy men making noise inside their mouth groaning, hearing the big girl's body screeching; screaming out like in pain; watching her body wriggling beneath the big boy man's body forcing him self down between the big girl's legs, watching the big boy man's backside pushing hard, down into the big girl's open legs, his backside jabbing up and down quick into the big girl's body, looking helpless; spaced out, hearing the other boy men's excitement, laughing, holding down the big girl's arms and legs, one of then ramming the piece of rag further into the big girl's mouth, hearing them shouting; me next, me next; feeling the body that I am frozen to the spot; shaking, watching the big boy men, all of them acting wild, raping the big girl of her self. My body trembling, eye water full up my eyes, scared for the girl child body that I am, not wanting the boy men them to see the body that I am, thinking in my mind going around fast; thinking, wondering what to do, frightened to move from the spot, feeling hurt for the big girl's body, raped, looking unable to help her self.

Here I am feeling frightened for the body that I am, feeling my girl's body form trembling, thinking the boy men them will rape me next, my mind rushing, thinking, knowing the act the boy men them do inside the big girl's body, just pleasuring themselves.

IAM®

CHAPTER 2

Here I am wondering in my mind, thinking about the body that I am, wanting to belong, wanting the man my papa, wanting the woman my mama.

Here I am wanting, not knowing what the body that I am is wanting, feeling my inside go round; thinking about the body that I am; the girl, the sister; feeling lone, wanting. I am speaking. Hazel; come here; quick. Your papa has sent the papers. Hensley send the money for you and your brother's to go to England. I must go to town and get your passports.

Here I am feeling my inside go round; thinking about England; wanting to know where England is; thinking in my mind realizing that my wanting is happening; I am going to England to be with my papa and mama. Me and Ruel and George are going to England; that is where we belong with our papa and mama and we will all be happy together; thinking in my mind; wondering what my mama look like; thinking in my mind; wondering what my papa look like; feeling good with myself, feeling glad, I am happy now; I am, I am; I am.

Here I am with my brothers Ruel and George; thinking of my mama and papa; feeling good inside the body that I am

Here I am; not knowing where I am.

Here I am not wanting to be where I am; feeling my inside go round; feeling sick to vomit; hearing the noise the thing name aeroplane is making; taking off; off the ground; rising up, up, going up into the sky; bouncing up higher, inside the clouds; feeling the body that I am rising off the seat; my insides coming up into my mouth; feeling scared; high off the ground in the air of the land that I am.

Here I am in the presence of many bodies; feeling something happening to the body that I am. The time is grey night time. The woman inside the aeroplane is holding my hand; walking me and George and Ruel off the aeroplane; feeling the air splash cold on my face; feeling the body that I am tremble all over; run walking along side the woman; making her way into the airport building; walking us up to the long chair seat; hearing her voice speaking; lifting my body onto the seat; her voice telling us to wait. Wait here sweetheart. Your father will be along soon.

Here I am feeling my insides going round; not knowing what to do with myself; wondering at all my eyes can see; feeling the water filling up my eyes; wanting my papa to come now; my mind wondering; wondering what my papa look like; wondering if my papa is going to find us; my eyes searching;

looking at the lot of bodies of all kind of shape and size and covered up in different kinds of clothes.

Here I am feeling what is happening; that I am not understanding; feeling the body that I am changing for the one time.

Here I am feeling the body that I am moving inside, turning, going round inside, looking for my papa; the man name Hensley.

Here I am not feeling good where I am.

Here I am looking at the body of a man like the colour on the body that I am.

Here I am wondering in my mind, thinking; looking for my papa; my mind wondering what my papa look like; wondering if the man coming towards us is my papa; the man with the sunshine expression; walking quick now; running with his arms and hands reaching towards us; the man looking down into the eyes I am; the man with the expression shining all over his face gathered my body up inside his hands; hugging my body and Ruel and George's body close to his body; kissing my face; making the body that I am feel good; feel happy being in my papa's arms; feeling his breath warm on my face; feeling my papa being glad to see me and Ruel and George; hearing my papa say; I am your papa; your father; feeling my body release its guard; resting my body head on my papa's body; holding my arms around my papa's neck; feeling my body bouncing up and down on my papa's arms; feeling his body walking, running to get where he is going. I am speaking. Ruel; you and George stick close to me. Come quick; the Taxi is waiting.

Here I am now in the care of the man my papa; seating my body between Ruel and George's body sitting on the back seat of the Taxi car; watching my papa's tall body bend down climbing into the front seat part of the Taxi car; watching the Taxi car driver; a white colour man; feeling the body that I am wanting sleep; sliding on the seat between Ruel and George's body talking and talking; sounding excited; feeling my body swaying with the movement of the car driving through the airport grounds; listening to my brothers laughing; making jokes with each other.

Here I am inside the Taxi car; hearing the Taxi car driver talking to papa; asking papa about his children; listening to my papa's voice sounding happy, pleased with him self talking about his children just come from Jamaica.

Here I am feeling the car moving faster; faster along the big wide road way.

Here I am feeling my eyes keep closing, wanting to sleep; wanting to stay awake; looking up at the lamp lightings along the road; my mind thinking;

IAM®

looking at the dark colour air; thinking about my brothers Ruel and George; wanting them to let me into their conversation; wanting to stay awake; wondering when we going to get where we going; wondering about my mama; feeling the car slowing down; frightening me out of sleep; feeling my inside go round; feeling the car moving slow; making ready to stop; under the lamp light on the road; looking at the long, long wall stone building with tree bushes and gates. I am speaking. Here man. This is our stop.

Here I am. Where am we? I am speaking. We must get out here.

Here I am standing on the road side pavement; feeling my body trembling in the grey light air drizzling rain; waiting for papa; watching his hand put some money into the Taxi man's hand. I am speaking. Thanks mate.

Here I am standing with my papa and my brothers Ruel and George; watching the Taxi car man driving the car away. I am speaking. Come.

Here I am with my brothers Ruel and George; following our papa walking through the gate way up to the stone wall house building. I am speaking. This is my house, your mother is inside.

Here I am feeling my insides turning over; going round; my eyes fixed on papa's hand turning the jingling thing inside the big wood door; pushing the door to open; hearing papa sounding pleased with him self; calling; Pearl; Pearl; here they are.

Here I am feeling papa's hand on my back; moving my body forward into his house; feeling the body that I am not want to be where I am; feeling my insides going round fast; hurting; not wanting to be where I am standing inside a big room; looking at the woman my mama's body sitting down on the chair; watching the little girl's body hiding her face behind the woman mama's chair; feeling something inside my body take over the body that I am; making my body not know what to do with it self; feeling the air keep changing about the body that I am; feeling the woman mama's presence; hearing papa's voice say; here is your mother; my eyes fixed on the woman mama's eyes wide open; just staring down on the body that I am not knowing what to do with myself; feeling the body that I am trembling; hurting inside. I am speaking. My God; where you get her from? Get her out of here.

Here I am; the body that I am hearing the woman my mama's voice for the one time; feeling her words echoing inside my head; vibrating inside the body that I am feeling my eyes flood with water pouring out; falling splash on my hands; my insides bursting shock pain; choked dumb; my mind in turmoil; bereft; wanting my mama; wanting the hurting to go away; wanting my

IAM®

mama; not knowing who my mama is; my mind thinking to run; my body rooted to the spot; wanting my head to stop hurting; my mind not wanting to accept that the woman papa said is my mama do not want the body that I am. I am speaking. Hush up your backside woman. What you mean telling me daughter that? Whose child is she then? Hazel is our child and you going to treat her right; you hear me.

Here I am hearing papa's voice gasp in disbelief at the woman's behaviour vexing him; her eyes blazing with scorn firing down on the body that I am.

Here I am hearing papa and the woman papa said is my mama shouting bad hurting words at one another; shouting, talking about the body that I am; she, her, daughter, child; the body that I am wanting the woman my mama to want the body that I am wanting my mama; wanting to belong; feeling outcast; abandoned; wanting to escape from the house; feeling rooted to the spot; unable to get away from the woman my mama's presence. I am speaking. I don't want her. Me don't know what you send for them for. I am speaking. Pearl; you hear what I say; hush up your mouth and stop that kind of chat in front of the children them. Me tired and my foot a hurt me. The food ready yet? Come; come me daughter; you come with me. Your mother don't know what she's talking about. If she hurt you, you tell me, you hear me.

Here I am feeling my papa take hold of my hand; leading the body that I am; listening to papa talking; making his way to the door way; beckoning Ruel and George's body to follow him out of the room; walking into the hall way; walking us along the long, long passage way; feeling my body insides hurting; wanting the water to stop coming into my eyes; listening to papa talking about the woman my mama; my mind wondering if the woman is really my mama. I am speaking. Hazel; don't pay any attention to what your mother say. I don't know what get up in her talking to you like that.

Here I am entering another room; listening to my papa talking to the body that I am; my mind wondering about what he said; feeling the body that I am not know what to do with it self; my eyes gazing around the room; looking on the big table top and the chairs spaced around the table in the middle of the room; feeling the body that I am hurting; tasting the food smelling in the air; feeling my skin wet inside my dress; feeling the body that I am not wanting to move from where I am standing; sensing the woman; feeling her presence coming; my body on guard; feeling the woman's body presence burst into the room; making everyone not know how to behave; her body talking out loud to her self; her body shoving the things aside; stamping her way across the room; out into another room; feeling my body on guard, rigid; hearing the

IAM®

woman that papa said is my mama; her voice talking aloud; my body hearing the noise she is making; banging things about; my eyes looking in papa's direction; watching papa shaking his head; his big back stature slumped on the chair; looking like he don't know what to do; his hands outstretched towards the body that I am; lifting the body that I am up, onto his knee; beckoning Ruel and George's body over at his side. I am speaking. Ruel; George; listen to me; over here you call your mama mother and you call me father. It is not mama and papa; understand; good.

Here I am hearing papa; feeling my body unable to release its guard; watching papa's eyes moving to rest on Ruel's body; moving to rest on George's body; watching papa's eyes fixed on the body that I am; looking into the eyes I am; papa's eyes making sure we understand his words; feeling his body rise off the chair; standing upright; resting the body that I am to sit down on the chair; watching papa's body walking towards the door to the room where the woman my mother is; watching his hand open the door; my body tasting the food smell rush into the room; scenting the air about the body that I am; trembling, feeling lone; wanting to belong; seeing Ruel and George whispering into each other's ears; making up faces at the body that I am; laughing behind their hands; feeling the body that I am hurting inside; my eyes wondering around the space; looking at the little girl's body the same height as the body that I am; looking at the little girl's body standing; leaning against the bed on wheels; her face turned towards the baby with the sunshine expression sitting up in the bed on wheels; playing with the thing making the rattling sound in his hands.

Here I am looking at the little girl's body; looking at her eyes fixed on the body that I am; her tongue hanging out; pointing her tongue at the body that I am; her face screwed up; my mind wondering; thinking; wondering at the girl's expression; thinking about the body that I am; feeling lone; hurting inside; wanting to belong; wanting the woman my mama to want the body that I am; hearing my father's voice raised; having words with the woman. I am speaking. You call yourself my wife? You watch me and you. If you do anything to hurt my daughter; me finish with you.

Here I am feeling the body that I am trembling; feeling my insides going round; feeling the woman's angry presence; hearing the door open and bang; feeling the body that I am fearing to look at the woman; hearing her feet stamping into the room; shoving the chairs aside; watching my father's body following after her; his voice raised; telling her to stop her antics. I am speaking. Can't you see the children them tired? Give them some food and get them into their beds.

IAM®

Here I am; the body that I am on guard; fearing the woman's angry presence shoving the chair out of her way; stamping out of the room; into the hall way; feeling the body that I am trembling; hurting inside; wanting to be near my father; my mind not knowing what to do with the body that I am wanting to run away from the woman's presence; my mind unable to accept that the woman my father said is my mother; is really my mama; knowing that the woman my mama does not want the body that I am near her body; feeling her presence making the body that I am scared; keeping the body that I am on guard; hearing her footsteps returning to the room where I am; hearing the door bang open; the woman's body rush come into the room; watching her body standing by the fire; hearing her body breathing quick; feeling her presence putting everyone on guard; feeling my father's eyes fixed on the body that I am head bowed facing the floor; thinking in my mind; not wanting my father to see the water inside my eyes; my mind thinking; wanting the body that I am to stop hurting. I am speaking. Hush Hazel. Come here Mavis. Come and say hello to your big sister Hazel.

Here I am; the body that I am on guard; feeling the woman's angry look fixed on the body that I am; engulfing my being; making the body that I am want to run; feeling that the woman does not want the body that I am near her body or the little girl's body; my sister Mavis's body standing at her side; screwing up her face at the body that I am; watching her body hiding behind the woman her mother's body not wanting to have anything to do with the body that Iam.

Here I am; one in the presence of many; looking; feeling; listening; hearing my father's body breathing; seeing his head moving side to side; hearing his body groan as if in disbelief of the woman and the girl's behaviour towards the body that I am; looking at my father's body; feeling his upset face fixed on the woman; his eyes staring into the woman mama's eyes; I am speaking. Pearl; why you acting like this? What have you got against my daughter? What Hazel done to you; you don't want her? I am speaking. Look at her; look how she looks. Send her back to where they pick her up from. She is not my child.

Here I am; feeling like dirt; hearing the woman talking about the body that I am; her body breathing loud; feeling her eyes fiery with scorn; boring into the body that I am; dashing the body that I am far from her side; demonstrating her will; not to have anything to do with the body that I am; rooted to the spot; desolate; hurting, thinking in my mind, realizing that it does not matter what papa say to the woman; he has no control of her thinking; feeling her words hurting the body that I am; her presence scaring my being; wounding my

IAM®

insides; worried for the body that I am realising that papa's not able to effect kindness from the woman; his wife; my mother.

Here I am; hearing my father and the woman my mother voices raised; shouting angry words; talking about the body that I am; wanting my father and mother to stop talking about the body that I am; wanting my mother to want the body that I am her girl child; feeling lone; wanting the little girl Mavis to want the body that I am her sister; wanting to belong; wanting the hurting to go away from inside the body that I am; thinking in my mind; wanting the body that I am to escape from where I am set to run; halted; frozen to the spot; feeling my father; his hands holding up the body that I am, off the floor, up against his chest, listening to my father's voice speaking to the body that Iam. I am speaking. Hush; never mind, never mind; hush my daughter; hush now. Look at Delroy. Look; see how your baby brother is smiling happy to see you. Hush; hush, I am here, hush.

Here I am; hurting; hearing my father's words; feeling the body that I am unable to release my guard; feeling the woman my mother's eyes fixed upon the body that I am; distancing her self far from the body that I am; her body ignoring my father's words; watching her body; her foot steps stamping her way past my father holding the body that I am out of the way of her body walking quick; hearing her body shouting angry words at the body that I am; trembling, not wanting to be in the woman's presence. I am speaking. You think him can stop me.

Here I am; the body that I am wanting to rest; unable to release my guard; hearing the woman's voice coming from the next room; my mind wondering about her words; hearing her banging the things about; feeling my insides going round; smelling the food; watching the woman entering the room with the plates of food in her hands; shoving the plates down onto the table; feeling the body that I am not know what to do with it self; tasting the food smelling inside my mouth; hearing my father telling us abut the food baked beans, sausages, bread and butter, tomato sauce and the chips on the plate before the body that I am feeling hunger; feeling the inside of my mouth feeling dry; thinking in my mind; wanting to eat; not knowing what to do; looking at the things on the table; thinking in my mind wondering. I am speaking. Hazel, pick up the knife and fork and copy me. Eat up now.

Here I am; the body that I am wanting to eat; watching my father's hands demonstrating his words; thinking in my mind; putting the beans inside my mouth eating; not liking the feel of the food inside my mouth; thinking in my mind; not wanting to be where I am; feeling the woman; my mother's eyes

IAM®

fixed on the body that I am. I am speaking. Pearl; I am going to my bed now; I am on early shift.

Here I am hearing my father's words; thinking in my mind; wondering; feeling the body that I am on guard; watching his body making it's way towards the hall way door; feeling my mother's body rise quick from the chair; snatch up Delroy's body from the bed on wheels; watching the little girl, Mavis body cramming the food bulging out the side of her mouth; watching the woman's body moving quick to follow my father's body disappearing into the hall way. I am speaking. Ruel; George; hurry up; finish eating and come upstairs.

Here I am eating; watching Mavis's body slide down off the chair; her body moving side ways towards the door; following after the woman; feeling the body that I am release it's guard.

Here I am wanting sleep; feeling my eyes keep closing; feeling hunger; wanting to eat the food; not liking the food; looking at my brothers Ruel and George; hearing them talking; watching them eating and laughing with each other; sounding like they like the food; seeing Ruel's eyes gazing on my plate; feeling the body that I am not know what to do with myself; hurting; thinking; not wanting to eat the food; wanting sleep. I am speaking. Don't you want your food Hazel? I will eat it for you.

Here I am in the presence of my brothers Ruel and George; feeling lone; watching Ruel holding out his plate towards the body that I am; my mind thinking; thinking about the body that I am and Ruel at Aunt Jane's house; realizing where I am; feeling the body that I am not belonging where I am; wishing the body that I am is with Aunt Jane in Jamaica; thinking abut the body that I am and Ruel at Aunt Jane's house; thinking about Ruel always hungry and the body that I am giving Ruel my food to eat; my mind wondering; thinking; wondering why my brother Ruel act different now; wondering why my big brother Ruel don't want to talk with the body that I am like he talks and play games with George; thinking in my mind; feeling lone by myself; looking at Ruel; emptying my plate of food onto his plate; thinking about the body that I am; thinking about the woman my mother; wondering if the woman is really my mother.

Here I am listening to the sounds inside the house; listening to Ruel and George's footsteps on the ceiling in the room above; my mind wondering; wondering what they are doing; thinking; wondering why the woman do not want the body that I am; wondering what to do with the body that I am; thinking; what to say to make the woman want my body.

IAM®

Here I am wanting to belong; thinking; feeling the woman's presence coming; feeling the body that I am on guard; trembling inside; hearing her footsteps stamping; coming down from the top part of the house; feeling the water stinging hot on my face; wanting the water to stop filling up my eyes; not wanting to be where I am standing in the presence of the woman; unable to stop my body shaking. I am speaking. You come with me.

Here I am following after the woman, my mother; her body walking fast towards the room where I saw the woman for the one time; hearing the woman's body talking to it self; her body bumping into the things; shoving the things about inside the room. I am speaking. Here; take your clothes off and put this on to sleep in.

Here I am; the body that I am trembling; shaking inside; wanting the water to stop filling up my eyes; my mind thinking; watching the woman's body; her hands holding the coloured bed-clothes; spreading the bed-clothes flat; covering the long chair like bed. I am speaking. Hang your dress there.

Here I am watching the woman my mother; my eyes following the movement of her hands resting on the back part of the chair. I am speaking. You; this is where you sleep; and stay in here; you hear me.

Here I am; my eyes fearing to look at the woman's face; my head bowed down to the floor; my eyes following her feet walking towards the open door; feeling her eyes fixed on my body; her body standing still; staring down on the body that I am; making my body not know what to do with it self; making the water keep flooding; poring out my eyes; splashing down on the body that I am; hearing the woman's clothes swish past the body that I am; hearing a click sound; seeing the light gone from the room where I am standing in the dark; feeling the woman my mother's presence; hearing the door slam shut; feeling scared; lone; fretting for the body that I am; thinking; wondering in my mind; taking off my dress; feeling the cold air on the body that I am trembling; looking up at the light coming through the window curtain; feeling my body wanting to sleep; crying; hurting; climbing onto the chair bed; crouched up under the bed clothes; lone inside the body that I am; crying; wanting the hurting pain to go away; thinking about the woman, my mama.

IAM®

CHAPTER 3

Here I am. The time is day light. I can feel the woman my mother's presence coming; entering the room where I am; her body standing over the body that I am; feeling the woman, my mother's hands pulling the bed clothes off the body that I am; hearing her voice. I am speaking. Get up; get up; get out of di' bed. I have things to do.

Here I am. Am..; am..; feeling my eyes full with sleep; puffed up sticky; feeling the body that I am trembling; remembering; feeling scared; hearing the sound of the woman my mother's raised voice; her presence making the body that I am not know what to do with it self. I am speaking. Put your dress on and fold up the bed things, quick, and get out of my way.

Here I am putting on my dress, feeling the body that I am moving inside.

Here I am folding the bed-clothes. The cloth is making my body hurt. I can feel my mother's presence coming near. I am speaking. Have you done yet? Come on.

Here I am not knowing what to do with my self; wanting my feet to get into my shoes; wanting to do what the woman my mother wants; the body that I am rushing to follow her body walking quick out of the room; making my body run to catch up with her body disappearing into another room. I am speaking. The room we just come from is the back bed-room.

Here I am feeling my body shaking; my mind in thought; my eyes scanning the room; my body moving quick away from my mother's body walking towards my body backing out of the room; following my mother's body walking fast along the long passage; her hand raised; pointing so I will understand the meaning of her words.

Here I am; now understanding the name of the high white walls; the room that I had to stay by my self.

Here I am standing on the ground of the front-room inside my father's house. I am speaking. Do not come inside here unless I tell you to. Do you hear me; good?

Here I am hearing every sound that the woman my mother is speaking.

Here I am feeling the body that I am shaking, thinking in my mind.

Here I am following my mother walking fast along the long passage way. I am speaking. This is the pantry; this is the cupboard for storing things and this room is called the dining-room.

IAM®

Here I am standing inside the room my mother call the kitchen; my eyes amazed; wondering; looking at all the differing things that I am seeing for the one time. I am speaking. Here is where we keep all the food in the house to cook for all of us.

Here I am listening to my mother sounding pleased with her self; watching my mother's hand on the big door handle; opening the tall door in the kitchen-room.

Here I am standing in the open air outside my father's house; following my mother; listening to her speaking; watching her hands demonstrating her words; my mind wondering; thinking; where's Ruel and George and Mavis and Delroy and my father? Where is everyone? I am speaking. Pay attention. This is the wash-house and this here is the outside toilet; you see.

Here I am looking at the toilet thing standing on the ground inside the little room. I am speaking. You sit on the toilet seat to do a wee-wee and then you pull the chain cord down like this to flush the bowl clean. You understand. Come; this is the coal house.

Here I am outside my father's house building. Here I am standing on the ground name England.

Here I am feeling the air feeling good on the body that I am.

Here I am hearing every sound the woman my mother is making, speaking, talking.

Here I am wondering in my mind, wanting to understand, wanting to remember; watching the woman my mother's hands on the coal house latch; pulling the door to open; her body stepping aside; her hands beckoning my body to her; my eyes looking into the room; heaped with pitch black stones and stick wood on the floor. I am speaking. Come; this is our ground space. This is our land betwixt the wood fencing is your daddy's land.

Here I am looking at the woman my mother's hand rising, pointing her finger forward, moving her hand across her body so I will understand the portion of the land that belong to my father.

Here I am; feeling my body standing rigid; feeling the air blowing up inside my dress; my eyes fixed on my mother; feeling the air blowing strong; making my mothers dress tail sway about her legs; flapping her apron up onto her face; her body turn; making its way back towards the house; my body running to catch up with her body standing inside the kitchen room; watching her body leaning forward; pressing against the kitchen door to shut; her hand turning

IAM®

the big key; locking the door tight; wiping her slipper shoe foot on the kitchen door mat; watching her hand wipe the water off her forehead; hearing her body breathing quick; making its way into the dining-room; into the hall way; pass the store-room; pass the pantry-room; making her way up one; up two steps; into the passage; her body resting itself at the beginning of the lot of steps; my eyes looking up; looking at the long line of steps disappearing up; going up to the top part of the house; following after my mother's body walking fast. I am speaking. This is called the stairway.

Here I am walking along another passage at the top of the stairway, following my mother's body walking quick.

Here I am standing inside a big room, looking on the body of my sister Mavis, watching her body on the bed. I can see another bed in the corner on the other side of the room. There are a lot of different wood things that I am seeing for the one time. I am speaking. This is your sister's bed-room. You can move into here, over there.

Here I am following my mother into the passage way. I am speaking. That room along there is mine and your father's bed-room. Along here is the landing and there is your brothers them bed-room.

Here I am standing inside my brother's bed-room.

Here I am watching my mother's body walking over to the window, hearing her making sounds to her self, making the sounds that I am not understanding.

Here I am wondering in my mind, looking at my mother, watching her body act. I am speaking. Ruel, you and George go and wash your self, and get dress now. Here are the clothes I want you to put on. You come with me Hazel. This is where we wash our body. This is the sink to wash your face, and here is the bath tub, and I want it keeping clean, do you understand.

Here I am looking around the space inside the room name bath-room.

Here I am inside my father's house, thinking in my mind. My father's house and everything inside my father's house looks good.

Here I am wondering in my mind, wondering about the woman that I am with; is she really my mother?

Here I am inside my father's big house with everything that I can think of and all the many things that I have never seen before I came to the ground name England. I am speaking. Here; wash your face with this. This is your face-cloth, and put it over here when you finish. Look; this is the tooth-brush and

IAM®

the tooth-paste. You put the paste on the brush and brush your teeth like this, understand.

Here I am wiping my face, looking at my mother standing at my side, demonstrating her words so I will understand.

Here I am brushing my teeth clean, looking at my mother standing at the bath-room doorway, looking down on the body that I am. I am speaking. Hurry up and come on down stairs to the kitchen. I want you where I can keep an eye on you.

Here I am inside my father's house.

Here I am with my brother Ruel and George and baby Delroy, and my sister Mavis, and the woman that my father said is my mother.

Here I am thinking in my mind; my brothers Ruel and George and my sister Mavis do not want anything to do with my body; and the woman my father said is my mama will not come close to the body that I am; thinking in my mind; feeling good thinking about the man my father; thinking; the presence of my father keeps everyone in order, even the woman my mother; thinking about the man my father; making the body that I am shine like my father shine the sunshine expression all over his body face.

Here I am; knowing that I am.

Here I am; wanting to understand the body that I am. Outside of what I am, the woman my mother and the man my father, I know not one thing.

Here I am inside my father's house.

Here I am with my family. The woman my mother gets up each day light before everyone. My mother cooks for each one present in my father's house. My mother washes all the clothes for each one present in my father's house, but not for the body that I am. My mother makes clothes to put on her body and Mavis her favourite body. My mother make all the good clothes Mavis have on her body; making Mavis body look good to the body that I am. My mother sort out some of Mavis's not so good clothes and give them to me to put one.

Here I am in the presence of my mother, watching her body doing all the things that she can do to care for Mavis and Delroy, and Ruel and George's body, even my father the big boy's body.

IAM®

Here I am wondering in my mind, wondering; why my mother do not help the body that I am to look good the way she wash and dress Mavis's body to look good; thinking in my mind; thinking about everyone.

Here I am. Mummy; where is daddy? I am speaking. What do you want to know that for? He went to work.

Here I am wondering in my mind, thinking, wondering about my father.

Here I am wondering in my mind, thinking. In all the time that I have been present here on the ground name England, not one body come to my father's house.

Here I am wondering in my mind, thinking about my father.

Here I am; not understanding the body that I am wanting my father to come home; thinking in my mind. I want daddy to come home now.

Here I am looking at my mother's body with the needle and cotton thread in her hand, sewing the two piece of cloth together. The time is grey light in the air outside my father's house.

Here I am sitting on the dining-room chair, looking at the body of the woman my mother; wondering in my mind, thinking about my father.

Here I am wondering; when is daddy going to come home? Thinking; in my mind; thinking about my father; gone to the factory again to work for the thing name money.

Here I am looking at my mother's face; thinking in my mind, wanting someone to come to my father's house, the building that the body that I am inside all the time; day in and day out.

IAM®

CHAPTER 4

Here I am hearing my mother's voice.

Here I am looking upon my mother's body standing over the body that I am lying down on my bed.

Here I am; wanting to stay in my bed and knowing that I have to get up now because mummy wants me to.

Here I am feeling hurt inside the body that I am; wondering what mummy wants me to get up for; at this time. The time is grey light and everyone is still sleeping in their beds. I am speaking. Hazel; hurry up. What is taking you so long?

Here I am inside the bath-room; washing my face; wondering in my mind, wondering; what mummy get up at this time for.

Here I am putting on my dress, feeling the body that I am moving around inside, feeling like I want to go back to my bed.

Here I am realizing that Mavis is in mummy and daddy's bed-room again.

Here I am making up my bed to look good, hearing my mother's footstep coming up the stairs.

Here I am standing by my bed, looking up at my mother's face looking down on the body that I am, making the body that I am not know what to do with it self. I am speaking. Come; I want you down stairs in the dining-room.

Here I am standing on the dining-room ground, looking at my mother's body sitting down on the chair, holding the thing name iron in her hand, pressing one of daddy's white cotton shirts.

Here I am mummy. I am speaking. You watch what I am doing.

Here I am looking at my mother holding the iron in her hand, pressing my father's white cotton shirt. I can hear the sound like my father's footstep coming down the stairway, coming into the dining-room. I am speaking. Pearl; what you wake up Hazel for? Why don't you let the child rest? I am speaking. How many pair of hands can you see me have? Hazel is a girl child. She must learn to do what I can do.

Here I am in the presence of my father and mother, feeling the air around me change; listening to my mother and father having words with each other; speaking about the body that I am as if my body was not here in their presence.

IAM®

Here I am listening to my father speaking up for the body that I am, making my body feel good; but here I am wanting my father to stop speaking up for the body that I am because mummy will only hurt my body when he is not at home.

Here I am watching my mother doing the ironing, realizing that daddy is getting ready to go to work at the factory.

Here I am wanting my father to stay home, not knowing what mummy is going to do with the body that I am when he is gone out of the house.

Here I am hurting, wanting to sleep, watching my father put on his work bag over his shoulder, feeling my inside go round. I am speaking. Later Pearl. Tata Hazel.

Here I am watching my mother pressing my father's shirt; hearing the front door slam shut. I am speaking. Here; press this pillow slip and these and make sure you iron them properly.

Here I am with the iron in my hand, pressing the cotton pillow case. The pillow case is not ironing.

Here I am feeling the body that I am trembling inside, knowing that my mother's eyes are looking down at what I am doing.

Here I am feeling the iron heavy in my hand, making the body that I am feel hurt inside, feeling my mother's eyes looking down at the body that I am, wanting my mother to leave the dining-room. I am speaking. Hold the iron like this and rest it like so when you are not using it, understand.

Here I am pressing the pillow case. The pillow case will not iron the way mummy can press the clothes and make everything she iron look like new.

Here I am watching my mother walking into the passage, listening to her footstep walking up the stairs.

IAM®

CHAPTER 5

Here I am standing inside the dining-room; looking at my mother changing the bed-clothes inside the bed on wheels; watching everything my mother is doing with her two hands; listening to the good sound coming from her body. I am speaking. It is Sunday today. I am taking you all to church.

Here I am thinking in my mind, wondering; what is my mother speaking of? What is Sunday?

Here I am feeling good thinking about going out of the house where I have been present from the time I came to the ground name England; thinking in my mind wondering; wondering what outside everywhere look like.

Here I am walking on the road with my father holding Delroy's body on his arm; walking with my mother holding Mavis's hand; walking with Ruel, walking with George.

Here I am feeling the air outside my father's house. The air is smelling good to the body that I am feeling good, walking forward to the place my mother call the church.

Here I am feeling good wearing my good dress; thinking in my mind; my mother and father and Mavis and Delroy and Ruel and George are all looking good to the body that I am.

Here I am looking at the lot of buildings of many different shape and size.

Here I am walking along the road, hearing the car, watching the car moving fast along the road, making my dress fly high up into the air, feeling the air inside my dress, touching my skin, making my body tremble.

Here I am standing outside the church, a big stone building.

Here I am looking at all the bodies of all kind of shape and size and form of many different colours; standing and talking to one another and holding hands together outside the building name church.

Here I am standing; just looking at everyone.

Here I am looking at one the same height as I am, looking at the little body making up it face, making my body not want to move from my father's side.

Here I am standing inside the church building, standing with my father and mother and Mavis and Delroy and Ruel and George and feeling my body inside changing.

Here I am; feeling the feeling that I am not understanding.

IAM®

Here I am following my mother and father to the front line of bench seat chair.

Here I am standing with my family, standing before one white man name Minister, the Preacher. The Minister put the water on all our heads and then said some words that I did not understand.

Here I am now of the understanding that Ruel and George and Mavis and Delroy and my body are christened in the name of our heavenly father God.

Here I am not understanding who I am, feeling the feeling that I am feeling inside the body that I am feeling good.

Here I am; knowing I am my mother and father's helper.

Here I am; understanding all that I can understand from everyone. Outside the body that I am, there is so much to know. I did not know that there is so many bodies of all kinds of shape and size, and so many colour shading with the form that is all it own, and stand it own height off the ground of the land that I am, just one.

Here I am inside my father's house.

Here I am; wanting to play a game with my brothers Ruel and George, wanting to play a game with my sister Mavis.

Here I am; wanting to do something; thinking in my mind thinking; everything here on the ground name England is not the same as on the ground name Jamaica.

Here I am wanting to be with Aunt Jane; remembering Aunt Jane, feeling good thinking about Aunt Jane.

Here I am wondering if I will ever see Aunt Jane again; thinking in my mind; Aunt Jane is far away from the body that I am here on the ground name England.

Here I am inside my father's house, the building that I cannot go out from.

Here I am doing for my mother.

Here I am wanting, wanting something good to happen to the body that I am.

Here I am at my mother's side, standing over the bath-tub, helping my mother wash the family clothes and things. All the clothes and things have different shapes and size and colour of all kind of names. One name is underpants that cover the lower part of Ruel and George and my father's body. One name is vest that covers the upper part of everyone's body. One name is socks that cover our feet. One name is petticoat slip that goes on top of the

IAM®

vest that cover Mavis and my mother's and my body. One name is shirt that goes on top of the vest that covers Ruel and George and my father's body. One name is dress that goes on top of the petty coat that covers the body of my sister Mavis and my mother's and my body. One name is trousers that go on top of the under pants that cover Ruel and George and my father's body.

Here I am scrubbing the piece of cloth in my hand; thinking in my mind; there is so many clothes to scrub clean every day.

Here I am looking at my mother ringing the water from the cloth in her hand; feeling the body that I am hurting. My hands are hurting me.

Here I am at my mother's side. I can see the water coming out from my mother's body all over on her face.

Here I am thinking in my mind; I am my mother's helper.

Here I am following my mother walking down the stairway, step by step, carrying the buckets of wet clothes in her two hands.

Here I am feeling the body that I am hurting; following my mother outside the back yard of the house.

Here I am standing on my father's land, looking at my mother holding the clothes line wire inside her two hands; looking at the line of wet clothes making the clothes line wire hang down to the ground.

Here I am looking at my mother pushing up the clothes line, hooked on the nail inside the long wood pole stick in her hand.

Here I am looking at my mother's body, hearing the hurting sound coming from her body, listening to her body talking to her self.

Here I am feeling good with myself, knowing that all the dirty clothes and things are clean; done for another day. I am speaking. Come Hazel; put these in the bath-room.

Here I am with the bucket and bowl inside my two hands.

Here I am walking through the kitchen door way, walking across the dining-room, looking at Ruel and George playing with something on the dining-room table, and making up noise with each other.

Here I am walking past the store-room, and the pantry, walking up the stairs, walking to the bath-room.

Here I am putting the buckets into the bowl, putting them down on the bath-room floor under the sink where they belong.

I AM®

Here I am walking along the landing, feeling good with myself, hearing the sound like my sister Mavis footsteps coming from mummy and daddy's bed-room.

Here I am walking down the stairway, thinking in my mind.

Here I am wondering; how come Mavis can go into mummy and daddy's bed-room whenever she wants, but I cannot?

Here I am wondering what my mother and father bed-room inside look like.

Here I am standing inside the dining-room, hearing my mother's body making the good sound, singing to her self, hearing the noise my mother is making, doing something inside the kitchen-room.

Here I am looking at Ruel, looking at George, watching them making up their face at my body. I am speaking. Come with me, you not done yet.

Here I am following my mother walking quick into the hall way, carrying some cloth in her hand, and singing the good sound; following my mother up the stairs; into the girl's bed-room. I am speaking. Watch me. This is how I want you to make the beds in future. You are in my house now.

Here I am standing in the girl's bed-room; looking at my mother's body making Mavis bed to look good, hearing my mother talking to her self.

Here I am hearing every word that is coming out from my mother's mouth; talking about my father. That my father does not realize how much work she one have to do, and that my father is not paying her to look after Ruel and George and me, and the money my father is giving to her is not enough. My mother does not realize that the body that I am is hearing every word that she is speaking, talking about my father. My mother does not realize that I can understand. I am speaking. Now make your bed to look like that. I am not going to live in a pig style because of you lot.

Here I am hearing my mother's every word, watching everything my mother is doing, and understanding every word that my mother is talking to her self. I am speaking. When you finish, polish the rest of the furniture and make sure the chamber pot is clean. Then go and do your brother them bed-room. Hurry up, you have not got all day. I don't know what your father's send for you for, making me not have no time for my self. I am going to show him. I don't know what he takes me for.

Here I am making up my bed to look like my sister Mavis's bed, hearing my mother talking about my father as if I was not here in her presence, talking of my father, making my body feel hurt, thinking about my father. I am speaking.

IAM®

Is that how me show you to make the bed? Pull the bed out from the corner off the wall and do it properly before me get mad with you, you hear me.

Here I am not feeling good inside my father's house. The woman, my mother is making my body hurt.

Here I am; not wanting to be in my mother's presence, hearing every word she is speaking.

Here I am watching my mother walking into the hall way, hearing her talking to her self, causing the air surrounding me to change, making the body that I am feel hurting inside.

Here I am; wanting my father to come home now; mummy is acting mad, wanting to hurt my body; always beating my body, hurting my body whenever daddy is not at home.

Here I am on my knees looking under Mavis's bed, looking for Mavis's potty. I can see that Mavis have done something in her potty and I have to empty it and wash it clean every time.

Here I am with the cloth and polish tin can in my hand.

Here I am wiping clean the thing name dressing-table, polishing it shine. The polish is making the air in the bed-room smell good to the body that I am.

Here I am standing on the chair by Mavis's wardrobe, wiping the polish all over the wardrobe, the tall wood thing that all Mavis's good dresses are hanging inside.

Here I am shining the wardrobe to look good, just like my mother make the wood things look shine.

Here I am standing still, looking all over the space inside the bed-room, making sure in my mind, looking at all the wood things in the room, making sure everything is clean, shining bright, just like my mother polish my sister Mavis's dressing-table to look as good as new; feeling good with myself, knowing that I am the one that is helping my mother to keep my father's house inside looking good.

Here I am walking to my brother's bed-room, thinking in my mind. I am the one helping my mother to do everything that I am told to do, but my mother keeps raising her voice at one.

Here I am thinking, Ruel and George and Mavis keep making the things inside the house look dirty, but mummy never shout at them. Mummy never beat Ruel or George or Mavis on their body the way she is always hurting the body that I am.

Here I am standing inside Ruel and George's bed-room. The air is smelling rank.

Here I am on my knees looking under the bed, wondering if Ruel or George have empty their potty. The air under the bed is smelling rank. The potty is full.

Here I am with the potty in my two hands.

Here I am walking slow, walking into the bath-room, feeling hurt inside the body that I am wondering why do I have to empty Ruel and George's potty when they are bigger than I am and older enough to use the toilet, just like I do?

Here I am washing the potty with the toilet brush.

Here I am standing on the toilet bowl, pulling the toilet chain down, making sure all the do-do go away.

Here I am cleaning, cleaning up Ruel and George's mess, feeling the body that I am hurting inside.

Here I am wondering; why won't mummy show Ruel and George how to keep them self clean? Why won't mummy show Ruel and George how to clean up their mess the way she show me?

Here I am returning the potty under the bed where it belongs.

Here I am pulling the bedclothes off the bed, wondering if Ruel and George are going to keep on wetting the bed. The bed is wet, smelling rank and I am hurting, knowing that I have to wash Ruel and George stinking wet sheet again.

Here I am hurting, dragging the dirty sheet to the bath-room. The body that I am is hurting, lifting the wet sheet into the bathtub.

Here I am turning the hot water tap on, watching the water coming into the bath.

Here I am leaning forward, down into the bath, pushing the plug into the hole. The water is coming hot with steam now.

Here I am turning the cold water tap on.

Here I am with the soap powder box, putting the powder over the sheet.

IAM®

Here I am turning off the hot water. My body is hurting.

Here I am with the washing stick in my hand, pushing the sheets under the water to soak out all the wee-wee stains.

Here I am standing on the bucket, reaching up, opening the bath-room window, wanting to let the clean air come in.

Here I am my mother's helper.

Here I am thinking in my mind.

Here I am in my brother's bed-room, standing on the chair pushing up the window, letting the clean air come into the room, making the room smell clean.

Here I am looking on Ruel and George's bed, looking at all the wet wee-wee stain all over the bed.

Here I am feeling hurt, thinking; when am I going to get to sit down?; knowing that Ruel and George is playing games with each other instead of learning to care for their body as I am caring for them.

Here I am on my knees with the hand brush sweeping the floor clean, the way mummy does.

Here I am under the dressing-table, sweeping, sweeping the dust forward to the bed-room door way, sweeping the dust into the dustpan, feeling good inside the body that I am.

Here I am with the cleaning cloth in my hand, polishing the dressing table clean, making it shine like new.

Here I am with the tin can of polish in my hand, spraying it up and down on the boy's wardrobe.

Here I am standing on the chair, rubbing the cloth over the wood, polishing it shine, making the wardrobe look good to the body that I am.

Here I am feeling the body that I am feeling good with myself; knowing that I can make everything shine as good as new, just like my mother make everything that she clean looks good like new.

Here I am inside the bath-room, looking down on the floor.

Here I am on my knees with the brush in my hand, sweeping the bath-room floor clean, sweeping the dust to the bath-room door way, hearing mummy raising her voice shouting at Ruel and George to keep the noise down.

IAM®

Here I am sweeping all the dust into the dustpan, realizing that I have the landing to sweep now and then the stairs.

Here I am walking to my mother's and father's bed-room door way.

Here I am standing outside my mother's bed-room, hearing the sounds like Mavis is playing with Delroy.

Here I am; wanting to go inside, and knowing that I cannot enter.

Here I am on my knees, sweeping the floor outside my mother's bed-room, sweeping along the landing, feeling the body that I am making water coming into my two eyes, feeling the body that I am hurting, working inside my father's house.

Here I am sweeping, wanting my body to stop hurting, wanting the water to stop coming into my eyes because mummy will only beat me again.

Here I am sweeping all the dust down the step, moving forward to the bath-room.

Here I am sweeping, wondering in my mind, wondering if daddy has gone to work at the factory again.

Here I am sweeping the floor outside my brother's bed-room, sweeping all the dust together at the bath-room door way, sweeping the dust into the dustpan.

Here I am sitting on the step, feeling the body that I am feeling hot.

Here I am thinking in my mind, thinking. Why must I the girl body that I am have to clean the house? Why won't mummy show Ruel and George how to clean the house the way she shows me?

Here I am; understanding that because my body is name girl, I must do the cleaning, but Ruel and George do not have to do the cleaning because their body is name boy.

Here I am understanding, realizing that the man, the one name father, the one name brother, the one name son, the one name boy, the child as I am, are all growing taller, believing that the mother, the one name woman, the one name sister, the one name daughter, the one name girl, is born just to care for the male form.

Here I am understanding that the boy and his father do not know how to do not one thing, because the woman their mother believe that it is the female duty to work to do everything for their born conception, the male child, the boy they call son; but at the same time, the woman believe that their other conception, born the image like her self, the daughter must work for the mother and the son.

Here I am one girl child, one daughter, one sister; thinking. What is the boy child born to do if not to help the woman his mother? She is his maker.

Here I am wondering; why did my father send for me and Ruel and George; knowing that the woman my mother do not want us?

Here I am knowing that I am my mother and father's helper and I am doing all that I can, but mummy keep raising her voice, shouting at me, making the body that I am not want to be in her presence. I can hear mummy asking for me, making my body move quick, gathering the dustpan and brush in my hand.

Here I am moving quickly; run walking to the top of the stair way, not wanting mummy to find my body not doing anything.

Here I am sweeping the dust down the stair.

Here I am on the ground floor of the house, sweeping the dust down on the bottom step, sweeping the step clean, hearing Ruel and George laughing out loud.

Here I am thinking about Ruel and George, wondering why Ruel and George do not want to talk to the body that I am their sister.

Here I am at the front door way of my father's house.

Here I am looking through the little box opening on the door.

Here I am looking into the air, wanting to go outside.

Here I am on my hands and knee, sweeping along the hall way, thinking in my mind, wondering what is happening outside my father's house.

Here I am at the beginning of the stairs, sweeping the dust together, sweeping the dust around the corner bend, around down the step, moving forward to the dining-room, sweeping past the store-room, past the pantry.

Here I am outside the dining-room, sweeping all the dust into the dustpan, wiping the dust off my face, shaking the dust off my dress and hands.

Here I am feeling good with myself.

Here I am walking into the dining-room. I can smell the fire in the air, smelling good.

IAM®

Here I am standing inside the dining-room.

Here I am looking down on the floor, looking, thinking in my mind; if I sweep the dining-room floor, mummy will not shout at me no more.

Here I am feeling good with myself, sweeping, hearing mummy doing inside the kitchen.

Here I am hearing my mother making the happy sound, making my body feel good.

Here I am. Excuse me please Ruel. I want to sweep under the table. I am speaking. Wait a minute.

Here I am. Ruel, move please. I am speaking. Have anyone seen Hazel?

Here I am. Here I am mummy. I am sweeping the dining-room floor. I am speaking. Hurry up and come here.

Here I am. Yes mummy.

Here I am sweeping under the dining-table, thinking in my mind, wondering what mummy wants me for.

Here I am sweeping the dirt into the dustpan.

Here I am walking into the kitchen, holding the dustpan and brush in my hand, feeling the body that I am trembling, wondering what mummy wants me for.

Here I am emptying the dust into the kitchen bin, returning the dustpan and brush under the kitchen sink where they belong. I am speaking. You finish yet?

Here I am. Yes mummy. I am speaking. Have you sweep everywhere?

Here I am. Yes mummy. I am speaking. You do your brother's bed-room.

Here I am. Yes mummy. Ruel and George have wet the bed again. I have put the wet sheets into the bath to soak. I am speaking. They keep wetting that bed. You watch me and them.

Here I am listening to my mother speaking, realizing that mummy is not shouting at the body that I am.

Here I am feeling good in my mother's presence; looking on the body of my mother, and feeling my mother's presence; wanting to be with my mother for the one time.

IAM®

Here I am standing on the kitchen ground, looking on the body of my mother and thinking in my mind; mummy you look good when you're not shouting at me; looking at my mother's body making the sunshine expression all over her face, making the body that I am feel good.

Here I am watching everything my mother is doing with her two hands, and hearing the good sound coming from her body. The air inside the kitchen is smelling good. I am speaking. Hazel; mind your self. That is the stove you are standing by. The food is cooking on top. Here; look. You can cook inside.

Here I am looking on my mother's body smiling all over her face, looking pleased with her self, demonstrating her words, so I will understand.

Here I am feeling good in my mother's presence.

Here I am learning from my mother, learning of all there is to know about the kitchen-room inside my father's house.

Here I am now of the understanding that the kitchen-room is the part of the house where my mother prepare and cook the food for the family.

Here I am learning from my mother, learning of everything she uses in the act of preparing and cooking the food for the family. The things my mother uses in the act of preparing and cooking the food; have each thing but one name. The thing is name, the sauce pan, the frying pan, the kettle, the fork, the knife, the spoon, the bowl, the jug, the plate, the chopping board, the colander, the mixing bowl, the chip pan, the dish cloth, the hand towel, and the name of all the many different things go on. I am now of the understanding of the things one use for the act of eating. The name is the different shape and size one use according to the nature of the food that my mother buys and cook for us to eat. The thing is name, the knife, the fork, the spoon, the cup, the mug, the jug, the glass, the plate, the tea-pot, the coffee-pot and the name of all the many different things go on.

Here I am watching my mother and understanding every word my mother is speaking.

Here I am feeling good knowing that I am the one that is learning. I am speaking. This is a box of matches; matches make fire; understand.

Here I am watching my mother demonstrate her words so I will understand; watching my mother put the burning piece of stick under the sauce-pan, watching her other hand turn the stove ring around, watching the fire sound light the flame all under the pan.

IAM®

Here I am realizing that one must be doing. One must use the body two hands to understand what the body is thinking.

Here I am of the understanding; that the one that is using the body one two hands; the one two hands working together; making and doing something of the self is the body that is creating.

IAM®

CHAPTER 6

Here I am standing on the front doorstep. The time is blue sky and brilliant sunshine.

Here I am feeling the morning air breezing warm on my face; drinking the air; feeling the air all about the body that I am; blowing up inside my dress; feeling my insides feeling good; making my face smile the sunshine expression.

Here I am on my knees; thinking about the body that I am; wiping the ox blood polish over the red brick step; rubbing the cloth hard on the stone; wanting it to shine; seeing the sunshine glistening on the front door step; feeling good with myself; gathering up the cloth and polish; pushing on the door to shut; wondering in my mind; thinking; making my way along the passage to the pantry; returning the cloth and polish in the box on top of the shelf where mummy keep them; thinking in my mind; wondering what to do next; not wanting mummy to find my body doing nothing; thinking in my mind; remembering the backyard.

Here I am standing on the back doorstep; holding the broom in my hand; thinking in my mind; breathing in the air; walking towards the top part of the yard beside the back bed-room of the house; looking down to the end of the garden; feeling good inside; sweeping the footpath; sweeping the dirt and leaves and stones away out of the corner wall; sweeping the dirt forward; pushing it down the yard; past the wash house; past the coal house; sweeping down towards the back fence gate; resting my body leaning on the broom stick; my eyes wondering about the yard; watching the birds flying about the yard; thinking in my mind; hearing voices on the other side of the garden fence; my body still; listening; sweeping the dirt forward; down towards the wooden house that mummy keep the chicken birds.

Here I am sweeping; pushing the pile of dirt together at the bottom part of the garden; feeling my insides go round; feeling my body on guard; frightened; hearing the chicken birds flapping their wings about inside the wooden chicken house; hearing the chicken bodies screeching; scaring my body; wondering at the noise; watching my mothers body coming down the yard; feeling my body go rigid; thinking; thinking in my mind; feeling my eyes fill up with water; my eyes fixed on the machete knife my mother have in her hand; her body moving quick coming towards where I am standing near the chicken house; my body frozen; my body not wanting to be where I am; watching my mother's hand reaching into the chicken house; hearing the screeching noise the chicken bodies are making; knowing something bad is happening.

IAM®

Here I am sweeping the dirt quick beside the garden heap; not wanting to be where I am; hurrying up; feeling my head hurting; my insides going fast; eyes fixed on my mother's body; hearing the chicken bodies sounding frightened; screaming to get away from my mother; watching the chicken wings flapping out its feathers; flying up into the air; running; zigzagging across the garden; running away from my mother's hand grabbing to catch the chicken; hearing my mothers voice shouting at my body. I am speaking. Hazel; come here; quick

Here I am feeling my insides coming up; my eyes fixed on the machete in my mothers hand; hearing all the chickens in the chicken house; their screeching sounds; my body wanting to help the chicken running about the garden; seeing my mother running after the chicken; my body feeling for the chicken; watching my mother's fist holding on tight around the chicken body neck; watching it's legs paddling; it's body flapping out its feathers about my mother's body wrestling the chicken body; trying to hold the chicken body down on the step near the house; watching the chicken body turning this way and that; wriggling; hearing the chicken body choking in breath. I am speaking. Give me the dustbin cover; quick.

Here I am feeling scarred; watching my mother; my body not wanting anything to do with what my mother is doing; hearing the chicken body screeching; the chicken body eyes rolling in its head; watching my mother's knee pressing down on the dustbin cover fixed on the chicken body neck; watching my mother's hand holding the machete raised up to the sky; taking aim; chopping the chicken head off its body; feeling the chicken life spirit soul jump out of the chicken body; into the body that I am; my body wanting the chicken life spirit soul to come out of the body that I am; feeling the chicken life blood smell engulf the body that I am; scenting out the air about the body that I am frightened; seeing my mothers act of killing; worried for the body that I am; feeling my insides hurting; watching the chicken life blood spatter red in all directions; covering my mother's body; her face and hands coloured red with the chicken life blood; watching the chicken body running over the garden; with no head on it's body; watching my mother's body running after the headless chicken; watching the chicken life blood red liquid pumping up out of it's neck; splashing all over my fathers land; my body rigid scared; unable to move from the spot; watching the chicken headless body twitching about on the ground; watching the heat rising out of the chicken life blood pumping out of the chicken headless body dying before the body that I am unable to stop the body that I am from crying; hurting pain for the chicken body that is no life no more. I am speaking. Go and fill the kitchen bowl with water and bring it come.

Here I am inside the kitchen; my body trembling; standing on the chair over the sink; turning on the cold water tap; watching the water filling up inside the kitchen bowl; thinking in my mind; wanting the smell of the chicken to come out of my body; my mind fretting; thinking about the body that I am.

Here I am lifting the bowl of water out of the sink onto the draining-board; my body standing on the floor; lifting the bowl of water down off the draining-board; feeling water splash up; down my dress; soaking my skin; my body trembling; walking slow; carrying the bowl of water outside; feeling the water running down inside my dress; cold on my skin.

Here I am resting the bowl of water down on the ground near my mother's body.

Here I am watching my mother's hands pulling the feathers out the chicken body; watching my mother's hands in the bowl of water; washing the chicken body blood and feathers off her hands; off the big cooking knife; washing the blood off the machete; emptying the bowl of blood stained water along the path way.

Here I am watching my mother's hands working; thinking in my mind; wondering where the water in the drain go; wondering about the chicken body that is no life no more; thinking in my mind. You can poor water over the ground to wash the chicken blood from your sight; but you can't wash away the act of killing; my mind thinking; you cannot give the chicken back its life; my mind thinking; wondering about the chicken body that is no life no more.

Here I am standing inside the kitchen; looking at the blood all over my mothers hand and dress and apron; looking at the knife in my mother's hand at work on the chicken body placed on the draining board; watching my mother's hand moving the knife down the front middle part of the chicken body; pulling the insides of the chicken out onto the newspaper spread out on the draining-board; my insides going round; watching my mother's hands separating the insides of the chicken body parts slipping about inside her hands; washing each piece under the cold tap water; washing the blood away from the chicken flesh. Two foot, two legs, two hips, two wings, two front pieces, one neck and arranging each piece of chicken flesh inside the meat bowl.

IAM®

Here I am watching my mother taking the skin off the big round vegetable onion, cutting it thin, slicing the pieces over the chicken flesh inside the big mixing bowl.

Here I am watching my mother, mixing everything in the bowl, mixing everything together with her hand; watching my mother placing the cover on top of the mixing bowl, watching her hand position the bowl down on the kitchen worktop inside the corner of the wall. My mother is washing her hands and the big cooking knife clean in the soap water inside the washing-up bowl standing in the sink. I am speaking. Finish cleaning up the kitchen please Hazel. Hurry and come up stairs.

Here I am inside the kitchen, standing on the chair, washing the dishcloth and smelling the chicken body flesh in all the air surrounding the body that I am.

Here I am wiping the worktop clean, making the kitchen look clean, like my mother make the kitchen room look good.

Here I am with the broom in my hand, sweeping the kitchen ground clean.

Here I am walking into the dining-room, walking into the hall way, walking up the stairs; hearing my mother's voice shouting at Ruel and George to hurry and get dress.

Here I am standing in the girl's bed-room, looking at my mother combing Mavis's hair. Mavis and Delray's body is looking good. I am speaking. Hazel; move yourself. Here; put these clothes on.

Here I am. Thank you mummy.

Here I am feeling good inside the body that I am, feeling good with my mother, knowing that I am going to look good, knowing that I have a good dress to put on.

Here I am taking my clean knickers and vest and my slip from the dressing-table drawer, and my white pair of socks, placing everything down on my bed.

Here I am looking at my shoes in my hand, wishing that I can have a pair of shoes that look good like Mavis's shoes look good; thinking in my mind; Mavis has a black shiny round bag to go with her pair of shoes that is shining bright.

Here I am wishing that mummy will dress my body to look as good as she dress Mavis's body to look good. I am speaking. Hazel hurry up. By the time I finish comb your brother's head, I want you ready.

IAM®

Here I am hearing my mother's voice, realizing that mummy is going to comb my hair.

Here I am standing inside the bath-room, wiping my face with my flannel, feeling good inside, knowing that I am going outside the house, into the open air.

Here I am wiping my body clean, thinking in my mind, thinking about the body that I am.

Here I am inside the bed-room, putting on my clean clothes, feeling good inside my good dress.

Here I am pulling out the plates in my hair, looking at Ruel, looking at George's body looking good. Ruel and George are wearing their white shirt and bow tie. I am speaking. Come Hazel.

Here I am on my knees, kneeling down between my mother's legs.

Here I am feeling hurt, feeling the way my mother is dragging the comb in my hair, making my head hurt.

Here I am wondering in my mind, wondering why my mother always hurt me whenever she is doing something for me, knowing that my mother always take her time whenever she is doing for Mavis.

IAM®

CHAPTER 7

Here I am ready to go to church with my brother's and sister and our mother. My mother's body is all dressed up, looking good.

Here I am walking along the road, walking with my mother pushing Delroy and Mavis in the pram, walking with Ruel and George, on our way to church.

Here we are walking towards the church building, the big tall place name Baptist church.

Here I am inside the Baptist church.

Here I am sitting on the bench seat, hearing every word that the preacher man is speaking.

Here I am; wanting to understand; not understanding one word that I can hear the preacher man is speaking.

Here I am; wanting to ask the preacher man what he is talking about; feeling not able to open my mouth because every other body is sitting in silence, just looking at the preacher man as if they know and understand all that the preacher man is saying.

Here I am looking at the preacher man looking into the big black book name Bible; speaking about all that I know not one thing of.

Here I am wondering why the preacher is not explaining what he is reading.

Here I am; wanting to understand.

Here I am surrounded by many the same as I am.

Here I am inside the church, inside the class-room, in attendance at Sunday school.

Here I am listening to the Sunday school teacher; a white colour woman reading the word written down inside the book, the Bible.

Here I am. Who is Jesus? I am speaking. Jesus is the son of God.

Here I am. Where is God and his son Jesus? I am speaking. God is in heaven. We are his children.

Here I am thinking about Jesus; thinking in my mind; wondering about heaven.

Here I am realizing the meaning of the words that I am hearing, listening to the teacher reading.

IAM®

Here I am thinking in my mind realizing that I am the daughter of God.

Here I am realizing that the preacher and the teacher and all the people here inside the Baptist church; they do not understand that I am the daughter of God as they themselves are sons and daughters, born of the one name God, even the body name mother and father, and the preacher man and the teacher woman.

Here I am; knowing that the body name Jesus is not the only child of God because I am as every living body and every plant is born of the one name God.

Here I am realizing that the people that come to Sunday school behave as if they are the only good people on the land.

Here I am listening to the teacher woman.

Here I am wondering in my mind, wondering; what is the meaning of the name church; thinking in my mind; everyone here is pretending to be something other than what the self know the self is.

Here I am not caring what anyone thinks that I am.

Here I am; knowing that I am the daughter of God and I am helping my mother and father to care for each one of my brothers and my sister, even my mother and my father.

Here I am now of the understanding that everyone think the self is better than the other, the neighbour.

The Baptist preacher man places himself higher than the Baptist teacher men, women and their children who think themselves better than every man, woman and child outside of the Baptist church.

Here I am realizing that my father and mother even place them self higher than their children, the child I am.

Here I am the girl child knowing that I am because God is the breath of life inside and outside the body that I am, just one.

Here I am; knowing that I am because God is.

Here I am walking on the road, on my way home, walking with my family. I can see all kinds of buildings along the roadside. I am feeling good, feeling the sun in the heaven shining down on me, making my body feel good, smelling the air tasting good inside the body that I am. I am speaking. That area is name Victoria Park. That is where the children go to play.

IAM®

Here I am having a good time, hearing my mother, understanding every word that my mother is saying. I can see all the children playing all over the ground name Victoria Park.

Here I am walking, on my way home to my father's house.

Here I am feeling the body that I am change, knowing that I have to start working again.

Here I am standing before the dressing-table.

Here I am looking at the body that I am; wondering about myself, thinking in my mind. What am I here for?

Here I am thinking about the body that I am.

Here I am inside my father's house.

Here I am with my brothers and sister and our mother.

Here I am feeling lone inside myself, thinking in my mind. Who am I?

Here I am taking off my good clothes, putting on my house clothes.

Here I am feeling the body that I am change, hearing the sound of Ruel and George sounding like they are having a good time, playing a game with each other.

Here I am; wanting Ruel and George to let me play the game with them, knowing that my sister Mavis does not want to play with me.

Here I am thinking; Mavis body think that her body is better than my body; all because mummy does everything to make her body look good.

Here I am walking down the stairway, walking into the dining-room and smelling something in the air smelling good, making my body want to eat. I can hear my mother doing inside the kitchen.

Here I am standing within the presence of Ruel and George sitting around the dining-table, playing the game of cards with each other.

Here I am looking on the body of my sister Mavis playing with her toy dolly, combing the dolly hair with her dolly hair comb.

Here I am looking on the body of my baby brother Delroy. Delroy is playing with his hands, making the good sound, hearing the music coming from the wooden box resting on the sideboard next to the television box.

IAM®

Here I am inside the body that I am; feeling lone, wanting; not knowing what my body is wanting, feeling hurt because my brother's and sister do not want to know me. I am speaking. Hazel; set the table.

Here I am listening to my mother, watching Ruel's body jump down quick off the chair.

Here I am opening out the dining-table; making it long.

Here I am standing on the chair by the cabinet, taking the knives and forks and the spoons from the drawer, placing them down on the dining-table.

Here I am looking inside the television table drawer, taking out the clean cotton tablecloth, smelling the food that my mother is preparing, making my body feel hunger, wanting to eat.

Here I am taking the cup and the saucer and the plate from the sideboard shelf, placing them down on the table, in order for everyone.

Here I am walking into the kitchen with the pile of plates in my two hands.

Here I am standing at the kitchen doorway, looking at my mother standing by the stove, turning over the dumpling food cooking in the frying pan.

Here I am placing the pile of plates down on the worktop, hearing my mother making the humming sound inside her body, making my body feel good to be in her presence. I am speaking. Bring me the can of milk and the sugar Hazel.

Here I am hearing my mother's order.

Here I am with the can of milk and the parcel of sugar, placing them down on the kitchen worktop.

Here I am watching my mother pouring the hot water from the kettle, pouring the water into the big tea-pot.

Here I am watching my mother pouring the milk from the can into the teapot, mixing it into the tea. Now my mother is putting the sugar into the teapot. One, and one, and one more, big spoon full, mixing everything together, making the tea for us to drink.

Here I am watching my mother holding the bowl full with fried dumpling, sharing the dumplings out on the plates. Now my mother is sharing out the sausages, eggs, bacon and the baked beans. I am speaking. Here, this is for Ruel and George.

Here I am taking the plates of food from my mother's hand.

I AM®

Here I am walking into the dining-room; placing the plates down on the table before Ruel, before George's body sitting around the table, ready to eat.

Here I am inside the kitchen, looking up at my mother's hand placing the cover on top of the pan on the stove. I am speaking. Here.

Here I am. Thank you mummy.

Here I am following my mother walking into the dining-room, carrying hers and Mavis's breakfast.

Here I am sitting around the dining-table, waiting for my mother to sit down before any one can begin to eat.

Here I am listening to my mother's voice, speaking, thanking our heavenly father for the food we are going to eat.

Here I am watching my mother holding her two hands together, and looking at her two eyes closed, listening to her talking to our heavenly father.

Here I am kneeling down on the chair seat.

Here I am washing the cups and plates and knives and forks, washing all the breakfast things clean, placing them down on the draining board.

Here I am wiping everything dry on the tea-towel in my hand, placing them down on the worktop. I am speaking. Hazel.

Here I am. Yes mummy. I am speaking. When you done, come in here.

Here I am. Yes mummy.

Here I am wondering in my mind.

Here I am wiping the worktop dry, wondering what mummy wants me for.

Here I am standing on the kitchen ground, sweeping the floor with the broom in my hand, sweeping all the dust into the dust pan, emptying the dust into the kitchen rubbish bin.

Here I am walking into the dining-room, carrying the pile of plates in my hand, placing them down on the dining-room table.

Here I am walking past my mother with the Bible book inside her two hands.

Here I am inside the kitchen.

Here I am getting the cups off the worktop, walking into the dining-room, thinking in my mind, wondering; what does mummy want me for?

IAM®

Here I am inside the dining-room, resting the cups down on the dining-table.

Here I am hearing Ruel and George playing a game with each other.

Here I am standing on the chair before the cabinet, putting the knives and forks and spoons away where they belong inside the drawer. I can see a little book and a pencil by my mother's hand resting on the table.

Here I am watching my mother's body, listening to her body making sounds to herself. I am speaking. What is taking you so long?

Here I am walking past my mother, listening to her speaking, feeling my body going around inside, thinking; what does mummy want me to do now?

Here I am standing inside the kitchen, putting the cooking knife and fork and spoon away inside the kitchen cupboard drawer. I am putting the saucepan and the little frying-pan, and the tea-pot into the cupboard where they belong.

Here I am standing inside the dining-room, looking at Mavis sitting on mummy's knee, making up her face, looking at me.

Here I am feeling the body that I am changing, not knowing what mummy want me for.

Here I am. I have finished mummy.

Here I am standing before my mother and my sister Mavis. My mother is not paying my body any attention.

Here I am wondering if mummy can hear me. I can see George's body making up his face at me, smiling behind his two hands.

Here I am. Here I am mummy. I am speaking. You think me deaf? Come over here. What is this?

Here I am. Am..; am..; hearing the words my mother is speaking direct to the body that I am.

Here I am wondering why mummy is asking me what the book is.

Here I am in the presence of my brothers and sister; feeling my insides going around, not knowing what to do with myself, feeling my mother's eyes just looking at one. I am speaking. Spell your name.

Here I am. Am..; am..; am..; feeling my body shaking; trembling inside; listening to the words mummy is saying; thinking in my mind; not knowing what to say; not understanding my mother. I don't know what mummy means.

IAM®

Here I am thinking, wondering in my mind, thinking; what do you mean?

Here I am feeling my mother's presence, making my body not know what to do with myself, not knowing what my mother expect from me. I am speaking. Hazel; spell your name.

Here I am; Am..; am..; am..; feeling the water full up my eyes; falling down my face; trembling inside the body that I am.

Here I am within the presence of my brother's and sister.

Here I am feeling lone, feeling hurt, not understanding the body that I am, not wanting to be where I am. I am speaking. H-A-Z-E-L, spells Hazel. H-A-Z-E-L, spells Hazel. Now spell your name. Your name is Hazel.

Here I am hearing the sounds my mother is saying.

Here I am feeling unable to open my mouth.

Here I am feeling my inside moving around, feeling the water falling from my eyes, feeling hurt, not wanting to look at my mother's face; listening; hearing the sounds my mother is speaking.

Here I am; wanting to remember the sounds my mother is speaking. I am speaking. Hazel, spell your name. Spell your name. Spell your name.

Here I am hearing my mother speaking to the body that I am; telling me how to spell my name.

Here I am; wanting to speak, feeling unable to open my mouth, feeling my mother's presence making my head hurt inside.

Here I am unable to move from the spot where I am standing.

Here I am feeling my mother moving fast across the dining-room, into the hall way, hearing her footstep walking, running up the stairway.

Here I am hurting, knowing that my sister is laughing at me.

Here I am unable to stop the water coming into my eyes.

Here I am listening to my mother's footstep coming towards the dining-room. My mother is making up her face looking down at me.

Here I am watching my mother winding my father's trouser belt around and around her hand. I am speaking. Move Mavis. Go and sit down. You come here. Now spell your name.

I AM®

Here I am. Mummy; don't beat me. I can spell my name. I can spell my name. I am speaking. Spell it; now.

Here I am; am... I am speaking. My God, Hazel; spell your name.

Here I am, the body that I am is hurting inside my head, inside my belly is hurting.

Here I am thinking in my mind; wanting to spell the name Hazel; wanting to remember the sounds, the letter sounds mummy make.

Here I am; wanting to do what my mother wants me to do.

Here I am feeling the body that I am feeling hot all over my body, feeling cold, feeling hot at the same time, feeling the water falling from my eyes, feeling hot on my hand, feeling my neck, my shoulders burning hot, feeling my legs inside hurting.

Here I am. Mummy; don't beat me mummy.

Here I am; wanting my father to come home.

Here I am; wishing that my mother is not my mother.

Here I am. Mummy; please don't beat me no more. I can spell my name. I can spell my name. H-A-Z-L. I am speaking. Was that the way you hear me spell your name.

Here I am. Am..; am..; am... I am speaking. Here; this is name exercise book and this is a pencil. Look at what I am writing. Look at how I am writing your name; look. This is how you write your name H-A-Z-E-L. Hazel is your Christian name and Grant is your sir name, understand. You understand.

Here I am watching my mother's hand writing.

Here I am feeling my body hurting.

Here I am; wanting to remember the letter sounds that my mother is saying; not wanting my mother to beat me no more. I am speaking. Repeat, after me.

Here I am listening to my mother sounding ever sound that I can hear her voice is making, remembering in my mind, watching my mother's hand writing every letter making up the word name Hazel. I am speaking. H-A-Z-E-L, Hazel. H-A-Z-E-L, Hazel.

Here I am; H-A-Z-E-L, Hazel; am..; H-A-Z-E-L, Hazel. I am speaking. Louder; so I can hear you. Louder I say. Now go and sit in the back bed-room and copy your name out. Properly; you hear me; good.

IAM®

Here I am walking into the hall way, listening to my mother raising her voice at me.

Here I am with the exercise book and pencil in my hand.

Here I am walking, speaking the letter sounds to myself; wanting to remember the sounds of the letters that make up the name Hazel; feeling hot all over my body, feeling my skin burning, stinging all over the body that I am hurting, skin bleeding; feeling the water falling from my eyes, feeling hot on my hand, feeling my neck, my shoulders burning hot, feeling my leg inside burning hot; stinging; hurting; thinking in my mind; wanting to remember how to write the name Hazel.

Here I am standing inside the back bed-room; hurting, feeling lone inside the body that I am; not understanding why my mother is beating my body.

Here I am on my knees, holding the exercise book on my lap, copywriting my mother's hand writing.

Here I am remembering the letter sound of the letter shapes I am writing, thinking about the name Hazel.

Here I am copywriting, thinking. Why; why am I writing the name Hazel?

Here I am. I can smell the food my mother is cooking, smelling in the air; thinking in my mind; wondering. What time is it?

Here I am wishing that my father is here; wanting someone to come to the room where I am; thinking; not one of my brothers and not my sister care about me; thinking in my mind; wondering why none of them have come to see how I am.

Here I am writing; hurting; thinking about the body that I am; feeling my mother's presence coming to the room where I am. I am speaking. Let me see what you have done.

Here I am looking at mother's face looking inside the exercise book; looking at what I have done; feeling the body that I am shaking, trembling; not wanting my mother to beat me no more. I am speaking. Spell Hazel.

Here I am. H-A-Z-L-E, Hazel.

Here I am hurting, feeling the belt across my back. My mother just keep beating and beating the body that I am and she don't know how hard she is beating the body that I am; making my skin bleed blood; making my body burn hot. I am hurting all over my body is hurting.

IAM®

Here I am; mummy; stop beating me. I can spell my name. I am speaking. You watch me and you. You're going to spell your name if it is the last thing you do.

Here I am; am…; am…; am….

Here I am inside my father's house.

Here I am with the pencil in my hand, copywriting in the exercise book.

Here I am; wanting to sleep. The time outside the house is dark grey light. I can hear the sound of knives and forks scraping the dinner plates.

Here I am thinking, wondering if mummy is going to give me any dinner.

Here I am; not wanting to be where I am, wishing that I can go away from my father's house and knowing that I cannot. I can feel my father, his presence is near. My father is coming home.

IAM®

CHAPTER 8

Here I am; wanting to see my father; knowing that I cannot leave the room where I am.

Here I am listening to my father's footstep stepping pass the room doorway.

Here I am listening to my father walking along the hall way, walking to the dining-room; hearing my father's voice say; where is my daughter Hazel?

Here I am feeling good inside myself, knowing that my father is home; feeling my father's presence coming to the room where I am sitting not knowing what to do with myself, feeling my eyes full with water, not wanting to look at my father. I am speaking. Come with me. I am here now. Come and have your dinner.

Here I am walking slow; following my father down the hall way into the dining-room light; feeling the light in the dining-room making my eyes burn.

Here I am standing behind my father.

Here I am; not wanting to see my mother's face. My mother's presence is making my body feel hurt. I am speaking. Pearl; what you have against my daughter? What she done you lock her up in the room like that? I am speaking. Who tell you to come in here? I am speaking. I tell her to come and have her dinner. The child must eat. You cannot keep Hazel working all the time without food. I am speaking. Go and get the exercise book let me see what you have done. I am speaking. Stay and have your dinner.

Here I am within the presence of my father and mother and brothers and sister; listening to my father and mother talking about me, making my body not know what to do with myself, feeling the air surrounding me change, just keep changing. I am speaking. Pearl, listen to what I am saying. Let Hazel have something to eat. Look at her. Look how my daughter looks maga.

Here I am listening to my father speaking up for me, defending the body I am.

Here I am thinking; I did not know my father thought about me until now.

Here I am realizing that my father do not understand the woman my mother and he does not know how she behave whenever he goes out. My father does not know the person my mother really is. I am speaking. Go and light the fire under the saucepan.

Here I am standing on the kitchen ground, lighting the stove with the burning match in my hand.

IAM®

Here I am standing on the chair by the sink, watching the cold water going into the kettle.

Here I am standing inside the kitchen, lifting the kettle up onto the stove, lighting the fire under the kettle, turning the flame up high.

Here I am listening to my father and mother talking about me. I can hear my mother saying that I must learn to do everything there is to do inside the house because I am a girl child.

Here I am; understanding all that I can hear.

Here I am thinking; what about Mavis? Mavis is the same as I am a girl child. How come Mavis never has to do anything? How come I alone have to do everything?

Here I am standing in the presence of my father and mother. My mother is looking down on me, making my body feel like I am doing something wrong.

Here I am; wanting to be somewhere, anywhere out of the sight of my mother.

Here I am walking around my mother, walking over to the cabinet.

Here I am opening up the tablecloth, spreading it out, moving it over the dining-table.

Here I am fixing the cloth over the table, feeling my father's presence over me, realizing that my father is smiling at the body that I am.

Here I am taking the knives and forks and spoons and cups and saucers and plates and the little tea-pot stand out from the cabinet, setting the table ready for my mother and father to eat their evening meal. I am speaking. I will dish out the food.

Here I am taking the can of milk from the fridge, placing it down on the table, hearing my mother talking to her self.

Here I am inside the kitchen with my mother, watching her sharing the food onto the dinner plates.

Here I am realizing that I am going to have to sit with my mother at the dining-table.

Here I am taking my plate of food from my mother's hand.

Here I am sitting at the dinner-table, before my mother.

IAM®

Here I am looking on the face of my father wanting to eat his dinner and having to stop and listen to mummy. My mother is holding her two hands together, praying; thanking God for our daily bread.

Here I am feeling the body that I am myself shaking inside.

Here I am sitting at the dining-table, face to face with my mother, and feeling my body feeling like I do not belong where I am.

Here I am, wanting to eat the food in front of the body that I am and feeling my mother's presence making my body not want to eat; feeling my body hurting; not wanting to be in my mother's presence. I am speaking. What is the matter with the food?

Here I am. Nothing mummy; my belly is hurting me. I am not hungry. I am speaking. Eat the food now. You must think that I have money to waste on something like you. I am speaking. Pearl, you hear me say, leave the child alone. Leave Hazel alone.

Here I am hearing my father raising his voice, feeling myself hurting, wanting to leave from the sight of my mother; feeling her presence all over me.

Here I am; not wanting to hear the name Hazel, spoken in my father's house; feeling my body keep hurting; hearing my mother talking about my body to my father.

Here I am eating the food, the chicken flesh, the meat. The food is making my insides hurt.

Here I am collecting the dirty dinner plates together. I can see my father with his back turned to my mother, as if not wanting to hear my mother talking to her self, talking about all the work she one have to do everyday.

Here I am walking into the kitchen carrying the pile of plates in my hand, resting them down in the bowl inside the kitchen sink.

Here I am standing on the chair by the sink, washing clean the dirty plates and things; hearing my father raising his voice, speaking to my mother. My father is talking about my body, talking about his daughter Hazel.

Here I am with the broom cloth and bucket of hot soap water.

Here I am pushing, pulling the broom cloth along the kitchen ground, wanting the floor to look clean.

Here I am washing the broom cloth clean inside the bucket of water.

IAM®

Here I am wiping the ground under my feet. The ground that I am standing on is looking good to the body that I am feeling pleased with myself.

Here I am standing on the ground outside my father's house, pouring the dirty water from the bucket into the drain.

Here I am returning the broom cloth and bucket where they belong, at the side of the stove on the kitchen ground.

Here I am looking down on the kitchen floor, looking at the water looking shine all over the floor.

Here I am standing lone inside the kitchen, feeling good inside myself; feeling good with the body that I am.

Here I am looking on my father's face; looking down at the body that I am; looking at my father standing at the dining-room doorway, just looking, looking down at me. I am speaking. Pearl; come here, quick. Look at what your daughter has done. Good Hazel. I am speaking. You see, didn't I tell you that Hazel can do anything she put her mind to.

Here I am within the presence of my father and mother, hearing my father praising my body, making me feel good, knowing that my father is feeling good with one, knowing that I can make my mother feel good.

Here I am looking at my mother's face, smiling the sunshine expression, looking like she is feeling good with herself, knowing that she is the cause that I can do as she can do, anything if I want to put my mind to it.

Here I am wanting my father and wanting my mother to stay feeling good with one.

Here I am feeling the presence of my father making the sunshine expression; making my body feel warm all over inside my body feeling good. I am speaking. Come and sit and watch the television.

Here I am by my father's chair, sitting down on the dining-room floor, looking at the television.

Here I am looking at the television, listening to the sounds, watching the picture not understanding anything.

Here I am looking into the grey light outside my father's house.

Here I am looking up into the sky, wondering in my mind.

Here I am wondering about me; thinking about the body that I am, wondering what is going on outside my father's house.

I AM®

Here I am; not knowing what to do with myself, feeling like I want to sleep; thinking in my mind; feeling like sleep; wanting to go to my bed.

Here I am. Can I go to my bed now please mummy? I am speaking. Go on if you want to.

Here I am. Good night mummy. Good night daddy. I am speaking. Good night mi daughter.

Here I am walking into the night-light, into the hall way, walking up the stairway, feeling my way into the girl's bed-room.

Here I am reaching up the wall, turning on the room light.

Here I am looking down on my sister sleeping in her bed, hearing the sounds coming from her body.

Here I am walking into the bath-room, with my nightdress on my arm.

Here I am hearing the sound of my mother's voice; hearing my father.

Here I am turning on the hot water tap, watching the water coming into the bath.

Here I am leaning forward into the bathtub, pushing the plug into the plughole; feeling the water feeling warm on my hand.

Here I am taking off my clothes, feeling my shoulders, my neck, my back, all over my body hurting, making water full up my eyes; feeling the air cold on my body; feeling my body tremble.

Here I am kneeling inside the bath, feeling the water all around my body.

Here I am rubbing the soap on my flannel; wiping my face with my flannel; feeling the belt marks sting on my face; my neck and shoulders, and my arms; wiping my flannel over my chest, and my belly and my bottom, and my two legs, and all under my two foot, feeling my body hurting; thinking in my mind; thinking about the body that I am; hurting; wanting sleep.

Here I am lying down on my back, feeling the water feeling good, feeling warm on my body.

Here I am standing up inside the bath; ringing the water from my flannel, wiping myself, wiping my body dry.

Here I am putting the cleaning powder on the bath sponge, pulling the plug out the bath, wiping the bath inside clean, quick before the water run out.

Here I am standing on the bath-room floor, wiping my feet dry.

IAM®

Here I am putting my nightdress on, feeling my body feeling good inside, feeling clean all over the body that I am.

Here I am putting my dirty clothes into the dirty clothes basket under the sink.

Here I am standing on the side of the bath, pulling the light switch off.

Here I am inside the girl's bed-room.

Here I am inside my bed. The body that I am is feeling wide awake, looking at the light shining through the window curtain; thinking in my mind.

Here I am wondering in my mind, thinking; what can I do? Knowing, that I cannot get up now; the time is night time.

Here I am touching myself, feeling my body, feeling the touch of one self, feeling myself for the one time.

Here I am touching myself, touching my skin, feeling my skin feeling warm on my hand, feeling my body feeling good inside myself.

Here I am moving my hands over my skin.

Here I am feeling good inside myself. The body that I am is moving around fast; feeling my body trembling, feeling good, feeling my insides moving, knowing that I am making myself feel good.

Here I am touching myself, thinking about myself, wondering in my mind, wondering if everyone feel the same as I am feeling, touching myself the way that I am, feeling good with myself.

Here I am lying still, hearing the sound of my mother and father footstep coming up the stairs.

Here I am pretending to be sleeping, looking over at my mother, watching her body bending over my sister, watching mummy's hands pushing the bedclothes around Mavis's body lying inside her bed. I can see everything my mother is doing; watching my father's body standing quite at the doorway.

Here I am hearing my father doing his wee-wee inside the toilet bowl, listening to my mother walking to her bed-room.

Here I am feeling good, knowing that everyone inside the house is in their bed-room now.

Here I am feeling the silence in the air, not hearing any sound inside my father's house.

IAM®

Here I am touching myself, feeling good inside myself, knowing that I can touch myself, anytime I want, and not anyone can stop me from touching the body that I am.

Here I am knowing that I belong to me; the body that I am is mine; knowing that I can touch myself and make myself feel good.

Here I am feeling myself, feeling my touch, touching my skin all over the body that I am.

Here I am feeling myself; thinking about the body that I am; thinking in my mind; knowing that the body I am is my own; the place where I belong.

Here I am feeling myself, feeling good, knowing that I belong; feeling good inside the body that I am; wanting to sleep.

IAM®

CHAPTER 9

Here I am looking over at my sister Mavis, lying still inside her bed, sounding like she is not ready to get up. The time is day light. I can feel the sun shining through the window curtain, shining over onto the body that I am.

Here I am feeling the sun all over my body, feeling wide awake, feeling good inside myself, not wanting to stay in my bed.

Here I am standing on the bed-room floor, looking at the body that I am, looking at myself inside the dressing-table mirror.

Here I am wondering at the face that I can see, remembering the feeling of myself touching myself, feeling good, thinking about the body that I am, looking at myself, looking into the eye I am, looking at me inside the dressing-table mirror.

Here I am walking to the bath-room, hearing Ruel's voice, hearing George's voice.

Here I am standing outside my brother's bed-room, knocking on the door, walking slow into the room, looking at Ruel holding something under the bedclothes, looking at George's face with his eyes wide open, just looking at one.

Here I am. Good morning Ruel. Good morning George. What are you doing? I am speaking. What do you want?

Here I am. I have just come to see you.

Here I am walking into the bath-room, thinking in my mind, wondering what Ruel and George have they do not want me to know about.

Here I am wiping my face, wondering why Ruel and George do not like the body that I am their sister.

Here I am walking to the girl's bed-room, hearing sounds coming from my mother's bed-room.

Here I am standing inside the girl's bed-room, standing before the dressing-table mirror, putting on my clean cotton house dress, feeling the body that I am moving inside, wondering if daddy is at home.

Here I am folding my night-dress, putting it under my pillow, making up my bed to look good.

Here I am looking around the space where I am, making sure that every thing inside the room is where it belongs.

IAM®

Here I am walking down the stairs, walking to the pantry.

Here I am with the floor polish and floor cloth, walking towards the front doorway.

Here I am on my toes, reaching up, opening the front door.

Here I am standing at the open doorway, feeling the air surrounding my body, smelling the air tasting good to the body that I am.

Here I am; smelling the air, feeling the sun shining warm on my body, feeling the morning air about the body that I am.

Here I am on my knees, wiping the cloth inside the polish, polishing the front doorstep. I can hear footsteps coming near to where I am inside the front doorway of my father's house.

Here I am looking at the body of a man walking pass the gateway of my father's house.

Here I am polishing the brick red doorstep, polishing it to look shine.

Here I am closing the door, walking to the pantry, returning the floor polish and cloth down on the shelf where it belong.

Here I am inside the kitchen, getting the broom, walking to the front doorway.

Here I am sweeping the hall way, sweeping the dust forward, sweeping it onto the dining-room floor.

Here I am inside the kitchen, taking the newspaper from under the kitchen sink.

Here I am with the shovel and bucket and newspaper in my hand.

Here I am inside the dining-room, placing everything down on the ground before the coal fire.

Here I am opening out the newspaper on the ground before the coal fire.

Here I am picking up the ashes with the shovel, taking time, emptying the ashes into the bucket standing on the fire hearth.

Here I am standing by the dining-room entrance, lifting the bucket of ashes onto the kitchen doormat.

Here I am turning the key inside the kitchen door, turning the kitchen door handle, opening the kitchen door.

IAM®

Here I am lifting the bucket of ashes down onto the ground outside my father's house.

Here I am looking over the ground.

Here I am lifting the bucket of ashes with my two hands, walking, dropping the bucket on the ground, lifting, walking, dropping the bucket, walking to the end of the garden by the chicken house; emptying the bucket of ashes along side the garden fence wall where my mother empty the ashes; feeling the air blowing the ashes up all over my hands and dress; onto my face.

Here I am looking over the ground, looking over the wooden fence that belongs to the other people, the neighbours surrounding my father's land on all sides.

Here I am looking into the chicken house, feeling the air surrounding my body, smelling good.

Here I am walking towards the house, walking along the footpath, walking to the coal house, carrying the bucket and shovel inside my two hand.

Here I am standing on my toes; reaching my hand; pushing up the lock on the coal house door.

Here I am shovelling up the coal with the shovel inside my two hands, filling up the bucket with coal, and some stick wood off the coal house ground.

Here I am lifting the bucket full with coal, dropping it down on the ground, feeling the bucket pulling down the body that I am walking towards the kitchen, feeling the bucket of coal making my body hurt, lifting it up onto the kitchen doorstep.

Here I am inside the kitchen, standing on the doormat, lifting the coal bucket onto the dining-room door step, lifting the coal bucket onto the fire hearth, remembering the coal house door is open.

Here I am outside the house, pushing the coal house door lock down, making sure the coal house door is shut tight.

Here I am standing inside the kitchen, remembering the match box and the coal light to light the fire.

Here I am standing before the open fire hole, making up the fire, putting the coal into the fire hole, placing the pieces of stick wood onto the coal.

Here I am rolling the pieces of newspaper tight together, placing it between the coals.

I AM®

Here I am making up the fire, placing the white brick coal light amongst the pieces of wood, and coal inside the fire hole, building the fire the way my mother make-up the fire, wanting the fire to burn just right.

Here I am lighting the coal light with the burning match inside my hand. I can see the fire flame burning the paper, lighting the wood, smoking the coal, making the fire burn.

Here I am holding up the newspaper over the fire hole, wanting the fire to burn even, just like my mother do to make the fire burn right. I can hear the fire sounding like it is burning, just like my mother make the fire burn bright, hot with flames.

Here I am with the broom in my hand, sweeping the dust from the fire hearth into the shovel, emptying it out on the fire, feeling the heat hot on the body that I am.

Here I am standing on the kitchen ground, putting the coal bucket and shovel by the stove where it belong in the corner.

Here I am standing on the chair by the sink, putting the washing up liquid inside my hands, rubbing my hands together, washing my hands clean under the cold water.

Here I am feeling good inside myself, wondering in my mind.

Here I am thinking; wondering what mummy is going to say when she sees the fire already made up and burning just right.

Here I am feeling good with myself.

Here I am; wanting to make everything inside the dining-room look good, wanting my mother to feel good with me, wanting to do everything that I can do to help mummy with her housework.

Here I am inside the pantry, getting the spray polish and cloth, wanting to polish everything inside the dining-room.

Here I am wiping the polish over the television box, rubbing it shine, polishing the dining-table, polishing the chairs, polishing the sideboard, polishing the fire surround, wiping it all the way around, down into the hearth, feeling the marble bricks under my hand, feeling hot, feeling the fire burning hot; making my face and hands feel hot.

Here I am polishing everything inside the dining-room, shining everything I can polish inside the dining-room. The air in the dining-room is feeling warm, smelling good.

IAM®

Here I am thinking; mummy can have a long rest now, everything is looking good.

Here I am inside the kitchen, standing on the chair, putting cold water inside the kettle.

Here I am with the burning match in my hand, lighting the fire under the kettle, turning the button control down low, making ready to make mummy a cup of tea when she get up. I can hear someone coming into the dining-room. I can hear everything that is happening here inside my father's house. I am speaking. Hazel.

Here I am. Yes mummy. I am speaking. A you make the fire?

Here I am. Yes mummy. I woke up early.

I am speaking. My God; who tell you to make the fire?

Here I am. Nobody mummy; I made the fire the other day when you were sleeping. I am speaking. It was you make the fire?

Here I am hearing my mother, looking at my mother's expression with the look that I am not understanding, looking like she is not feeling good inside herself, looking like she do not know what to do with herself, making the body that I am feel for my mother, wanting to understand, wanting to help my mother.

Here I am inside the kitchen putting the tea into the little teapot, thinking in my mind, thinking about my mother, wondering what is happening to my mother now.

Here I am standing on the chair by the stove, holding the cloth over the kettle handle, pouring the hot water into the tea-pot, making the tea for mummy; thinking in my mind; mummy is acting different now.

Here I am standing inside the kitchen, lifting the chair over by the sink.

Here I am standing on the chair with the kettle in my hand, watching the cold water falling inside the kettle; thinking about my mother. My mother is making the noise that I am not; understanding.

Here I am wondering what is happening to my mother.

Here I am returning the kettle on top of the fire, wondering if mummy and daddy have words with each other again, to make mummy change her way of acting.

IAM®

Here I am inside the dining-room, standing on the chair by the cabinet, taking out one cup and saucer and the teaspoon and teapot stand, resting them down on the dining-table, and feeling my mother's presence not shouting at one.

Here I am looking at my mother's body just sitting by the fire, looking lone inside her self.

Here I am taking the sugar bowl from the cabinet, placing it down on the table, hearing my mother speaking to herself.

Here I am looking inside the fridge, taking the can of milk out of the fridge, placing it down on the dining-table.

Here I am inside the kitchen, walking into the dining-room, carrying the pot of tea, thinking in my mind, thinking; mummy is not acting like herself this morning.

Here I am pouring the tea into the cup, feeling my body wanting to help my mother, wanting mummy to feel good.

Here I am. Here is a cup of tea mummy. Is there anything wrong mummy? Are you sick mummy? I am speaking. No; I am pregnant; I am going to have a baby.

Here I am talking with my mother, understanding the reason why my mother is behaving different now.

Here I am thinking about my mother, feeling good, knowing that mummy is pregnant; going to have a baby.

Here I am looking at my mother, thinking in my mind, wanting mummy to have a girl baby so I can have someone to talk to and play with inside the house.

Here I am in the presence of my mother and wondering, wondering what it is like to have a baby. I am speaking. Hazel. I am going to have a lie down. Look after your brother them.

Here I am. Yes mummy. Shall I bring daddy a cup of tea? I am speaking. Your father is at work. He is working shift work. He will be home after lunch.

Here I am listening to my mother's voice talking to me.

Here I am realizing that my mother is sick.

IAM®

Here I am; understanding that the baby mummy is having is making mummy act different. My mother is moving slow, walking across the dining-room, into the hall way, dragging her foot along the floor.

Here I am standing by the fire, thinking about my mother; pregnant; thinking; mummy is having a baby.

Here I am returning the sugar bowl inside the cabinet, realizing that I am my mother's helper.

Here I am returning the milk can inside the fridge.

Here I am feeling the feeling that I am feeling, feeling good, understanding and knowing that I can do everything there is to do inside my father's house.

Here I am wondering in my mind, wondering what would happen to mummy now, if I was not here to help her; knowing how she is feeling, looking like she cannot help her self; pregnant; having a baby and daddy has gone to the factory to work.

Here I am; understanding the body that I am is feeling for my mother; knowing that it is my mother that makes the body that I am feels the way that I am feeling; feeling for her body.

Here I am walking into the kitchen with the tea-pot and cup and saucer in my hand.

Here I am; understanding my mother and her body feelings.

Here I am; knowing that my father does not realize how much work to do inside his house.

Here I am; knowing how much work to do each day, just to make the house inside look clean and tidy.

Here I am walking up the stairs, walking into the girl's bed-room; looking at my sister Mavis looking wide awake now.

Here I am. Guess what Mavis? Are you getting up now? Guess what? Mummy is pregnant and going to have a baby.

Here I am looking at the body of my sister, looking at my body; just looking at one.

Here I am wondering if Mavis understands me, looking at her body running out from the room, as if not wanting to speak to the body that I am her sister.

IAM®

Here I am feeling good, walking to Ruel and George's bed-room.

Here I am standing outside my brother's bed-room, knocking on the door, wanting to tell Ruel and George about mummy; pregnant; going to have a baby.

Here I am. Ruel, George, Ruel; can I come in? I am speaking. Wait a minute Hazel. You can come in now.

Here I am feeling good, wondering what Ruel and George have to hide now.

Here I am looking at Ruel; looking at George.

Here I am. Guess what? Mummy is pregnant; going to have a baby. She is lying down. You have to get up now. Your room smells. I am speaking. So what?

Here I am. Are you glad? I am. I hope mummy have a girl baby. You and George better keep quiet. Mummy is not well. She is having a lie down and daddy is at work. What is the smell? Have you wet the bed again? Have you George, Ruel? Come on Delroy. I am going to get you dress and then make the breakfast.

Ruel; you and George get up now and clean up your room as well. Mummy said I must look after us.

IAM®

CHAPTER 10

Here I am in the bath-room with Delroy.

Here I am taking off Delroy's wet clothes. Delroy is smelling rank with wee-wee.

God Delroy. Your do-do stinks. Delroy, we are going to have a new baby. Mummy is having a baby.

Here I am holding the nappy full of do-do, shaking the do-do into the toilet bowl.

Here I am putting the nappy into the nappy bucket, realizing the nappy bucket is full of dirty nappy.

Here I am standing on the toilet seat, pulling the chain down, hearing Delroy singing to him self, lying on the bath-room floor.

Here I am putting water into the bowl.

Here I am wiping Delroy's body clean, wiping the flannel all over his body, making Delroy's body smell clean.

Here I am on my toes, reaching into the hot water tank, wanting a towel, wanting to wipe Delroy's body dry.

Here I am spreading the towel on the bath-room floor, lifting Delroy's body on top, wiping Delroy's skin dry.

Here I am remembering the baby oil and powder, and clean clothes for Delroy to put on.

Here I am. Stay there Delroy; I am going to get you some clean clothes.

Here I am inside the boy's bed-room taking the baby powder and oil, and Delroy's baby clothes from his cupboard drawer.

Here I am inside the bath-room, kneeling down before Delroy, wiping the olive oil on Delroy's skin, feeling Delroy's body feeling warm on my hand, rubbing the oil into Delroy's skin, watching Delroy's body lying down on his back, smiling up at one.

Here I am looking at Delroy's body looking clean and shine.

Here I am folding the nappy halfway, pushing it under Delroy's fat bottom. Delroy's bottom is bleeding around his do-do and we-we.

I AM®

Here I am rubbing some vaseline over the red sore bumpy rash marks on Delroy's bottom. Delroy's body is hurting from my hand rubbing vaseline onto his sore bottom.

Here I am putting the baby powder over Delroy's bottom, making Delroy's body smell good.

Here I am putting on Delroy's clothes; watching Delroy moving his body about on the floor, and smiling up at me; making my body feel good.

Here I am looking down on Delroy's body; thinking in my mind, thinking you; look good Delroy.

Here I am putting all Delroy's dirty clothes into the basket with all the other dirty clothes; folding up the towel, returning it into the hot water tank where it belong.

Here I am feeling good with myself, returning the oil and vaseline and powder inside the cupboard drawer where they belong.

Here I am. Come on Delroy, I am going to make you a drink now.

Here I am with Delroy inside the girl's bed-room.

Here I am making up Mavis's bed, making it look good.

Here I am pulling the window curtain open, letting the day light shine into the bed-room, making everything look good.

Here I am on my knees, looking under Mavis's bed, looking for the potty. The potty is full again.

Here I am. You stay there Delroy.

Here I am looking at Delroy's body sitting down on the bed-room floor, looking up at me, smiling all over his face.

Here I am walking into the hall way; carrying the potty, walking to the bath-room.

Here I am standing at the bath-room doorway, looking at Ruel with my flannel in his hand.

Here I am. That is my flannel you are using Ruel. Where is yours? I am speaking. It's only a cloth.

Here I am. Give me my cloth then. You have one of your own. This one is mine. Thank you. You can go and find yours where you put it.

IAM®

Here I am putting water into Mavis's potty, washing away the smell, listening to Ruel talking to himself.

Here I am standing on the toilet seat, pulling the toilet chain down.

Here I am walking to the girl's bed-room, holding the potty in my hand, returning it under Mavis's bed where it belongs. Come on Delroy, we are going down stairs now.

Here I am walking down the stairs, watching Delroy's body coming down on his hands and body sliding backwards down the stairs.

Here I am inside the dining-room with Delroy.

Here I am lifting Delroy's body up into his pram.

Here I am looking at the fire, looking like it is going out.

Here I am inside the kitchen, lifting the coal bucket, walking into the dining-room, resting it down on the hearth.

Here I am shovelling the coal on the fire, wanting the fire to stay alive and warm for daddy to come home to.

Here I am lifting the coal bucket and shovel, walking inside the kitchen, resting it down on the ground by the stove where it belongs.

Here I am with the brush and shovel, walking into the dining-room.

Here I am sweeping away the coal dust from the fire surround, emptying it onto the fire, wanting to keep the dining-room looking clean for my mother.

Here I am returning the brush and shovel under the kitchen sink where it belong.

Here I am hearing Delroy's voice making to cry; remembering Delroy haven't had his milk yet.

Here I am taking the little saucepan from the kitchen cupboard, resting it down on the worktop.

Here I am walking into the dining-room, getting the milk bottle from the fridge, hearing Delroy making noise as if he is wanting; his milk now.

Here I am standing on the chair pouring the milk from the bottle into the little saucepan.

Here I am standing inside the kitchen, lifting down the saucepan of milk of the worktop, resting it down on top of the stove.

I AM®

Here I am with the burning match in my hand lighting the fire under the saucepan. I can hear Delroy crying out wanting his milk.

Here I am. I am here Delroy. Look; I'll open the door so you can hear me inside the kitchen.

Here I am standing on the chair by the sink, washing Delroy's bottle clean, putting it down on the draining-board, ready to put the milk inside.

Here I am hearing the milk boiling, turning off the fire quick; not wanting the milk to boil out over the pan.

Here I am standing on the kitchen ground, lifting the saucepan down off the stove, walking slow, walking over to the draining-board, placing it down on top.

Here I am lifting the pot of tea down off the stove, placing it down on the draining-board, making ready to make Delroy's milk-tea.

Here I am standing on the chair by the sink, pouring the tea into the bottle, pouring the milk into the bottle, watching the milk fill up to the top marking inside the bottle.

Here I am screwing the top onto the bottle, shaking the bottle, mixing the tea, making Delroy his morning drink.

Here I am turning on the cold water, resting the bottle inside the saucepan, filling the pan with cold water, running over the bottle, wanting the milk to cool just right for Delroy to drink.

Here I am Delroy. Here; your milk is ready now.

Here I am looking at Delroy drinking down his milk, drinking, quick. I can see Delroy is thirsty, the way he is drinking the milk down fast.

Here I am walking into the kitchen, opening the dining-room door wide for Delroy to here me doing inside the kitchen.

Here I am taking the big saucepan from the kitchen cupboard placing it down on top of the stove.

Here I am standing on the chair putting water inside the kettle.

Here I am standing on the chair by the stove, pouring the water from the kettle into the big saucepan.

Here I am getting everything to make oats porridge for our breakfast.

IAM®

Here I am with the burning match in my hand, lighting the fire under the saucepan.

Here I am walking into the dining-room, looking at Delroy playing by himself, playing with his hands; hearing Delroy making the happy sound making my body feel good just looking at my baby brother. Delroy.

Here I am taking the bottle of milk from the fridge; and the margarine.

Here I am looking inside the bottom of the cabinet safe, looking for the box of oats.

Here I am walking into the kitchen with everything in my hand, placing them down on the worktop.

Here I am walking into the dining-room, picking up Delroy's feeding bottle off the dining-room floor where Delroy has dropped it.

Here I am standing on the chair by the stove, pouring half the milk into the saucepan, wanting the milk to boil with the water.

Here I am standing on the chair by the worktop.

Here I am pouring the oats into the cup, emptying it into the little saucepan; measuring out; one, two, three, four cup full of oats into the pan, preparing to make the porridge for our breakfast.

Here I am pouring the balance of milk from the bottle into the little saucepan, pouring it on top of the oats; mixing the milk and the oats the way I see my mother prepare the porridge.

Here I am standing on the chair, standing over the stove, holding the saucepan of porridge mix, pouring the porridge into the big saucepan of hot milk, mixing everything together with the big wood spoon.

Here I am looking; standing on the chair over the stove; looking into the saucepan of porridge; looking at the porridge; looking like it is set hard in the pan.

Here I am feeling myself feeling hot, feeling the water coming out onto my face, feeling the heat from the fire all over me.

Here I am thinking; thinking; wondering what to do; looking at the porridge set hard in the pan.

Here I am remembering what mummy does when she is making porridge; mummy pours hot water into the pan.

IAM®

Here I am standing on the chair, winding the dishcloth around my hand, lifting the kettle off the stove, pouring the boiling water onto the porridge; watching the porridge popping bubbles inside the pot.

Here I am mixing the water into the porridge, stirring, mixing the porridge around and around with the big wood spoon; watching the porridge looking good now, looking like the porridge is full up inside the pan; looking just like the porridge I see mummy make.

Here I am with the tub of margarine in my hand.

Here I am standing on the chair with the knife in my hand, marking off about a table spoon of margarine; the way I see mummy do it; putting it into the saucepan with the porridge; mixing the margarine into the porridge; watching the porridge looking good; ready to eat.

Here I am sharing out the salt onto the little teaspoon, putting it into the saucepan, mixing it into the porridge.

Here I am walking into the dining-room, standing on the chair by the cabinet, getting the parcel of sugar.

Here I am inside the kitchen, standing on the chair over the stove, holding the big cooking spoon in my hand, putting one, two, three and another one big spoon full of sugar into the saucepan, stirring the porridge around, mixing everything together, making the porridge to eat for our breakfast.

Here I am blowing on the spoonful of porridge, tasting the porridge, burning my lip, tasting the porridge, tasting good.

Here I am feeling good with myself, standing on the chair, stirring the porridge around, and around with the big wood cooking spoon, stirring the porridge around, thinking in my mind; feeling good with myself knowing that I can make the porridge just like mummy can.

Here I am standing on the kitchen ground, putting the dirty milk pan and things into the washing-up bowl, realizing to myself. I can do everything that mummy want me to do. I am speaking. What you doing Hazel?

Here I am. I am making the porridge for our breakfast. Look George. I am speaking. It looks good Hazel. I am hungry.

Here I am. Have you and Ruel clean your room? I am speaking. I have clean my part of the room.

Here I am listening to George speaking, listening at the sound like someone coming into the dining-room. I am speaking. Is breakfast ready yet Hazel?

IAM®

Here I am. Yes, I have made porridge; have a look Ruel. George, will you butter the bread and set the table for us. I nearly finish. Put those things away please Ruel.

Here I am standing on the chair washing clean the dirty cooking things, wanting the kitchen to look clean again.

Here I am walking into the dining-room, standing on the chair by the cabinet, getting the porridge bowls, placing them down on the dining-table.

Here I am walking into the kitchen, carrying the bowls, lifting them up onto the worktop.

Here I am with the spoon like cup, standing on the chair with a bowl in my hand, filling the spoon cup full with porridge, pouring the porridge into the bowls.

Here I am. Ruel; will you come and help me please. I am speaking. Here I am. What you want me to do Hazel?

Here I am. Take this one for me please and pass me another bowl. I am speaking. The porridge looks good Hazel. Who is this one for Hazel?

Here I am. Yours if you want it. Do you want some more. I am speaking. Yes please, I am hungry.

Here I am pouring the porridge into the bowl.

Here I am feeling good with myself.

Here I am remembering Mavis.

Here I am. Has anyone call Mavis? I am speaking. Mavis is in the dining-room.

Here I am putting the cover on the saucepan, looking at the buttons on the stove, making sure all the stove buttons is turned to the off mark.

Here I am putting the chair at the side of the stove where it belongs.

Here I am walking into the dining-room, carrying my bowl full with porridge.

Here I am sitting down at the dining-table with Ruel and George and Mavis, watching everyone eating their porridge. I can see Delroy is awake sitting up in his pram looking over at us eating. Delroy is making up noise wanting his porridge now. The porridge taste good.

Here I am eating, listening to George sounding like he is liking the porridge. I am speaking. Is there any more Hazel?

IAM®

Here I am. Yes, I made too much. Go and have some more. We have to finish it now.

Here I am giving Delroy his porridge. Delroy is sounding like he is liking the porridge. Delroy is swallowing every spoon full as soon as I put it into his mouth and acting like he wants more.

Here I am. Is mummy still sleeping Mavis? I am speaking. No; mummy is lying down.

Here I am walking into the kitchen with the empty bowls in my hands, placing them down in the washing-up bowl inside the sink.

Here I am feeling the feeling that I am feeling, wondering if mummy is getting better.

Here I am standing on the chair over the sink, turning the hot water tap on, pouring the washing-up liquid into the bowl, washing up the dirty things, putting them down on the draining-board.

Here I am. Bring your dirty things here please.

Here I am washing the dirty breakfast things, thinking in my mind; thinking. I am speaking. Where do you want them Hazel?

Here I am. Put them inside here. Is there any more? I am tired now.

Here I am wiping the breakfast things dry.

Here I am listening to Ruel and George laughing out loud.

Here I am listening to the sound of my brothers playing; feeling the body that I am hurting; wanting to stop working now but knowing that I cannot.

Here I am putting everything away where they belong inside the kitchen cupboard.

Here I am returning the chair by the stove where it belongs.

Here I am walking into the dining-room, carrying the bowls into the dining-room, placing them down on the table.

Here I am standing on the chair by the cabinet, returning the bowls inside the cabinet where they belong.

Here I am walking into the kitchen, gathering up the spoons off the worktop, carrying them into the dining-room, standing on the chair putting them away inside the cabinet drawer where they belong.

IAM®

Here I am within the presence of my brothers, watching my sister, watching Mavis walking away from me, looking as if she does not want to be in my presence. My body is hurting.

Here I am looking at Ruel, looking at George playing the game of cards with each other; looking at Delroy lying on his back; gone into sleep again.

Here I am, just one.

IAM®

CHAPTER 11

Here I am standing inside the dining-room.

Here I am standing by the fire, listening to the sounds coming from my brother's bed-room on top of the dining-room.

Here I am thinking in my mind, wondering what to do with myself. I can hear the sound like my mother's breathing, coming towards the dining-room.

Here I am feeling my inside go round, feeling my mother's presence at the dining-room entrance. I am speaking. What are you standing there looking at? Go and do something.

Here I am hearing my mother.

Here I am feeling hurt inside, feeling the water full up in my eyes.

Here I am walking quick, not wanting to stay in my mother's presence.

Here I am walking into the hall way, thinking in my mind, thinking, wondering what to do now.

Here I am inside the pantry.

Here I am looking around the room, looking at all the things on the floor making the pantry look dirty.

Here I am taking the things off the shelf, placing them down on the floor.

Here I am; wanting to make the pantry room look good. I can hear mummy speaking to Mavis.

Here I am looking at all the things on the floor, looking at all the things making the pantry look untidy.

Here I am walking through the dining-room, feeling my mother's eyes on me.

Here I am inside the kitchen, looking for the dustpan and hand-brush.

Here I am walking pass my mother and Mavis. I can feel their eyes just looking at me.

Here I am inside the pantry, sweeping the dust off the shelf; thinking about the body that I am, wondering why my mother never likes to see my body doing nothing.

Here I am putting everything in its right place on the shelf.

Here I am putting all the old clothes into the big plastic bag.

IAM®

Here I am sweeping the pantry floor, wanting the room to look good.

Here I am putting everything where it belongs.

Here I am inside the little cupboard next to the pantry. I can see my father's old work jacket hanging on the hook in the wall; and my father's shoe on the floor; and some of mummy's old house shoes beside it. The cupboard is looking clean again. I am speaking. Move out of my way.

Here I am feeling hurt with my mother the way she just shove pass me with Delroy on her arm; watching Mavis's body following after her.

Here I am thinking; mummy behaves like she does not like me.

Here I am feeling hurt inside, thinking in my mind; wondering.

Here I am thinking about school, wanting to be at school, wanting to be out of my mother's presence, away from my father's house. I can hear someone at the front door. I can hear my mother coming down the stairs; someone is knocking on the front door of my father's house.

Here I am standing at the corner of the hall way, listening to my mother speaking to someone sounding like a woman's body speaking. I can hear my mother calling her to come into the house.

Here I am hearing everything my mother is saying to the woman. I can hear them walking into the back bed-room.

Here I am wondering in my mind, wondering, who is she?

Here I am wondering, what is she here for? I am speaking. Hazel, Ruel, George, come here, hurry.

Here I am standing at the bottom of the stair, listening to my mother talking to the woman. I am speaking. Who is it Hazel?

Here I am. A woman I think.

Here I am with Ruel and George, walking into the back bed-room, looking at the body of the woman sitting down on the chair, holding her hand-bag on her lap, leaning forward, looking; just looking with a smile on her face.

Here I am wondering; who are you? I am speaking. Come closer and let the woman take a good look at you.

Here I am looking at the white woman smiling all over her face.

Here I am listening to the woman talking about Ruel and George to my mother. The woman is talking about getting some clothes for me. I can see

I AM®

my mother making up her face at the woman. My mother is raising her voice shouting at the woman. The woman is standing up now, looking like she doesn't know what to do with herself, hearing the words my mother is saying to her. I am speaking. Get out of my house. Who do you think I am? bringing all your dirty old things here. Get out and don't you come back.

Here I am looking at the woman's body moving fast into the hall way.

Here I am watching my mother with her hands raised; watching the woman walking, running out of the house.

Here I am wondering what the woman done to make mummy angry at her like that. I am speaking. You, you see you, I am going to kill you.

Here I am feeling my mother's hand across my face.

Here I am hurting, hearing my mother's words.

Here I am wondering in my mind, thinking; what have I done?

Here I am wishing that my father will come home. My mother is acting sick again; wanting to kill me.

Here I am hurting, not knowing why my mother is always taking her anger out on me.

Here I am wondering; what have I done? What have I done to make mummy act out of control again. I am speaking. Come up here Hazel. Come and tidy up the things in the tank.

Here I am inside the bath-room.

Here I am looking at my mother's body, her face looking mad, looking like she is ready to kill me.

Here I am standing on the toilet seat, taking the clothes out of the tank.

Here I am folding up the clothes, knowing that it is Ruel and George that keep making everything their hands touch look out of place, messy; but I am the one that my mother keep blaming for the mess the house is in.

Here I am inside the bath-room, listening to my mother talking to herself, listening to her hands rubbing the wet clothes, washing the clothes over the bath.

Here I am putting everything where they belong inside the hot water tank.

Here I am hearing every word my mother is speaking to herself.

IAM®

Here I am wondering if mummy realizes that I can hear every word that she is saying; and that I can understand every word that I am hearing. I am speaking. The sooner you get out of my sight the better.

Here I am; the girl body that I am is hurting; hearing the words my mother is speaking, talking about one.

Here I am; wanting my father to come home.

Here I am hurting, not knowing what to do with myself, feeling unable to stop the water coming into my eyes, not wanting my mother to see me crying. I am speaking. Shut up, shut up, you hear me. Shut up before I box you; give you something to really cry for.

Here I am feeling my mother's hand on my face, feeling my mother's hand beating my body, just beating me.

Here I am hurting, wanting to get away from my mother; my body is burning, hurting, my mouth is bleeding.

Here I am hurting, knowing that my mother is the cause of all her hard work, knowing that all she has to do is show Ruel and George how to do the things she show me to do.

Here I am hurting, knowing that my mother does not realize that she is the cause of all that is happening here inside my father's house, the building where I am present day in and day out.

Here I am walking down the stair, walking into the dining-room.

Here I am hearing my mother doing inside the kitchen, feeling my body inside feeling lone, looking at my sister.

Here I am sitting down on the chair, sitting by the dining-room window, looking out into the air, wondering about the body that I am.

Here I am thinking, feeling my mother's presence coming into the dining-room, feeling my body inside go round, changing, moving round fast. I am speaking. You sitting down again?; isn't there anything you can do? Go and get the ironing board and bring it in here.

Here I am inside the pantry, lifting the iron-board feeling heavy in my hands.

Here I am walking into the dining-room, dragging the ironing-board down the step, standing the board up to the height that I am, ready to do the ironing.

Here I am inside the pantry, lifting the iron down off the shelf, walking into the dining-room, resting the iron down on the board.

IAM®

Here I am walking along the hall way, walking into the back bed-room, lifting the washing basket off the floor, walking, falling; carrying the basket full with clothes.

Here I am standing before the iron-board.

Here I am looking into the washing basket, looking at all the things that I have to iron.

Here I am on my knees, under the television table, pushing the iron plug into the socket on the wall.

Here I am sorting the clothes inside the basket, thinking what to iron first.

Here I am thinking in my mind. Daddy believes that mummy is the only one cleaning and doing everything there is to do in his house.

Here I am thinking. Daddy do not realize that mommy only clean the parts of the house she want to clean and order my body to clean and do every other thing that she does not like her hands to touch.

Here I am walking towards the kitchen, walking pass my mother. I am speaking. Where are you going?

Here I am hearing my mother's voice; moving my body quick away from my mother's raised hand; feeling my mother hands keep hitting the body that I am.

Here I am. I am going to the kitchen to get the clothes peg-bag to put the clothes peg in mummy.

Here I am inside the kitchen; taking the peg-bag off the hook on the kitchen wall; thinking in my mind; wondering why my mother never say that she is sorry when she hit my body for no reason.

Here I am on my knee, kneeling before the washing basket, putting the clothes peg into the peg-bag, feeling my mother's eyes; just looking at me.

Here I am thinking; mummy thinks that her body is the only body that can feel hurt.

Here I am hurting, hurting inside; feeling lone. I am speaking Hurry up and start the ironing so I can see what you are doing. It cost money to burn the electric you know.

Here I am walking fast into the kitchen, returning the clothes peg-bag on the wall hook where it belongs.

IAM®

Here I am feeling my body shaking, walking into the dining-room.

Here I am standing before the iron-board, feeling the presence of my mother looking at one.

Here I am pressing the pillow case.

Here I am feeling hurt, feeling the hot iron burn on my hand.

Here I am hurting not wanting my mother to see the water coming into my eyes. My hand is hurting; the iron mark is burning my hand.

Here I am pressing the pillow case, hurting inside, knowing that my sister is standing by mummy, making up her face, holding out her tongue at me, making my body hurt. I can hear my father outside at the kitchen door.

Here I am feeling my inside go round, feeling good, knowing that daddy's come home.

Here I am looking up on the body of my father walking into the dining-room. Daddy is smiling down on the body that I am, watching my body doing the ironing.

Here I am feeling glad; daddy's home; knowing that mummy will stop shouting at me now daddy is here. I am speaking. Pearl. How many times must I tell you; Hazel is too little to iron the clothes? I am speaking. Granti; you leave Hazel to me. Hazel is a girl child. Look; Hazel can iron. Look at what she done. I am speaking. Never mind that.

Here I am hearing my father, listening to my mother, watching my mother making up to my father.

Here I am putting George's shirt flat on the iron-board, wondering; how to iron the shirt. I am speaking. This is how you iron the shirts.

Here I am looking at my mother demonstrating her words; watching her hand moving the shirt top around the iron-board corner, watching her press the shirt top, watching her hand moving the shirt around on the ironing board, pressing all the different parts of the shirt, making the shirt look like new.

Here I am thinking; mommy can make things look good.

Here I am looking at the shirt that my mother just finished ironing. There is no iron mark on the shirt, no creasing on the shirt, the shirt look like new.

Here I am with the other shirt, ironing it the way mummy show me how to press away the creasing out of the cloth.

IAM®

Here I am feeling good with myself, ironing the shirt, wanting it to look as good as mummy iron the shirts to look good.

Here I am pressing my dress with lots of folds in it, causing me to spend time on it, wanting it to look good. Ouch; feeling the iron burn hot on my hand; feeling my hand burning hot, making my body feel wet inside my clothes.

Here I am ironing, hurting inside, feeling the burn mark on my hand holding the iron feeling heavy in my hand; feeling myself wanting to cry out loud; crying inside; not wanting my mother to see me crying, not knowing what to do with myself. I am speaking. Pearl, you see what I mean. I am speaking. How else she going to understand? Where do you think all these marks on my hands come from? She will learn to be careful. Go and run the cold water on your hand.

Here I am inside the kitchen, standing on the chair over the sink, holding my hand under the cold water, feeling my body hurting, feeling tired.

Here I am feeling lone, looking at the burn mark changing colour on my skin; puffing up; feeling the burning feeling going away.

Here I am inside the dining-room, standing before the ironing-board, pressing my dress, hanging my dress over the chair back.

Here I am pressing the pillowcase. I am speaking. Pearl; how come Hazel is looking like that? Where are all Hazel's clothes? Every time me see my daughter, she always have on the same old frock.

Here I am under the television table, pulling the plug out the wall socket.

Here I am listening to my father talking about my body, talking to my mother.

Here I am listening to my mother sounding like she does not want to answer my father.

Here I am under the television table, positioning the iron to sand up on the floor to cool down.

Here I am making the iron-board flat, resting it on the wall, opening the dining-room door, lifting the ironing-board up the step, lifting the ironing-board into the pantry, resting the board against the pantry wall.

Here I am walking into the dining-room, picking up the pile of clothes off the dining-room table, feeling the presence of my mother and my father making my body not know what to do with itself, not wanting to be where I am.

IAM®

Here I am holding the pile of ironed clothes against my body, opening the door, walking along the hall way, walking up the stairs, on my way to the girl's bed-room, resting the pile of clothes down on my bed, sorting them into different piles.

Here I am putting Mavis's clothes into her dressing-table drawer; putting my clothes into my dressing-table drawer.

Here I am walking towards my brother's bed-room, hearing the sound like daddy and mummy is coming up the stairs.

Here I am standing outside my brother's bed-room, knocking on the door, hearing Ruel's voice.

Here I am walking into the bed-room, looking at Ruel, looking into the comic book, looking at George stretched out on the bed, pretending to not know that I am in their presence.

Here I am putting my brother's clothes away inside their dressing table drawer where they belong.

Here I am looking at Ruel and George ironed clothes all scrambled up inside the drawer; making my body feel hurt; wondering why I have to keep ironing their clothes when they cant be bothered to keep them tidy in the drawer.

Here I am walking away, walking into the hall way, walking down the stairs, hearing my mother's voice talking to my father; realizing that mummy and daddy always go into their bed-room whenever they want to talk about us.

Here I am inside the dining-room, getting the washing basket, carrying it to the pantry where it belongs.

IAM®

CHAPTER 12

Here I am inside the dining-room, sitting down on the chair at the window; looking at my sister looking at me, looking at her. I am speaking. What you looking at?

Here I am watching Mavis run across the dining-room floor, moving quick into the hall way.

Here I am thinking in my mind; Mavis does not like being in the same room as the body that I am. Mavis does not like being alone with me.

Here I am thinking in my mind, thinking about me and my sister Mavis, knowing that Mavis is up stairs in mummy and daddy's bed-room.

Here I am thinking, hearing footsteps coming towards the dining-room; watching Mavis coming into the dining-room; looking like she is crying.

Here I am. What is the matter Mavis? I am speaking. None of your business.

Here I am looking at Mavis sucking her finger, looking like she does not know what to do with herself, not wanting to be in my presence.

Here I am looking into my hands, thinking about myself.

Here I am looking at the colour of my skin, looking at the colour of Mavis's skin a different colour shade than the colour of my skin.

Here I am wondering why my skin is a different colour to Mavis.

Here I am thinking; how come Mavis skin is a different colour shade than the skin on the body that I am.

Here I am looking into the palm of my hands, looking at all the lines inside my palm; looking at all the knife cut marks in the palm of my hand; looking at all the burn marks on the back part of my hand.

Here I am looking at my hands, thinking about myself, thinking about my sister, knowing that Mavis hands look soft like Delroy's hands and body look smooth and soft.

Here I am thinking about myself, looking at my sister playing with her big toy dolly. The dolly looks the colour like the white woman that came to the house. The toy dolly, with long hair, coloured like the sun and two big round blue colour eyes.

Here I am watching Mavis playing with her toy dolly, talking to the dolly, playing with the dolly instead of playing with me.

IAM®

Here I am thinking about the toy dolly; thinking in my mind; thinking; the dolly can't talk like I can; thinking; Mavis prefer to talk to the dolly instead of talking to me her sister.

Here I am watching Mavis, listening to her talking to the dolly.

Here I am; wanting to know my sister, wanting Mavis to like me.

Here I am watching my sister Mavis playing with her dolly as if not noticing me.

Here I am thinking; looking; hearing the sound like my mother's footsteps; feeling her presence coming to the dining-room. I am speaking. Hazel, come and help me get some potatoes to peel for the dinner.

Here I am. Yes mummy.

Here I am walking, following my mother, walking into the kitchen.

Here I am standing over the big bag of potato, taking out the potatoes; putting them into the washing bowl.

Here I am lifting the bowl into the sink, lifting the chair by the sink, kneeling on the chair, turning on the hot water, watching the water filling up the bowl, watching the potatoes floating in the water.

Here I am rubbing the dirt off the potatoes, washing them clean for my mother to peel for our dinner.

Here I am with my mother. My mother is standing at my side, holding the big saucepan under the cold water, lifting the pan on the stove. I am speaking. Hazel; what is this meat name?

Here I am. I don't know mummy. I am speaking. This meat is call, ox-liver.

Here I am standing on the chair by the kitchen worktop.

Here I am with the little knife in my hand, peeling the skin off the potato.

Here I am; wanting to see what my mother is doing with the ox-liver flesh. My mother is preparing the ox-liver flesh to cook for dinner.

Here I am watching my mother pouring hot water over the ox-liver inside the meat bowl. I am speaking. Hazel; look at what I am doing.

Here I am watching my mother holding the big cooking knife, stripping the shiny skin off the ox-liver flesh in her hand. The ox-liver flesh looks soaking wet, dripping with blood. I can smell the ox-liver flesh smelling in the air making my insides go round; making my body feel like it want to vomit up sick.

Here I am watching my mother's hand holding the ox-liver flesh tight in her hand. I am speaking. Leave the potato Hazel. Watch what I am doing, you have to know how to cook the meat if I am not here.

Here I am listening to my mother, wondering in my mind thinking, where are you going to mummy? I am speaking. Never you mind, just watch what I am doing. You see; make sure all the water is drain from the meat. Now you put some salt on it; you see and the pepper to season it.

Here I am watching my mother demonstrate how much salt and pepper she means; one teaspoon full so I can understand. My mother does not realize that I know what she is doing, knowing that I have watched her cooking all the other times and I watch Aunt Jane doing the cooking.

Here I am watching my mother peeling the skin off the big onion, slicing the onion into the bowl. Now my mother is peeling two clove of garlic herb, cutting it into little pieces falling on top of the ox-liver flesh inside the bowl. My mother is washing a little bunch of the thyme herb under the cold water, dropping it into the bowl with the ox-liver flesh and onion.

Here I am watching my mother's hand inside the meat bowl, mixing everything together.

Here I am inside the kitchen, watching everything my mother is doing, preparing the ox-liver flesh for dinner today.

Here I am feeling good inside, knowing that I am with my mother, learning everything there is to know about cooking.

Here I am looking at my mother's body, looking at her face smiling to herself, washing her hands clean, wiping them dry on the clean dishcloth in her hands. I am speaking. You see; now put the cover on top and leave it to season for a time. Come now; bring the bowl with the potato into the dining-room with the other knife.

Here I am feeling good with my mother.

Here I am; wanting to be with my mother, helping my mother prepare the food for our dinner.

Here I am putting water into the medium size saucepan, carrying it into the dining-room, resting it down on the table where my mother is sitting.

IAM®

Here I am walking into the kitchen, lifting the bowl full of potatoes down on the worktop, and the little cooking knife.

Here I am walking into the dining-room, resting the bowl down on the table before my mother smiling at me, making my body feel good to be in my mother's presence.

Here I am inside the kitchen, taking the old newspaper from under the kitchen sink, walking into the dining-room, opening it out onto the table before my mother.

Here I am kneeling up on the chair at my mother's side, holding the little potato in my hand, peeling the skin off the potato, feeling good with myself, feeling good with my mother. I am speaking. Pearl; how do I look?

Here I am looking up on my father's body wearing his good brown suit, looking good all over, smiling all over his face. I am speaking. Turn around let me see your back. Mavis; run up stairs; look on your daddy's dresser, you see the clothes brush; bring it come, quick.

Here I am. Daddy you look good. Where are you going? I am speaking. I am going to the school building to see the Headmaster about you and your brothers.

Here I am looking at my father; his body is looking good wearing his white cotton shirt and tie.

Here I am looking at my father's brown shoe, polished shine, looking like new. My father is looking good. I am speaking. Here is the brush mummy.

Here I am looking at my mother's hand holding the brush, moving it up and down on my father's jacket back.

Here I am looking at the height of my father standing tall like the door; smiling all over his face; watching my mother's hand making sure my father is looking good from his head all the way down his trouser edge.

Here I am looking at my father with his two hands around my mother's body, leaning forward with his lips on my mother's lips, making my mother smile, giggling to her self, looking please with my father. I am speaking. Thank you. Later now. I am speaking. Put the brush where you find it please Mavis.

Here I am. Goodbye daddy.

Here I am with the potato in my hand, watching my father's body turn towards the dining-room door, walking away, watching my mother following after him, walking with my father to the front door.

IAM®

Here I am with my mother peeling the potato, realizing how quick mummy's hands move, peeling the potato. Mummy finish peeling two big size potato and I am still on the same one. I can see Delroy getting up from his sleep, raising his head, looking around the room, making to cry; looking at mummy smiling at him. I am speaking. Hazel, go and put the kettle on.

Here I am. Yes mummy.

Here I am walking into the kitchen, realizing that the kettle is already on the fire and it is boiling.

Here I am. The kettle is on the fire mummy. It is boiling. I am speaking. Good; make Delroy a drink of milk.

Here I am inside the fridge, getting the milk bottle looking half full.

Here I am inside the kitchen, preparing to make the milk tea for Delroy.

Here I am resting the little milk saucepan down on top of the stove.

Here I am standing on the chair by the stove.

Here I am with the tea towel in my hand, lifting the kettle off the fire, pouring the hot water into the milk pan, watching the water filling up; half way up the inside.

Here I am taking a tea-bag from the tea-box, placing it into the saucepan of hot water.

Here I am looking around the kitchen, looking for Delroy's bottle.

Here I am standing on the chair inside the dining-room, looking into the cabinet, looking for Delroy's bottle on the shelf.

Here I am walking into the kitchen with Delroy's bottle, and the sugar packet in my hand.

Here I am standing inside the kitchen, turning off the fire under the kettle, lifting down the saucepan off the stove, placing it down on the draining-board.

Here I am standing on the chair by the draining-board.

Here I am with the big cooking spoon in my hand, taking out the sugar, mixing one half spoonful of sugar into the tea, pouring the milk into the tea, mixing everything together; taking out the tea-bag; not wanting the milk to get too strong.

Here I am turning on the cold water tap, putting the saucepan of milk-tea into the sink, wanting the milk-tea to cool down ready for Delroy to drink.

IAM®

Here I am pouring the drink into Delroy's bottle, putting on the top, testing the milk-tea drink on the back of my hands; feeling just right for Delroy to drink now.

Here I am walking towards Delroy sitting in his pram reaching out his hands stretched to me. I am speaking. Here you are Delroy.

Delroy is drinking quick, swallowing with his eyes wide open, looking into the eye I am. I am speaking. Come now Hazel. Bring the potato peel in.

Here I am rolling up the newspaper, rolling up the potato skin, walking into the kitchen, putting it into the kitchen dustbin. I am speaking. Pick out about five of the carrots. Put them on the side.

Here I am with my mother, hearing her say five.

Here I am wondering how many carrots make five; sorting the carrots inside the vegetable rack; thinking in my mind; five.

Here I am. Is this enough mummy? I am speaking. Get out two more.

Here I am getting to more carrots from the vegetable rack, placing them into my mother's hand and understanding to myself, understanding the numbers counting up to five and knowing how many ones make five.

Here I am watching my mother peeling the skin off the carrot, slicing it down the middle into half, and half again, putting the pieces into the colander on the draining-board; watching every-thing that my mother is doing with her two hands. I am speaking. Go and bring the lard come Hazel.

Here I am hearing my mother speak.

Here I am inside the dining-room, looking inside the fridge, taking out the packet of lard.

Here I am handing the lard into my mother's hand.

My mother is standing over the stove, opening out the packet of lard cooking oil, marking the lard into half, and half again, holding down her hand so I can see how much she means to use.

Here I am watching my mother placing the lard into the dutch-pot resting on the stove over the fire.

Here I am watching my mother's hand holding up a piece of ox-liver flesh, scraping off all the onion and garlic and thyme seasonings. I am speaking. You must make sure the oil is hot before you put the meat in or it will cook hard, understand.

IAM®

Here I am. Yes mummy.

Here I am watching my mother's hand holding the big cooking fork; turning the ox-liver flesh over inside the pot; hearing the ox-liver flesh frying inside the hot oil; watching the oil bubbles in the air; bursting pop; smelling in all the air surrounding the body that I am. I am speaking. You must keep stirring the meat to stop it from sticking to the pan bottom, or it will burn.

Here I am watching my mother's every action, understanding her words. I am speaking. Go and get me the biggest tomato from inside the fridge and the margarine.

Here I am inside the dining-room, looking inside the fridge, looking into the bowl full of tomato, looking for the biggest one.

Here I am inside the kitchen, standing on the chair, washing the tomato under the cold water tap, wiping the tomato dry on the dishcloth.

Here I am holding the tomato, watching my mother emptying all the seasoning from the meat bowl into the dutch-pot.

Here I am; smelling the meat cooking, tasting the smell inside my mouth.

Here I am looking into the dutch-pot. My mother is holding the pot down before me, so I can see and understand her words.

Here I am watching my mother holding the knife and tomato over the dutch-pot on the stove, slicing the tomato, letting the tomato slices drop onto the meat cooking in the pot. I am speaking. Now a little margarine to make it taste sweet; and some hot water. Remember the water must boil up to make the gravy. Look how much water I am putting in.

Here I am watching, looking inside the pot. I can see the ox-liver flesh and the onion, and the tomato cooking in the water and tasting the smell rising in the steam scenting out the kitchen.

Here I am watching my mother's hand turning up the fire under the pot. I can hear the water boiling inside the pot. I can see the steam pushing the pot cover up, boiling bubbles steaming out the pot cooking the ox-liver for our dinner. I am speaking. You must let the water boil until it is half way down, then turn the fire down low and let it simmer and cook the meat slow.

Here I am listening to every word my mother is saying, understanding ever word, watching everything my mother is doing, preparing the dinner.

Here I am watching my mother cutting the big round cabbage into half, washing it under the cold water, cutting it into little pieces, cutting up the cabbage into the middle size saucepan. My mother hands are moving fast cutting up the cabbage. I am speaking. Hazel. Finish cleaning away everything. Leave the margarine and bring me the jug with water and the salt.

Here I am watching my mother walking into the dining-room carrying the mixing bowl in her hand. Mummy is going to sit down to make the dumpling now.

Here I am standing on the chair watching the cold water falling into the plastic jug.

Here I am inside the dining-room, resting the jug down on the dining-table next to my mother standing over the table measuring the flour into the bowl. I am speaking. Where is the salt?

Here I am walking fast into the kitchen; looking for the salt pot.

Here I am inside the dining-room, resting the salt pot down on the table for my mother to see.

Here I am inside the kitchen, putting all the dirty things into the washing-up bowl inside the sink.

Here I am kneeling down on the chair over the sink, washing clean the cooking things, turning the things down on the draining-board.

Here I am wringing the water out of the dishcloth.

Here I am standing on the floor, lifting the chair over to the worktop, standing on the chair, reaching over the worktop, wiping it clean.

Here I am standing on the chair by the sink, holding the tea towel in my hand, wiping everything dry; leaving the big cooking spoon and fork inside the white enamel bowl that mummy is using to prepare the food.

Here I am returning the cooking things inside the cupboard where they belong.

Here I am watching my mother putting the potato into the big saucepan. I can see the steam rising out of the pot. I can see my mother's face look wet. My mother is putting the carrot into the pot. Now mummy is making the piece of dumpling to look round inside her palm, placing each portion into the hot water on top of the vegetables cooking inside the big cooking pot.

Here I am watching my mother preparing the food for our dinner. My mother is pouring some salt into the little teaspoon in her hand, holding the spoon

IAM®

over the pot, emptying the salt into the pot full of vegetables cooking for our dinner.

Here I am watching my mother returning the cover on top of the saucepan, wiping the stove surround clean with the dishcloth in her hand, making everything in the kitchen look good.

Here I am watching my mother tasting a piece of the cooked meat; turning off the fire from under the dutch-pot, pushing the dutch-pot over to the back part of the stove; thinking in my mind; following my mother into the dining-room.

IAM®

CHAPTER 13

Here I am inside the dining-room, sitting down on the chair, looking at Delroy looking at the television picture cartoon show.

Here I am looking at my sister sucking her fingers in her mouth, watching the television, holding onto her toy dolly resting on her lap.

Here I am looking at each one present in the dining-room.

Here I am thinking, wondering in my mind, wondering about my father, wondering what my father is doing at the school building.

Here I am wondering if I can go to school with Ruel and George.

Here I am watching my mother sitting on the chair over by the dining-room window. My mother is looking at the cotton string thing inside her two hands.

Here I am watching my mother's hands using a little long metal like needle hook, hooking the cotton string around the metal needle, making the round netting thing in her hand.

Here I am wondering in my mind, watching my mother's hands doing.

Here I am wondering what the thing is for. I can see my mother is taking her time, hooking the cotton around the needle hook.

Here I am. What are you doing mummy? I am speaking. I am crocheting.

Here I am listening to my mother, watching her hands working, making a crocheting thing.

Here I am; wanting to do some crocheting like my mother is doing.

Here I am feeling something bite me on my head; feeling my head itching.

Here I am thinking, wandering in my mind wanting to remember the time I last washed my hair.

Here I am. Can I go and wash my hair please mummy? I am speaking. Go and wash your head if you want. You don't have to ask me that.

Here I am walking up the stair, walking into the bath-room, hearing Ruel and George talking with each other inside their bed-room.

Here I am inside the bath-room.

Here I am leaning down inside the bath, pushing the plug into the plughole.

I AM®

Here I am turning on the hot water tap, taking the shampoo from the hot water tank cupboard.

Here I am standing inside the bath-room, pulling out the plates in my hair, feeling my head scratching.

Here I am bending forward into the bath, putting the water on my head.

Here I am squeezing the shampoo into my palm, rubbing the shampoo into my hair, rubbing my hands hard on my head, wanting my hair to be clean.

Here I am holding my flannel, washing the soap out my hair.

Here I am putting the water over my head, feeling my dress top sticking around my neck, feeling the water on my skin, running down on my body.

Here I am feeling the soap water burning my eyes, making me wring the water out my flannel quick, wiping my face, wanting my eyes to stop burning with shampoo. I can see all the dirty soap suds frothing, foaming dirty grey colour on the water top.

Here I am thinking; looking at how dirty my hair was.

Here I am squeezing some more shampoo into my hair, scrubbing my head hard, wanting my hair to be clean; feeling my neck and hands hurting; scrubbing my hair; wanting my body to be clean.

Here I am watching the dirty water going down the hole, watching the cold water coming into the bath.

Here I am with the bath jug in my hand, pouring the clean water on top of my head, wanting to rinse away the shampoo suds; wanting my hair to look clean.

Here I am wringing the water from my flannel, wiping my face dry, wiping the flannel over my hair, wringing out the cloth, wiping my neck; feeling my dress feeling wet down into my navel, making my body tremble cold.

Here I am screwing the top on the shampoo bottle, returning it inside the tank where it belongs.

Here I am trembling inside my wet dress; standing inside the girl's bed-room.

Here I am feeling the water falling off my head, splashing on my hands; splashing on feet; dropping around my body; onto the floor.

Here I am walking down the stairs, carrying the vaseline and comb in my hand, walking into the dining-room.

IAM®

Here I am kneeling down on the dining-room floor, resting the comb and vaseline on my lap.

Here I am rubbing the towel over my head, wanting my hair to get dry. I can see mummy is still doing her crocheting.

Here I am; wanting to rest my hands.

Here I am looking at Mavis and Delroy watching the television.

I am speaking. Come; bring the vaseline and comb here.

Here I am kneeling on the floor before my mother's body sitting down. Mummy is rubbing her hands over my head, feeling my hair, rubbing the towel hard on my head; dragging the comb through my hair.

Here I am feel my hair pulling inside the comb.

Here I am; wanting to cry, feeling myself hurting, feeling the water coming into my eyes.

Here I am wondering why mummy will not take her time and stop dragging the comb through my hair. I am speaking. Hush up. I have to comb out your natty hair before I can plait it.

Here I am feeling my mother's hand holding my hair tight, pulling it from the root, feeling her hand parting the hair, slapping the vaseline on my scalp all over my head.

Here I am feeling hurt inside, feeling my mother's hand pulling my hair, plaiting it, dragging my head into position. I am speaking. Here; me finish. Go and put the vaseline and comb down.

Here I am. Thank you mummy.

Here I am feeling my hair feeling tight on my head, feeling clean.

Here I am walking up the stairs, walking into the girl's bed-room, returning the comb into the hairbrush and hair oil on top of the mantle.

Here I am standing before the dressing-table, looking into the mirror, looking at my hair looking clean and shine, feeling tight on my head. I am feeling better now.

Here I am on my way to the bath-room; folding the towel.

Here I am standing on the toilet seat, leaning into the hot water tank, spreading the wet towel over the tank to dry.

I AM®

Here I am walking down the stair, walking into the dining-room. I can see my mother is doing her crocheting again.

Here I am standing by the fire-side, looking at the television picture; thinking in my mind, wondering if daddy is on his way home.

Here I am thinking about myself, wanting to go to the school with Ruel and George when they are going.

Here I am; not wanting to stay at home; thinking about Ruel and George going to school; wondering in my mind; thinking about the body that I am. I am speaking. Hazel; go and get the exercise book and pencil let me see if you can write your name as yet.

Here I am hearing my mother.

Here I am thinking in my mind, remembering how to write my name.

Here I am on my way to the back bed-room.

Here I am walking, thinking how to spell my name.

Here I am inside the back bed-room, feeling my inside go round, wanting to remember how to write my name.

Here I am looking inside the little table drawer, looking for the exercise book and pencil.

Here I am running up the stairs, knocking on my brother's bed-room door, wanting to find the exercise book and pencil.

Here I am. Ruel; George; have any of you got a writing book and pencil I can use? Mummy wants me to write my name again.

I am speaking. You can use mine Hazel. It's in the dressing-table drawer. Have this pencil.

Here I am looking in the direction of my brother George's hand pointing. Here I am looking inside the dressing-table drawer, turning over all the things, looking for the exercise book.

Here I am holding George's exercise book, turning over the leaf, looking for a clean page to write on.

Here I am remembering how to write my name, remembering each sound, talking to myself, writing the name Hazel.

Here I am. Have I write my name right George. I am speaking. That's right Hazel. Write Grant now.

IAM®

Here I am hearing my brother George, remembering the sounds of the word Grant, thinking in my mind, writing the word Grant.

Here I am. Look George. Have I got it right? I am speaking. You can write your name. You learn quick Hazel. Mummy is going to have a surprise.

Here I am. Thank you George. Here me spell it now. I am speaking. Go on then.

Here I am speaking the sounds of the letter of the name Hazel.

Here I am speaking, looking at Ruel and George's face, looking as if surprise and happy with me, spelling out the name, Hazel and Grant. I am speaking. You have done it Hazel. I am bored. I wonder why we can't go outside and play like the other children next door.

Here I am hearing my brother George, and knowing the reason why my mother stops them from playing outside is because they make their clothes dirty, and mummy and I am fed-up of washing dirty clothes. I am going down now before mummy come and get me. Thanks George.

Here I am walking down the stairs, walking into the dining-room, feeling good with myself, knowing that I can spell and I can writ my name now.

Here I am standing before my mother, watching her hands doing the crocheting. I am speaking. Write your name Hazel for me.

Here I am sitting down on the chair, resting my book down on the dining-table.

Here I am with the pencil in my hand, writing each letter sounding like my name Hazel.

Here I am feeling good with myself writing my handwriting to look good. I am speaking. You write your name as yet?

Here I am. I am writing it mummy. I am speaking. What is taking you so long? Let me see what you do.

Here I am standing before my mother, watching my mother's eyes looking down inside the exercise book.

Here I am watching my mother's face changing, smiling to herself; watching her face looking up at one. I am speaking. You see. You can write your name. Come over here. I am going to write down the name of this house. Give me the pencil. You have to know where you live if you want to go to school with your brother's.

IAM®

Here I am listening to my mother's every word, watching her hand writing the number of my father's house and understanding every word that I can see my mother's hand writing. I am speaking. This is how you write the name of this house. This is our address, understand. 17 Wellington Road, Smethwick, Warley, West Midlands, England. Now go and copy it. Keep writing it till you can remember how to write it down properly.

Here I am feeling good with myself, copy writing my mother's hand-writing of my father's house building address.

Here I am writing, understanding what I am writing, understanding that my father's house have its own name. My father's house name is 17 Wellington Road, Smethwick, Warley, West Midlands, England. I can hear the front door bang shut. Daddy is home.

Here I am looking at the dining-room door, waiting for it to open, looking at my father's body; his face smiling entering into the dining-room.

Here I am writing, listening to daddy speaking to mummy.

Here I am looking at my mother's face smiling, hearing my father say that they can go to school in a week's time. My father is talking about his visit to the school, talking about Ruel and George and me.

Here I am feeling good; daddy said that I can go to school with Ruel and George in a week's time.

Here I am feeling good inside, knowing that I am going to go to school with Ruel and George.

Here I am writing, and wanting to go and tell Ruel and George what daddy said; we are going to school in a week's time.

Here I am writing wondering in my mind, thinking; how long is a week's time?, wanting the time to come quick. I am speaking. What are you writing Hazel?

Here I am. I am writing the name of our house daddy. I am speaking. You mean the address.

Here I am looking at my father's face smiling, looking down at one.

Here I am. Yes daddy, I am writing the address, the name of our house. I am speaking. You and your brother's will be going to school soon. I had to talk hard with the Headmaster man to let you go at the same time.

Here I am listening to my father, feeling good inside.

IAM®

Here I am. Thank you daddy. Do you want a cup of tea now? I am speaking. Thank you Hazel. My foot a hurt me in these shoes. I am going up to change.

Here I am. Do you want a cup of tea mummy? I am speaking. Never mind a cup of tea. I better look about your school things. I never expect you to go as yet.

Here I am hearing my mother.

Here I am inside the kitchen, standing on the chair over the sink, putting cold water into the kettle; lifting the kettle up onto the stove, lighting the gas with the burning match in my hand. I am speaking. Go and set the table for your father and I, and Mavis.

Here I am listening to my mother, watching her standing over the stove, lighting the fire under the saucepans.

Here I am inside the dining-room, spreading the tablecloth over the dining-table. I can see daddy is coming into the dining-room; wearing his house clothes.

Here I am standing on the chair by the cabinet, taking out the knives and forks and teaspoons, resting them down on the table.

Here I am getting the cup and saucer, and one dinner plate each for daddy, and mummy and Mavis.

Here I am setting the table correct for my father and mother and sister Mavis to eat their dinner.

Here I am inside the cabinet getting the sugar bowl, and teapot stand, resting them down on the dining-table.

Here I am looking inside the fridge, getting the tin of milk, resting it down on the dining-table, watching my father looking at the television picture.

Here I am walking into the kitchen, holding the three dinner plates in my hand, resting them down on the worktop, looking at my mother standing over the stove, stirring the meat inside the dutch-pot; smelling ready to eat.

Here I am inside the kitchen cupboard, getting the teapot, putting two tea-bags into the pot, resting the teapot down on the kitchen worktop.

Here I am watching the steam coming out from the kettle, listening to the water boiling up inside.

Here I am with the tea-cloth in my hand.

IAM®

Here I am standing on the kitchen ground, lifting the teapot off the stove, resting it down on the draining-board.

Here I am lifting the chair over by the draining-board, standing on the chair, pouring the boiling water into the teapot.

Here I am waiting for the tea to mix into the hot water.

Here I am watching my mother sharing the food out onto the big dinner plate in her hand.

Here I am walking into the dining-room, carrying the teapot on my hand, resting the teapot down on the teapot stand, standing in the centre of the dining-table. I am speaking. You all right?

Here I am. Yes thank you daddy; I am.

Here I am standing inside the dining-room; looking at everyone present inside the dining-room.

Here I am thinking, thinking in my mind, wondering about the school building; thinking about going to school.

Here I am thinking about school, wondering about school, feeling my inside go round, not wanting to go to school, not knowing what I am going to wear, wanting my body to look good.

Here I am thinking, wondering about school, wondering if Ruel and George know about the place name school.

Here I am wondering, thinking. What am I going to wear to go to school? I can hear my mother and father talking to each other, eating their dinner. Mummy is telling daddy about all the things she have to buy for Ruel and George and me to go to school. I am speaking. I will have to go shopping on Thursday to buy every-thing.

Here I am. Can I go with you shopping mummy? I am speaking. I will think about it.

IAM®

CHAPTER 14

Here I am looking at Ruel and George standing at the dining-table, watching mummy and daddy eating their food. Ruel and George are looking on mummy and daddies plate, as if wanting to grab the plate first, knowing that mummy and daddy always leave some of their food for us.

Here I am standing inside the dining-room, looking at everyone, watching my mother feeding Delroy some food. I am speaking. The food taste good Pearl. You sure can cook good. I am speaking. Come Hazel; lay the table for you and your brothers. Mix some orange juice.

Here I am listening to my mother, watching her body walking into the kitchen, carrying the dinner plates for Ruel and George and me.

Here I am standing on the chair by the cabinet, taking the knife and fork from the cabinet drawer, resting them down on the dining-table. I am speaking. Which one of you can speak your A, B, C: alphabet?

Here I am making the table ready for our dinner, listening to daddy speaking.

Here I am wondering in my mind, thinking about the word my father just said; alphabet.

Here I am; wanting to understand what daddy means. I am speaking. I know daddy. I know my alphabet.

Here I am looking at George holding his hand up, reaching high above his head, smiling all over his face, looking please with him-self, wanting daddy to acknowledge him. I am speaking. I know my alphabet daddy. I am speaking. Speak George. Speak it let me hear.

Here I am standing in the presence of my father and Ruel, and George, and Mavis and Delroy.

Here I am listening to George's voice speaking the sounds, saying the alphabet. George is speaking out loud, saying the alphabet. I am speaking. A, B, C, D, E, F, G, H, I, J, K, L, M, N, O, P, Q, R, S, T, U, V, W, X, Y, Z.

Here I am hearing George's voice speaking something good, talking good; saying the alphabet.

Here I am listening to George speaking about something that I now nothing about the word my father calls the alphabet.

IAM®

Here I am listening to my brother George sounding good. I am speaking. What about you Ruel? I am speaking. I can speak the alphabet. I am speaking. Go on then, let me hear you say it then.

Here I am listening to Ruel speaking the letters sounding the alphabet. Ruel voice sound good like George's voice speaking the alphabet.

I am speaking. A, B, C, D, E, F, G, H, I, J, K, L, M, N, O, P, Q, R, S, T, U, V, W, X, Y, Z. I am speaking. What about you Hazel?

Here I am listening to my father talking to me.

Here I am looking at my father, feeling my inside go round, knowing that I don't know how to say the alphabet like Ruel and George can.

Here I am. I don't know the alphabet daddy. I am speaking. Granti; you see now why I am down on Hazel to read and write her name. I know they never show her how to do anything back home. I am speaking. You leave the child alone. Hazel is not school age as yet. I am speaking. Go and get your dinner.

Here I am listening to my mother and father having words with each other, talking about me.

Here I am pouring the orange juice into the jug, listening to every word that I can hear my mother saying to my father.

Here I am inside the kitchen, standing on the chair over the sink, watching the cold water falling into the jug, mixing the orange juice to drink with our dinner.

Here I am walking into the dining-room, carrying the jug of juice, resting it down on the table. I am speaking. George; pass the glass them out of the cabinet please.

Here I am. Come and get your dinner Ruel, it's ready inside the kitchen.

Here I am walking into the dining-room, carrying mine and George's dinner plate, resting them down on the dining-table.

Here I am sitting down around the dining-table.

Here I am looking at Ruel eating down his food, not wanting to wait for George and me to start. I am speaking.

Hazel, wash up the dinner plate when you finish and keep down the noise. Your father has gone to bed.

Here I am eating my food, watching my mother walking into the hall way, carrying Delroy on her hip.

IAM®

Here I am eating, thinking in my mind, wondering if George will show me how to write and speak the alphabet like he can.

Here I am looking at George eating his food.

Her I am. George; will you show me how to write the alphabet when we finish our dinner? I am speaking. Yes, easy. I can read and write, and I can count up to one hundred. I know everything about school. I am speaking. Yes, you can talk. You went to school.

Here I am listening to Ruel talking about George, saying how George had everything good when we were back home in Jamaica.

Here I am. We will play hand-writing when I finish all the washing-up. I am speaking. Do you want all of your dumplings Hazel?

Here I am. Here then. I am going to start the washing-up. Clear the table for me when you finish please Ruel.

Here I am walking into the kitchen. I can see that mummy has cleared away everything. All I have to do is wash mine and Ruel and George's dinner things.

Here I am standing on the chair over the kitchen sink, putting hot water into the washing-up bowl, and some washing-up liquid.

Here I am. Ruel and George, bring the dirty things come. I am speaking. Where do you want them Hazel?

Here I am. Put them in here. Can you pull the table down please George?

Here I am washing-up the dirty dinner plates, resting them down on the draining-board. I can hear Rule's voice talking to George, talking about the time when we were back at home on the ground name Jamaica.

Here I am wiping the plates dry on the tea-towel, resting them down on the worktop.

Here I am emptying the bowl of water, wringing the water out from the dish-cloth, wiping the water off the draining-board, wiping the water tap dry, making everywhere look good, just like mummy leave everywhere looking good.

Here I am walking into the dining-room, carrying the pile of plates and saucer in my hands, resting them down on the dining-table.

Here I am inside the kitchen, collecting the glasses into my two hands.

100

IAM®

Here I am inside the dining-room, resting the glasses down on the dining-table.

Here I am. Can you put these away please George?

Here I am walking into the kitchen, collecting the knives and forks and spoons off the worktop, carrying them into the dining-room; standing on the chair by the cabinet, putting them away where they belong inside the drawer.

Here I am. I am ready George. I am speaking. Let me write the letters first and then say them so you can understand when I am speaking them.

Here I am standing by my brother, watching George's hand writing, watching George's eyes moving across the paper, understanding every word that I am listening to George speaking.

Here I am on the chair next to George positioning the exercise book, so I can see his hand-writing the sounds of each letter sounding the alphabet. I can see George hand-writing looks good.

Here I am watching the way George's hand is writing each letter, forming the alphabet signs, A, B, C, D, E, F, G, H, I, J, K, L, M, N, O, P, Q, R, S, T, U, V, W, X, Y, Z. George's hand-writing look good.

Here I am watching George's finger on the letter sounding A, pointing his finger to each letter, listening to every sound coming out of George's mouth, wanting to understand the alphabet letters.

Here I am listening to George saying the alphabet, listening to Ruel speaking with George, talking out loud, saying the alphabet letters so I can understand.

Here I am; understanding the sounds that I am hearing, realizing that I can say the alphabet, I can hear myself speaking the sounds, copying Ruel and George speaking the sounds, feeling myself remembering the sounds that I am hearing.

Here I am; wanting to remember all that I can hear Ruel and George is speaking the sounds of the alphabet.

Here I am with the pencil in my hand, writing, copying each letter making up the alphabet. I am writing the letters on a clean page, testing myself, wanting to remember, wanting to remember the alphabet like George and Ruel remembers how to speak the alphabet.

Here I am realizing that I can read and write because I want to. I can hear, and I can speak; now I can write because I want to. I want to know everything there is to know about reading and writing.

IAM®

Here I am feeling good inside, feeling pleased with myself.

Here I am remembering the sounds of the alphabet.

Here I am hand-writing the alphabet, copying George's hand-writing, saying the sounds to myself, writing the signs, wanting to remember the alphabet. I am speaking. Let me show you the little letters that sound the same as the big letters sound.

Here I am listening to George speaking, wondering in my mind, thinking; what is George talking about.

Here I am looking at George's hand writing what he means so I can understand.

Here I am watching George hand-writing, and understanding the meaning of what I can see, a little letter a, the same sound as the big letter A. I am speaking. This A is name capital A, and you write it when you begin the words that begin a sentence. Look; you see the beginning of the story. The word begins with the capital letter, and the rest of the words are written in small letters.

Here I am looking at the words inside the picture story book George is holding in his hand, showing me what he means so I will understand.

Here I am. Yes George.

Here I am; understanding what George means.

Here I am; wanting to read the words that I am looking at inside the story book. I want to read. I am speaking. Read to me please George. I want to read good like you can.

Here I am looking at the picture inside the book. I can see a big animal in the picture, and another big animal the same, and one little animal the same.

I can see three bowls full of porridge and three spoons on the table inside the picture. I can see three chairs in the picture.

Here I am looking at the writings inside the book, looking at the colour pictures, wanting to know what the words mean, wanting to read. I want to read. I want to read. I want to read. I want to read.

Here I am; wanting to read the words that I can see, wanting to understand about all the pictures that I can see.

Here I am. What is this word please George? I am speaking. This is the once upon a time story.

IAM®

Here I am listening to George speaking, reading the sounds of the words written inside the picture book.

Here I am watching George's hand pointing his finger at each word on the page, and hearing the sounds of every word, making me picture the word sounds inside my mind. I can see the sound sounding each word, making the picture that I can see inside my mind inside my eyes. The word sounding picture is moving inside my mind. I can see the picture is moving in my mind.

Here I am; understanding what reading is.

Here I am; knowing how to read. All I have to do is speak the word out loud so I can hear what I am saying. I can read. I can see the picture of every sound that I can hear George is speaking.

Here I am feeling good, knowing how to read.

Here I am. Thank you George. I want to read. I want to read good just like I hear you can read to sound good.

Here I am; understanding everything that is happening to the body that I am.

Here I am; knowing that I can read, because I am speaking the words so I can hear the sounds I am making.

Here I am with George, reading with George, speaking the words as I am hearing George speak, watching his finger pointing to each word so I can understand.

Here I am speaking. Once upon a time there were three bears. I am speaking. You can read Hazel. You can read by yourself now. I want to watch the television.

Here I am. Can I have the book George? I want to read some more. I am speaking. Cause you can. It isn't mine.

Here I am sitting down on the dining-room floor, holding the picture book on my lap.

Here I am looking at the pictures inside the book, turning over the pages, looking at the words written inside the book, looking at the pictures, wanting to understand what the words mean to say, speaking the letter word sounds in my mind, wanting to read. I can hear mummy's footsteps coming down the stairs, coming towards the dining-room. I am speaking. Turn off the television now, and get to your beds.

IAM®

Here I am looking on the body of my mother, shouting at us, telling us to go to bed.

Here I am listening to Ruel and George, moaning, wanting to watch the television.

Here I am putting the book under the television table, making sure that I can find it in the morning. I am speaking. Move yourselves, quick.

Here I am running into the hall way, following after Ruel, walking up the stairs.

Here I am inside the girl's bed-room.

Here I am turning on the light. I can see Mavis is sleeping inside her bed. Mavis eyes are wide open, looking still, not moving, just looking still inside her face, sleeping, causing my body to jump up inside.

Here I am walking along the hall way, walking into the bath-room, hearing my mother's footsteps coming up the stairs.

Here I am standing on the bath, turning on the light.

Here I am turning on the hot water tap, pushing the plug into the plughole.

Here I am standing inside the bath, turning off the water, feeling the water feeling cold on my foot.

Here I am standing inside the bath, taking off my clothes.

Here I am wiping soap on my flannel, wiping my face, wiping my neck, wiping my shoulders, wiping my arm and under my arms into my armpit.

Here I am washing myself, rubbing more soap on the flannel, standing up inside the water, wiping all around my bottom, into my wee-wee, wiping my legs all the way down under my foot.

Here I am sitting down inside the water, splashing the water over me, washing off the soap, washing my body clean, feeling myself feeling good inside.

Here I am ringing the water from my flannel, wiping the water off my body, climbing out the bath, feeling myself trembling inside.

Here I am leaning over the bath, rubbing soap onto my knickers, scrubbing my knickers clean.

I AM®

Here I am pulling the plug out of the bath, putting the cleaning powder on the sponge, leaning into the bath, wiping the bath inside clean, washing the soap marks off the bath inside.

Here I am turning on the cold water tap, washing away all the dirty soap suds, making the bath inside look clean.

Here I am standing on the toilet seat, reaching inside the hot water tank, spreading my knickers over the hot water tank, wanting my knickers to dry ready to wear in the morning.

Here I am putting on my night-dress. I can hear someone's footstep walking along the hall way, coming towards the bath-room.

Here I am standing looking at my father's body standing at the bath-room doorway, looking down on me. I am speaking. Hurry up Hazel and get to your bed.

Here I am listening to my father, watching my father's body standing over the toilet bowl, listening to my father wee-weeing. I can hear my father's wee-wee splashing inside the toilet.

Here I am thinking; daddy take a long time to do his wee-wee. I am speaking. Good night.

Here I am. Good night daddy. I have nearly finished now.

Here I am walking into the girl's bed-room, carrying my dress over my hand. I can see my mother's bed-room light shining at the bottom of the door.

Here I am inside the bed-room, spreading my dress over the end of my bed.

Here I am listening to the sounds inside my father's house.

Here I am thinking about every-one, thinking about my mother having the baby, wanting mummy to have a girl baby.

Here I am lying down inside my bed; feeling wide awake, not wanting to sleep; looking into the darkness; wondering in my mind.

Here I am touching the body that I am; feeling myself getting hot, feeling my insides moving around fast, feeling my heart beating quick, feeling the body that I am wanting to sleep, feeling my eyes wanting to close, wanting to sleep, feeling myself not wanting to move, lying still, feeling my heart beating quick, hearing the body that I am inside breathing fast; feeling good.

IAM®

CHAPTER 15

Here I am feeling wide awake. The time is day light and my eyes are wide open looking at the light coming into the bed-room window curtain, making my body feel like it want to get up out of bed.

Here I am looking at Mavis smiling, looking at me.

Here I am. Good morning Mavis. I am getting up now.

Here I am making up my bed, straightening out all my bedclothes, making my bedding look neat on my bed.

Here I am. Did you use the potty Mavis?

Here I am looking at Mavis, her body lying still in her bed under the blanket, as if pretending not to hear me speaking to her.

Here I am on my knees, looking under Mavis's bed, looking for the potty, smelling the smell like do-do under the bed.

Here I am walking to the bath-room, walking slow, holding the potty away from me. Mavis do-do is smelling, all around my body, making my body feel sick; hurt; knowing that I have to clean up after Mavis.

Here I am standing on the bath-room floor, emptying the potty into the toilet bowl.

Here I am standing over the bath, watching the water coming into the dirty potty, washing the potty clean, brushing away the do-do with the toilet brush.

Here I am pulling up my night-dress over my bottom, sitting down on the toilet seat, wanting to do a wee-wee.

Here I am wiping my bottom on the piece of toilet paper.

Here I am emptying the water from the potty into the toilet.

Here I am standing on the toilet seat, pulling the chain down, wanting to flush the toilet bowl clean.

Here I am rubbing soap on my flannel, wiping my face, wiping the sleep from the corner of my eyes, washing my face, hearing sounds coming from down stairs.

Here I am putting tooth-paste on my tooth-brush, brushing my teeth, washing my mouth clean.

IAM®

Here I am rubbing the soap onto my flannel, wiping my bottom, washing my flannel clean, ringing out the water, hanging it over the railing under the sink where it belong.

Here I am putting cleaning powder on the bath-sponge, wiping the sink inside clean, washing away the dirty soap marks, rinsing the sink clean with cold water.

Here I am standing on the toilet seat, reaching down into the hot water tank, getting my knickers.

Here I am walking along the hall way, walking into the girl's bed-room, feeling my mother's presence.

Here I am looking at my mother standing at Mavis's bed-side, looking down at my body, making my body not know what to do with myself.

Here I am. Good morning mummy.

Here I am on my knees, returning the potty under Mavis's bed, wondering in my mind, wondering what mummy is doing just standing there. I am speaking. I am glad you get up. I am taking all of you with me shopping today. Go and tell your brothers to get up now. Hurry Hazel.

Here I am walking to the boy's bed-room, thinking in my mind, wondering if today is Thursday, feeling myself feeling good, knowing that mummy is going to let us go shopping with her.

Here I am outside my brother's bed-room, knocking on the door, wanting to go inside. I am speaking. You can come in Hazel.

Here I am. Good morning George. Good morning Ruel. Where is Delroy? Guess what. I am speaking. What. Tell us. Go on then, guess what.

Here I am. We are going out shopping with mummy today. Mummy said you must hurry up and get ready now. I think we are going to get our new clothes to wear when we go to school.

Here I am running along the hall way, walking into the girl's bed-room.

Here I am standing at the bed-room entrance, looking at mummy wiping Mavis's bottom with the flannel. I can see mummy is getting Mavis ready, wiping Mavis's body clean all over. Mummy is putting on Mavis white vest and petticoat slip, and her white cotton socks with the yellow line around the top, making Mavis body look good.

IAM®

Here I am watching my mother getting Mavis ready to go shopping. Mummy is putting on Mavis shiny black shoes.

Here I am watching my mother standing by the girls wardrobe, taking out one of Mavis dress on the clothes hander; looking at all Mavis dresses hanging up inside; just looking. I am speaking. That dress on the bed is for you Hazel.

Here I am looking on the bed, looking at the green dress spread out on the bed.

Here I am. Thank you mummy. Are these things for me mummy? I am speaking. Everything on the bed is for you to put on. Here is a pair of socks and the pants.

Here I am feeling good with my mother. Now I have a new pair of socks, and new knickers to put on with my new vest, and new petticoat slip, and my new dress. I am speaking. Go and get the polish and polish your shoes first.

Here I am running down the stairs, on my way to the pantry.

Here I am inside the pantry, looking on the shelf, looking for the polish and some cloth to clean my shoes.

Here I am walking up the stairs, carrying the polish and cloth into the bed-room.

Here I am on my knees, wiping the cloth inside the polish, wiping the brown polish over my shoes.

Here I am rubbing the cloth hard on my shoe, wanting my shoes to shine like Mavis shoes look shine.

Here I am thinking in my mind, thinking about shopping, thinking. I am speaking. Hazel; empty this bowl of water please and hurry up get dress and come on down stairs.

Here I am putting the top on the polish tin.

Here I am walking down the stairs, carrying the polish tin and shoe cloth, returning them inside the pantry where they belong.

Here I am running up stairs, running into the girl's bed-room.

Here I am lifting the bowl of dirty soap water off the chair, walking along the hall way, walking slow, feeling the water splashing over the sides.

Here I am inside the bath-room, resting the bowl down on the floor.

I AM®

Here I am kneeling down over the bowl, rubbing soap inside my hands, rubbing the soap into the polish on my hands, wanting the polish to go away, not wanting anything to dirty up my new clothes I am going to put on.

Here I am lifting the bowl of water up off the floor, emptying the water into the toilet, returning the bowl down on the floor under the sink where it belong.

Here I am on my way to the girl's bed-room.

Here I am thinking in my mind, thinking, feeling, I am going to look good today.

Here I am standing before my dressing-table, looking at myself inside the mirror, putting on my clothes, feeling myself feeling good inside, just looking at myself wearing my new dress.

Here I am putting on my shoes, hearing mummy raising her voice, shouting at Ruel and George, telling them to go and wash their skin.

Here I am feeling good with myself, knowing that my body is clean, smelling good.

Here I am walking down the stairs, hearing Ruel and George inside the bathroom, talking about our mummy.

Here I am standing inside the dining-room, feeling the warm air on my face; looking around the room; looking at everything mummy has done. Delroy is dressed looking good. Delroy is smiling all over his face. Mummy has made-up the fire. The fire is burning bright, smelling in the air. I can see the saucepan on the dining-table, and the cereal bowls and spoon with the big box of cereal set out ready for our breakfast.

Here I am sitting at the table, eating my breakfast, watching my mother plaiting Mavis's hair. Mummy is tying a white ribbon bow on the plait in Mavis hair.

Here I am watching my mother making Mavis hair look good, watching her hand sliding the hair slide inside Mavis hair, one at each side of Mavis head. Mavis is looking good. I am speaking. Hurry Hazel. I want your head next.

Here I am walking into the kitchen, carrying the empty bowl and spoon, putting them down into the washing-up bowl inside the sink. I am speaking. Come on Hazel.

Here I am hearing my mother's voice.

IAM®

Here I am on my knees, kneeling down on the floor between my mother's legs.

Here I am feeling my mother's hands on my head. I can see Ruel and George coming into the dining-room. I am speaking. Your breakfast is on the table. Hurry up now and eat. Ruel; go and wipe the sleep out of your eyes, and go and put some oil on your face. I can feel my mother tying a ribbon in my hair. I am speaking. Hazel, watch Delroy; I am going to get dress now.

Here I am looking at Ruel and George, and Mavis and Delroy looking good, ready to go out shopping with mummy.

Here I am folding down the dining-table.

Here I am looking around the dining-room, looking out through the window, into the air outside my father's house. I can see the sky is looking blue.

Here I am thinking; it is a good time now to go out shopping; feeling the sun shining on the body that I am; making my body feel good.

Here I am watching my mother's body coming into the room.

Here I am thinking my mother looks good, dressed in her blue suit and her white hat on her head. My mother is wearing her white gloves on her one hand, holding her white handbag. My mother can dress-up her body to look good, wearing her white high heel shoe.

Here I am feeling my inside go round, not understanding why I am feeling the way I am feeling. I am speaking. George, Ruel; come over here. Where is the comb? This is how you comb your head.

Here I am looking at my mother holding the comb in her hand, dragging the comb through Ruel's hair. I can see Ruel's face looking like he is making to cry. I am speaking. Right; every one; ready now? Hazel, you pull the trolley for me. Hold my bag Mavis. Ruel; you and George come help me lift the pram to the front door.

Here I am holding the door open, watching my mother with Ruel and George lifting the pram, carrying Delroy inside. I am speaking. You all wait here one minute let me go and check the house.

Here I am standing outside my father's house; standing inside our front garden, feeling the air on my skin. I am speaking. Close the gate shut Ruel.

Here I am walking with my mother and Ruel and George, following our mother pushing the pram with Delroy and Mavis.

IAM®

Here I am looking at Delroy sitting up inside the pram, smiling all over his face and looking around, looking up at our mother. I am speaking. Ruel, you and George behave yourselves. Come and walk in front so I can see you. Walk away from the roadside before a car come and knock you.

Here I am walking with my mother, watching everybody move out of my mother's way. I am speaking. Hold your head up. There is nothing on the ground. Hold up your head when you are walking out with me. Stand still. Look to your right; now look left and make sure no car is coming. Come on. Walk quickly now. This is the road you are crossing. I am going to the shoe shop up Cape Hill.

Here I am on my way shopping with my mother. I can see all the men and women walking out together. I can see a lot of children walking out with big people like my mother and father.

Here I am; wanting to look inside all the shop windows, wondering in my mind, thinking about the shoe shop, wondering what a shoe shop look like. I am speaking. This is the newsagent shop where your daddy buys the newspaper from.

Here I am walking with my mother, feeling my inside turn over, feeling the man looking down on the body that I am. I am speaking. This is a clothes dress shop. Come, here is the shoe shop. Hazel; you stand by the pram and watch Delroy. Ruel and George come inside this shop with me.

Here I am standing outside the shoe shop, looking into the shop window, looking at all the many different shape shoes, and all the colours on all the shoes.

Here I am looking, wanting to have a new pair of shoes like the one I can see in the window-box.

Here I am standing outside the shop, wondering why the woman is looking at me, wondering what the woman want, smiling at me like that, just looking. I am speaking. Look Hazel. I have got a new pair of shoes and George. I think you are going to have one as well. Mummy wants you to go inside the shop now.

Here I am pushing the shop door forward, walking inside the shop, feeling my inside go round, changing; looking at my mother standing in the middle of the room.

Here I am standing at the shop doorway, feeling everyone's eyes on the body that I am making my inside go round, not knowing what to do with myself. I

IAM®

am speaking. I want a pair for her. I am speaking. Come and sit her sweetheart. I am speaking. Hazel, move yourself sharp and take off your shoes.

Here I am inside the shoe shop, sitting down on the chair, watching the shop woman coming close to me.

Here I am looking down on the woman putting the shoe on my foot.

Here I am looking at the shoe on my foot.

Here I am thinking in my mind; I don't like this one. I am speaking. It's a good fit madam. There is plenty of growing room. I am speaking. I will take that one. That is all. How much do I owe you?

Here I am watching the woman putting the new pair of shoe into the box into the plastic carry bag.

Here I am not feeling good with myself.

Here I am thinking about the shoes inside the shop window; the one that look like Mavis's shoes that don't need any polish on them to shine.

Here I am watching my mother standing by the woman, speaking to the woman and putting some paper money into the woman's hand. I am speaking. Hazel, come and take the bag from the woman. Here George. Come on Mavis. Come we are going to the clothes dress shop.

Here I am standing outside the shop with all kind of man and boys clothes hanging up inside the window box.

Here I am standing outside the shop, holding onto the pram with Delroy lying down sleeping inside. Mummy and Mavis is coming out of the shop with George and Ruel is carrying two more bags; smiling all over his face looking please with himself. I am speaking. Come on now. Hold on to each other. Quick, cross the road, quick.

Here I am on the other side of the road, walking with my mother and Ruel and George and Mavis, listening to mummy's voice talking to her self. I am speaking. You lot walk up. Everything is so expensive. One shoe cost so much money. We got to make the money stretch. This one; Ruel, you and George wait here and look after Delroy. Come Hazel.

Here I am walking into the shop, following after my mother holding onto Mavis's hand.

IAM®

Here I am inside the shop looking all around the space where I am looking at the shop cupboard drawers with glass front showing off all the clothes things that women and girls wear on their bodies. I am speaking. Let me have a look at the girl's underwear.

Here I am looking at my mother's hand holding up something, talking to the woman standing on the other side of the shop counter; looking at my mother buying some new vest and petticoat slip, and new white colour socks for me.

Here I am watching my mother's hand inside her hand-bag, taking out some paper money, placing it into the shop woman's hand. I am speaking. Take the bag from the woman Hazel.

Here I am. Thank you. I am speaking. I am going to get the coats now before the money run out.

Here I am standing outside the big, big shop mummy call Woolworth. I am speaking. Hold open the door let me push the pram inside.

Here I am inside the Woolworth shop; looking around at all that I can see, wondering at all the different kinds of food and things making me want to want some of everything that I can see. I am speaking. Come on and stop gazing on the food.

Here I am looking at all the different colour sweets, feeling my mouth inside watering, looking at all the cakes and biscuits; thinking in my mind, wondering what do they taste like, wishing that mummy will buy some. I am speaking. Hold my hand-bag Mavis. Put this coat on Hazel.

Here I am putting on the coat, feeling the weight of the coat dragging my hands down; watching mummy looking at me; looking up and down at the body that I am wearing the coat, understanding the meaning of the word coat. I am speaking. Turn around Hazel. Good, come over here Ruel and put this one on. George, you try on this one. You are lucky. We have everything. Take them off and bring them to the woman over there behind the counter. I am speaking. These three coats thank you.

Here I am standing at the side of my mother, standing by the shop counter.

Here I am watching the woman putting the coat inside a bag; one in each bag; watching the woman press her fingers on the big metal money box standing on the counter.

Here I am watching my mother's hand inside her hand-bag, sorting out some more paper money, handing the paper money into the shop woman's hand; watching the woman give my mother some money; counting the money into

IAM®

my mother's hand. I am speaking. Here; carry the bag. I am going into the market hall now. Hold each others hand, and walk close by me.

Here I am walking running after my mother walking quick.

Here I am on the road feeling myself hurting inside, feeling the people bodies knocking me on my body and stepping on my foot.

Here I am walking on another road, feeling my hands hurting inside, pulling the trolley bag, following my mother. I am speaking. Hazel, this is the meat shop name the butchers and there is the vegetable shop over there.

Here I am hearing every word that my mother is saying, pointing her hand to each shop so I can understand and realizing the meaning of her words.

Here we are walking into the big market shop with the doorway as high as the shop and bigger than the Woolworth shop. I am speaking. Stand on their foot if they cannot say sorry.

Here I am standing at the cloth stall, looking at my mother's hand holding up the colour flower cotton cloth, watching my mother looking at all the many colour cloths spread out on the bench stall. I am speaking. Hazel, choose one of these pieces of cloth. I am going to make you your school dress. Which one do you like?

Here I am looking at the cloth in my mother's hand.

Here I am looking at all the other pieces of cloth mixed up together on the bench stall, wondering in my mind, thinking which piece must I have, not knowing which piece of cloth to choose, feeling my mother's eyes looking down at one, wanting my body to choose a piece of cloth. There are so many different pieces of cloth that look good.

Here I am thinking which one I must have. I am speaking. Which one? This one?

Here I am. This piece mummy; I like this one. I am speaking. What about this piece?

Here I am. I like that one and this one please mummy. I am speaking. Good; we will have these three pieces; yes?

Here I am watching my mother's hand handing the pieces of cloth over into the hand of the man standing on the other side of the bench stall.

Here I am looking at the man smiling all over his face, watching his hands folding the cloth smaller and smaller; wrapping the cloth together into a sheet of brown paper; watching my mother put some money coins into the man's hand; paying the man for the pieces of cloth. I am speaking. Thank you darling. Come again. I am speaking. I am not your darling.

Here I am taking the cloth parcel from my mother's hand, putting it into the trolley bag, feeling please with myself, thinking about the new dress mummy is going to make for me.

Here I am now of the understanding that my mother pay out less money to buy the tree pieces of cloth to make three dresses. The three pieces of cloth cost my mother less money to make three dresses, less money than it would cost mummy to buy a dress already made up from the shop.

Here I am; understanding the cost of money, knowing how much one can buy for the same amount of money, and how many more things we can have if we have a talent like my mother have.

Here I am; knowing that my mother's talent can make three dresses for the same price it cost to buy one.

Here I am pulling the trolley bag, following my mother pushing the pram with Delroy and Mavis; walking with Ruel and George inside the market building.

Here I am watching my mother doing the shopping, feeling good with my mother, knowing that I am going to have a new dress because mummy can sew.

Here I am feeling pleased with my mother, thinking in my mind, thinking; now I can have lots of good dresses, just like Mavis have lots of good dresses hanging up in her wardrobe. I am speaking. I want some sewing threads and things. Come we are going to the cotton stall now. Where are Ruel and George? All of you keep close, you hear.

Here I am standing at the cotton stall, watching my mother's hand picking up some different colour threads wound around round wooden reels. I can see a lot of different kind of bright shiny colour ribbons, and cord strings, and elastics and buttons and things that I am seeing for the first time. I am speaking. Two yard of this please, and four yard of the bias binding. How much is this ribbon? I am speaking. Everything in that box is half price. I am speaking. I want two and a half yard of these two, thank you.

Here I am watching my mother, listening to her speaking to the woman, watching the woman holding a long wooden stick, measuring the white cloth ribbon reeling it off the big round paper card reel.

IAM®

Here I am watching the woman, measuring out the things my mother want, understanding in my mind, knowing that we can buy anything we want from a shop. We can buy everything, anything we want inside the market full of the things that all the other shops have and it cost less money to buy the things we need from the people inside the market.

Here I am watching my mother sorting out, counting up the number of buttons and some elastic that mummy use to make knickers with.

Here I am watching my mother's hand inside her hand-bag, sorting out the money coins, counting up the money inside her hand, counting it into the palm of the woman's hand. I am speaking. Put these into the trolley please Hazel. I have one last stop to make before we can go home.

Here I am following my mother walking up to the stall where all the sweets and cakes and biscuits are stacked up in rows.

Here I am looking at the biscuits, smelling the biscuits in the air making my mouth water.

Here I am watching my mother moving her eyes across the counter, wanting mummy to buy some of everything. I am speaking. Two pound of the mix please, and not all the broken ones and one pound of the mix quality streets; and these three cakes. Let me have half of that one; watching my mother's hand pointing to the brown colour cake with a white top. Yes; that piece there.

Here I am; wanting to get home now; wanting to have some of the cake that mummy is buying. I am speaking. How much you want? I am speaking. Is that all love? I am speaking. Do not call me love. I am not your love.

Here I am listening to my mother and the man having words with each other, watching the man's smile disappear from his face. I am speaking. I want them in a bag. I am speaking. I am just being friendly darling. Can't you take a compliment?

Here I am watching my mother, watching her eyes fixed on the man's face, watching my mother accepting the bag of shopping from shop man's hands; watching the man's mouth shut tight. I am speaking. You all come on now.

Here I am inside the market; shopping with my mother, watching my mother looking at the tomatoes on the vegetable stall; watching my mother holding up the tomato in her hand. I am speaking. Two pound of tomatoes please. How much is this cabbage? Yes; I will take it and a pound of these apples and six of the large oranges.

IAM®

Here I am watching my mother doing the shopping for us. I am speaking. Come. We are going home now before the money done.

Here I am; wanting to reach home, feeling the trolley bag pulling, feeling my neck and hands hurting, pulling the trolley full to the top with food; watching Ruel and George playing in the market, getting mummy angry.

Here I am following my mother, listening to her speaking to herself, saying how tired she is, saying everything is getting more and more expensive. Every week the price of food go up.

Here I am; wanting to reach home, walking quick, dragging the trolley behind me, feeling my body hurting inside, feeling my feet hurting inside my shoes.

Here I am thinking about myself, wanting to put on my new school clothes, wondering how I am going to look inside my new clothes. I am speaking. Open the gate George.

Here I am standing on the ground outside my father's house, watching my mother put the key inside the front door; feeling my arms dragging off; feeling my body wanting to sit down; wanting to get inside the house; wanting to take off my shoes now. I am speaking. Hold the door wide open George. Come Ruel; help me with the pram.

Here I am inside the house, feeling good with myself.

Here I am feeling good to be home; thinking' all the people on the street never say sorry when they step on my foot.

Here I am thinking in my mind, thinking; it is hard work to do the shopping. I am speaking. Go and change into your house clothes.

Here I am pulling the trolley bag into the dining-room, placing the plastic bags down on the floor next to it.

Here I am walking into the hall way, walking up the stair, feeling the weight coming off my body, making my body feel light.

Here I am inside the girl's bed-room.

Here I am pulling my shoes off my feet, taking off my socks.

Here I am taking off my dress, putting it on the clothes-hanger, hanging it inside the wardrobe, putting my shoes under the dressing-table where it belong.

Here I am putting on my house dress, hearing my mother's voice talking inside her room.

IAM®

Here I am walking down the stairs, walking into the dining-room.

Here I am inside the dining-room.

Here I am looking at all the plastic carry bags full with new clothes, and food for all of us. I can see Delroy is still sleeping inside the pram.

Here I am wondering in my mind, thinking what to do, watching my mother's body entering the dining-room. I am speaking. Hazel; put the kettle on and make Delroy a bottle.

Here I am hearing my mother's voice, watching Ruel and George and Mavis following each other into the dining-room, gathering around mummy, just looking.

Here I am inside the kitchen, lifting the chair by the sink.

Here I am putting cold water into the kettle, resting it down on top of the stove.

Here I am with the burning match inside my hand, lighting the gas under the kettle, turning the flame up high.

Here I am standing inside the dining-room, standing in the presence of Ruel and George and Mavis; all of us standing around our mother sitting down on the chair, taking the things out of the trolley bag, putting them down on the dining-table.

Here I am watching my mother's hand emptying the bags.

Here I am taking the bottle of milk from the fridge, carrying it into the kitchen, resting it down on the worktop.

Here I am standing on the chair with the tea-towel in my hand, lifting the kettle off the fire, pouring the hot water into the saucepan, half full.

Here I am pouring the milk into the water. I can hear my mother telling Ruel and George to put on there new clothes for her to see.

Here I am inside the kitchen, standing on the chair, putting the tea-bag into the saucepan, making the milk-tea for Delroy.

Here I am lifting the chair over to the sink, lifting the saucepan off the stove, resting it down on top of the draining-board.

Here I am standing on the chair, pouring the milk-tea into Delroy's bottle. I am speaking. Hazel; what is taking you so long? Come and put these on let me see how you look.

IAM®

Here I am hearing my mother's voice feeling my inside jump up, feeling the hot milk on my hand, burning into my skin, making water come into my eyes.

Here I am remembering how the cold water stop the iron burn marks hurting.

Here I am holding my hands under the cold water, feeling the hurting going away, feeling the cold water turn warm on my hands. I am speaking. Hazel.

Here I am hearing my mother's voice, calling out my name.

Here I am wiping my hands dry, putting the top onto Delroy's feeding bottle.

Here I am mummy.

Here I am looking at Ruel, looking at George's body dressed in their new school clothes. Ruel and George look good, smiling all over their face. I am speaking. You come here Hazel. Put these on let me see if they fit.

Here I am. Thank you mummy. I am speaking. Put the shoes on now let me see you walk in them Hazel.

Here I am putting on my new brown colour shoes the same as Ruel and George's new shoes.

Here I am tying the shoe lace, thinking in my mind, realizing; my new shoes look good on my foot. I like my new pair of shoes that I am wearing.

Here I am walking across the dining-room floor, walking so mummy can see me wearing my new shoes. I am speaking. Good; you look good in them Hazel. Right, go and put your clothes up in your room and come help me put the food away. Ruel, you and George go and hang up your clothes in the wardrobe properly; quick now.

IAM®

CHAPTER 16

Here I am walking up the stairs, carrying my new clothes; feeling good knowing that my body is having everything new to put on to wear to school.

Here I am standing before my dressing-table, putting away my two new knickers pants, and white vest, and petticoat slip, and two pairs of white socks, and a cardigan to wear over my dress.

Here I am walking down the stairs, wondering in my mind thinking; when is mummy going to make me my dress.

Here I am standing in the presence of my mother, watching her taking the food from the trolley bag. I am speaking. Mix the jug full of orange drink for you lot. Move quick now. I have to make you a dress before Monday morning come.

Here I am standing on the chair taking the big glass jug out of the cabinet, resting it down on the table.

Here I am looking inside the cabinet cupboard, looking for the bottle of orange drink, resting it down of the table.

Here I am walking into the kitchen, carrying the jug and orange drink, resting them down on the draining-board.

Here I am lifting the chair over to the sink.

Here I am standing on the chair pouring the orange drink into the jug.

Here I am watching the cold water falling into the sink, waiting for the water to come clean, wanting to mix the orange drink.

Here I am walking into the dining-room, carrying the jug of orange drink.

Here I am wondering in my mind, thinking; what is mummy going to give us to eat.

Here I am standing on the chair by the cabinet, taking out the glasses, resting them down on the table, making ready to eat our lunch. I am speaking. Hazel, wash one apple and pour me a glass of milk please. Make sure the glass is clean.

Here I am standing the chair by the cabinet, getting a long glass, resting it down on the table.

Here I am looking at the apples and pears and oranges in the fruit bowl, choosing an apple for mummy, carrying it into the kitchen with the glass.

IAM®

Here I am inside the kitchen, standing on the chair over the sink, washing the glass under the warm water, wanting the glass to look clean for mummy.

Here I am washing the apple under the cold water, wiping it dry on the clean dishcloth.

Here I am wiping the glass dry, wiping my hands dry, drying the glass, making the glass look shine.

Here I am inside the dining-room, taking the bottle of milk from the fridge.

Here I am inside the kitchen, standing on the chair, pouring the milk into the glass.

Here I am walking into the dining-room, carrying the glass of cold milk and the apple to my mother.

Here I am standing before my mother, wondering in my mind.

Here I am. Here is the apple and milk mummy. I am speaking. Is that how you are serving me the apple? Go and put it on a plate and bring the little cooking knife with you.

Here I am feeling my inside go round, changing, listening to my mother's voice.

Here I am standing on the chair, taking the side-plate out of the cabinet, walking around my mother on my way to the kitchen to get the little sharp knife.

Here I am inside the dining-room, placing the apple on the plate on the table, pushing the plate near to mummy.

Here I am; understanding in my mind, the way mummy wants me to serve food on a plate and not from my hands.

Here I am standing inside the dining-room, watching mummy emptying the paper bags of biscuits into the biscuit tin.

Here I am. Here it is mummy. The milk and apple is ready for you mummy. I am speaking. Thank you and don't you ever give anyone any food from your hands again.

Here I am. Yes mummy. I am speaking. Pass me some side-plates. Mavis, you go and call your brothers down.

Here I am watching my mother's eyes looking down into the biscuit tin on her lap. I am speaking. Take three and put them on the plate.

IAM®

Here I am looking down into the biscuit tin, looking at all the different kinds of shapes, and all the colours of biscuits I can see.

Here I am looking, wondering what the different biscuit taste like, thinking in my mind, wondering which one must I have, wanting to try them all.

Here I am sitting at the table, eating my biscuit. The biscuit taste nice.

Here I am eating my biscuit, watching Delray's body moving inside the pram. Delroy is waking up, raising his head looking around at us eating, looking like he is making to cry. I am speaking. Give this to Delroy. Did you make Delroy his milk Hazel?

Here I am. Yes mummy.

Here I am inside the kitchen, getting Delroy's bottle of milk off the kitchen worktop. I can feel the bottle is feeling warm on the back of my hands; feeling just right for Delroy to drink.

Here I am inside the dining-room, watching Delroy pushing the balance of biscuit into his mouth, reaching out his hand to me, wanting his milk.

Here I am sitting at the dining-table, licking the cream chocolate off the biscuit, thinking in my mind, not wanting the biscuit to finish, wanting the taste to stay inside my mouth.

Here I am eating, looking at each one present inside my father's house.

Here I am thinking, wondering in my mind.

Here I am realizing in my mind; understanding that there is many more buildings of the one name house and the names of the other buildings are different, according to its use.

Here I am realizing in my mind, understanding that every house has its own number, and some houses have a name. The shop buildings look like my father's house, and the shops all have a number and a name, according to the thing that the people sell inside their shop. The things inside the shops have a number on them to show how much money the owner of the things will sell it for. Everything has a number on it. The shops have all kinds of name. The fruit and vegetable shop name is greengrocer. The shop that sells tins and packets, and bottles, and boxes and jars of food is name grocery shop. There are so many different kinds of shops. The yarn shop that sell wool and ribbons, and knitting and crocheting pins, sewing needles, sewing cotton and all kinds of things to make clothes with. The men's shop that sells clothes for men. The ladies shop that sells clothes for women. The baby shop that sells babies and little children's clothes and all the things that mother's use for babies. The children shop that sell boys and girls clothes, and toys and all the things that mother and fathers buy for little boys and girls. The shoe shop that sells shoes and boots and socks and shoe polish. The bag shop, that sells all kinds of shape bags and money purses and things. The flower shop, that sells flowers and plants. The newsagent shop, that sells newspaper and books, and magazines and sweets, and cigarettes and other things. The butcher's shop, that sells all kind of animal flesh meat that people eat. There is even a shop that sells shops and houses, and a shop name Post Office that people go and get money from.

Here I am thinking in my mind, understanding all that I can remember about everything happening outside my father's house.

Here I am remembering all the different buildings and the names people call the places like the church and the market and the factory like the big tall long building that does not have any windows for us to see inside.

Here I am thinking in my mind, understanding in my mind, learning about the place where I am on the ground name England.

Here I am realizing that a house is a building that a man and woman set-up home together and have babies. The house inside is where the man and the woman sleep with their children. The house inside is where the man and his wife act out their plans. The house is where the man goes out from to work for the thing name money, and give some to the woman; his wife to look after the man and all the children his wife borne.

Here I am thinking, wondering in my mind, thinking of myself, understanding all that I can remember about shopping with my mother. I am speaking. Hazel, wash-up everything then come on up stairs.

Here I am. Yes mummy.

Here I am collecting the plates off the dining-table, watching my mother's body walking into the hall way, carrying Delroy on her side, watching Mavis pushing her way in front of mummy.

Here I am walking into the kitchen, thinking in my mind, wondering what mummy wants me for.

Here I am standing on the chair over the sink, washing the dirty plates and glasses, resting them down on the draining-board.

Here I am wiping everything dry, resting them down on the worktop.

IAM®

Here I am putting everything where they belong inside the cabinet cupboard, feeling good inside myself, thinking about going to school, wishing Monday is here.

Here I am wondering about the school, wondering what they do at school.

Here I am. Ruel; how many more days before Monday school day come Ruel? I am speaking. Three more days and night then the next morning is Monday.

Here I am listening to Ruel and understanding every word that Ruel is saying. I am speaking. Seven days make one week.

Here I am thinking in my mind, remembering the day names, knowing that this day is name Thursday and the next two day is Friday and Saturday is the day that mummy always go out shopping for food. Then Sunday, church day.

Here I am. Ruel; what is the name of the day next to Sunday? I am speaking. Monday; that's the day we are going to school. Tuesday is the next morning we get up and the next morning is Wednesday and then Thursday again like today; then Friday and Saturday and Sunday again.

Monday, Tuesday, Wednesday, Thursday, Friday, Saturday, Sunday. Seven days make one week. Do you get it?

Here I am listening to Ruel sounding good speaking the names of the seven days making one the week.

Here I am; wanting to understand.

Here I am. Say the names again Ruel. Please, so I can remember. You sound good. I am speaking. George knows everything about school and how to read and write properly. I am speaking. Monday, Tuesday, Wednesday, Thursday, Friday, Saturday, Sunday.

Here I am remembering mummy wants me up stairs.

Here I am. Ruel; will you write the names of the week in the book for me please Ruel. I just remember, mummy want me up stairs now. Will you Ruel. I am speaking. Where is the book then?

Here I am on my knees, looking under the television table, looking for my exercise book.

Here I am. Here it is Ruel. Write on this page please. Say it again; please Ruel; then I will remember. I am speaking. Monday, Tuesday, Wednesday, Thursday, Friday, Saturday, Sunday.

IAM®

Here I am. Thank you Ruel.

Here I am remembering the sounds of Ruel's voice speaking the names of every day making one week; counting the names on my finger; remembering the sound of all the days and feeling good with myself knowing that I can speak the names of ever day making up one week.

Here I am walking up the stairs, saying out loud. Monday, Tuesday, Wednesday, Thursday, Friday, Saturday, Sunday.

Here I am at the top part of our house, walking into the girl's bed-room. I can see all the bedclothes are gone from Mavis's bed. Mummy is changing the bed-clothes again.

Here I am walking along the hall way, on my way to my brother's bed-room. I can hear my mother pulling the bed away from the wall.

Here I am mummy. I am speaking. Come help me change the bed them; the boys them nasty.

Here I am within the presence of my mother, watching my mother making up her face, looking at the blanket on Ruel and George's bed. The blanket and sheet smells rank. I am speaking. Put them on the bathroom floor.

Here I am pulling the dirty sheets and blanket along the floor, walking into the bath-room, thinking in my mind.

Ruel and George can't even get up and use the toilet.

Here I am with my mother, making-up Ruel and George's bed. I am speaking. Go and get the broom and sweeping brush.

Here I am walking down the stairs, walking into the dining-room, walking into the kitchen, getting the broom and sweeping brush, and the dustpan.

Here I am on my way up the stairs, carrying the broom and sweeping brush and the dustpan up the stairs. I can hear the front door key hole sounding like daddy is home.

Here I am standing on the step, looking at the front door opening, watching my father's body coming into the house.

Here I am looking at my father's body walking coming towards me, making my body feel good inside.

Here I am. Hallo daddy.

I am speaking. Hallo daughter. Where is your mother?

IAM®

Here I am. Mummy is up stairs cleaning out the boy's bed-room. I am helping mummy.

Here I am walking up the stairs, hearing my father's footstep walking towards the dining-room. I am happy now; daddy is home.

Here I am standing in the boy's bed-room, looking at my mother's body on her hands, kneeling on the floor, reaching her hands under the bed, dragging out all the things from under the bed.

Here I am. Daddy is home mummy. I am speaking. Your daddy's come home? Pass me the bin. Look at all the things Ruel and George got under the bed. I am going to beat them back-side. Look at the food crumbs in the place. Rat will cover the house. Look at the food from under the bed. My God, what am I going to do with them?

Here I am listening to every word I can hear my mother saying, looking at all the different things that I can see on the floor inside Ruel and George's bed-room. I can see the apple heart, dirty underpants, orange skin, bread crumbs, dirty socks and clothes, magazines and the games board. I am speaking. Hazel. Put these inside the bath-room.

Here I am walking into the bath-room, carrying Ruel and George's dirty underpants, and dirty clothes, putting them into the clothes basket under the sink.

Here I am inside the bed-room, feeling the clean air coming from the open window. The air is smelling good; making the room smell clean again. I am speaking. Finish sweeping the rubbish, please Hazel.

Here I am on my knees with the hand-brush in my hands sweeping the floor. I can see my mother is standing before the boy's wardrobe, sorting the clothes hanging down off the hangers inside the wardrobe.

Here I am sweeping the floor, listening to my mother talking to herself. I am speaking. What am I going to do? I am tired of cleaning up house. The boy's them nasty. They believe there daddy have plenty of money to waste. Look how Ruel and George treat their clothes.

Here I am inside the bed-room doorway, sweeping the dust together, brushing the dust into the dustpan, listening to every word my mother is saying aloud. I am speaking. When you done. There are some clean sheets on Mavis's bed. Go and change your bed clothes and carry the dirty ones come.

IAM®

Here I am listening to my mother, realizing that she is doing a house clean-out again.

Here I am walking into the girl's bed-room, thinking in my mind, thinking about my mother having a baby.

Here I am; knowing that mummy spends a lot of time on cleaning.

Here I am; knowing that my father, one man and the boys expect mummy and I to clean-up after them. My mother and I have to do all, the house cleaning or stay inside a pig-sty as mummy say.

Here I am making-up the bed, thinking in my mind, feeling hurt for my mother's body, hearing her hands washing the dirty clothes in the bath-room.

Here I am thinking, wondering in my mind, thinking of my mother's body having a baby.

Here I am wondering what mummy would do if I was not here to help her to do all the cleaning and cooking and ironing work.

Here I am thinking; if I was not here mummy would have to do all the work herself or show Ruel and George how to care for their bodies and help each other, or she would have to work and work and do everything herself or live in a pig-sty.

Here I am; knowing that Ruel and George never help mummy to keep the house inside clean and daddy is always at the factory or sleeping when he is home and Mavis and Delroy are too small to do anything.

Here I am feeling pleased with myself, knowing that I am my mother's helper.

Here I am thinking; mummy should show Ruel and George how to keep their room clean and how to wash their clothes just like I have to do the washing and cooking and cleaning. All Ruel and George do is play games and watch television until they are bored and then they go to bed.

Here I am standing outside the bath-room doorway, holding the dirty bedclothes in my hand.

Here I am standing listening to my mother's body breathing, sounding louder, sounding out of breath; like the women do when they are washing clothes on the ground name Jamaica.

Here I am standing over the bath, helping my mother to wash the clothes. I can hear my mother's body sounding tired now, hearing her breathing change. I am speaking. God knows what I would do without you.

IAM®

Here I am watching my mother's face, looking at the water coming out of her face onto her nose and over her eyebrow; watching the water falling off my mother's face. I am speaking. Where is the pillow-slip and sheet them from off your bed?

Here I am lifting the sheets into the water, looking at my mother resting her hand on the side of the bath.

Here I am thinking in my mind, watching my mother's face looking wet with water running down the sides of her face.

Here I am. Mummy; I will wash the balance of the clothes. You should go and rest now. You are having a baby. I am speaking. Hazel; I wish I could stop to rest. Let me finish off these big things. Here; hold this end and help me wring out the water. My hands are falling off. Your father does not realize what it is to wring water out of wet clothes with your bear hands. I am speaking. Pull out the plug.

Here I am watching my mother sort the balance of clothes out on the floor. I am speaking. Turn on the hot water.

Here I am watching my mother putting the sheets back into the bath, and some disinfectant, and the clothes conditioner to make the clothes feel soft. I am speaking. Only the Lord God knows how long and hard I work and what I am suffering.

Here I am hearing every word that my mother is speaking; watching everything my mother is doing.

Here I am helping my mother to wash the bedclothes. My mother is always doing something, even when she is sitting down.

Here I am; knowing what my mother means; knowing what my mother does with her time. I am speaking. Scrub that piece for me.

Here I am helping my mother rinse the clothes inside the clean smelling water.

Here I am watching my mother's hand twist and twist the sheet clothe around and around it self; wringing out the water, putting the sheet into the bowl on the bath-room floor. I am speaking. Wash those things out Hazel. I am going to peg these out now to dry before the evening comes. Help me down stairs with these first.

Here I am putting the balance of dirty clothes into the bath, pouring the soap powder into the bath, pushing everything down under the water.

128

IAM®

Here I am walking down the stairs, carrying the bucket of wet clothes, feeling my body hurting, feeling the bucket of wet clothes pulling down on me, lifting the bucket down on each step.

Here I am walking lifting dropping the bucket down, resting my hands, carrying the bucket into the dining-room, walking across the dining-room, into the kitchen, dropping the bucket down on the doormat, lifting the bucket outside, carrying it to my mother standing in the garden pegging out the sheets along the wire clothes line. I am speaking. Hold these for me Hazel.

Here I am standing by my mother, holding up the wet sheet off the ground, holding it with my mother, watching my mother pegging the sheet out along the line. I can see that my mother has just washed the two long clothes line full of clothes and sheets looking good, moving with the air, flying high up off the ground where I am standing looking at my mother's body, her face looking tired.

Here I am collecting the bucket and bowl off the ground following my mother into the house.

Here I am standing at the kitchen dining-room doorway, looking at Ruel and George and Mavis, and my father sitting down with their eyes wide open watching the television. I am speaking. Pearl; come and sit down a minute. I am speaking. Sit down what; you going to cook the dinner? I am speaking. What; me tired, me just come in from work. I am speaking. Work; you know what name work. I have not stopped yet from morning.

Here I am walking into the hall way, hearing my mother and father having words with each other. I can hear my mother telling my father about himself and Ruel and George who are just like he is.

Here I am walking up the stairs, thinking in my mind.

Here I am standing inside the bath-room, standing over the bath, washing the little clothes, the dark colour clothes me and Ruel and George wear inside the house.

Here I am scrubbing the cloth in my hand, feeling the body that I am hurting.

Here I am; understanding and realizing that the bodies that do nothing to help them self; makes work for another.

Here I am washing Ruel and George dirty clothes and knowing that their bodies would not have any clean clothes to put on if mummy and I didn't wash their clothes clean. Ruel and George never wash their clothes, not even their dirty underpants that are always dirty with do-do marks. Ruel and

IAM®

George cannot be bothered to use the toilet paper and wipe their bottom clean.

Here I am washing, thinking in my mind, realizing that the man like my father appear to keep a woman to wash and cook and clean up after their bodies that do not understand how much work, extra work they make, all because they cannot be bothered to clean up after them self.

Here I am knowing that Ruel and George is a child as I am and Ruel and George is older than I am, but the girl child that I am is expected to clean-up after them; all because they are born the image of their father one man.

Here I am knowing that from the time I came to the ground name England, Ruel and George have not done anything of the self to help them self to help mummy or daddy.

Here I am the girl child, doing all that one can to help my mother and father.

Here I am knowing that my father is the cause of Ruel and George not helping themselves because daddy is not showing Ruel and George how to do for them self, like mummy is always showing me how to do all the things that she can do.

Here I am wondering what my father do in the factory where he goes to work.

Here I am rinsing the clothes inside the clean water, thinking in my mind.

Here I am wringing the water out the clothes putting each piece into the bucket.

Here I am rubbing the sponge on the inside of the bath, washing it clean, thinking in my mind.

Here I am walking down the stairs, carrying the bucket of clean clothes, lifting the bucket down on the steps, walking down the stairs, sitting down on the step, resting the body that I am; feeling my body hurting inside my hands are hurting.

Here I am walking past my father, walking into the kitchen. I can see mummy is still working. Mummy is preparing the food for our dinner. I am speaking. Good Hazel. Hang them out on the little line by the coal house.

Here I am getting the clothes peg-bag off the hook on the kitchen wall. I can feel the body that I am hurting, just hurting me inside.

Here I am standing outside the house, stretching my body reaching up, pulling the clothes line down, holding it down in one hand, pushing the

IAM®

clothes peg into the clothes, pegging each piece of cloth out, just like my mother peg the clothes out along the wire clothes line.

Here I am hanging the boy's trouser pants by the two legs, and the shirt from the collar and my house dress and all the house cardigans.

Here I am wringing out the water from the socks, pegging them together along the clothes line, and Ruel and George's under pants, and the last piece, my knickers. My neck is hurting at the back inside the body that I am hurting.

IAM®

CHAPTER 17

Here I am standing on the land, looking out from myself, looking all over my father's land, looking up into the air, looking at all the clean clothes moving inside the air, moving high off the ground of the land that I am standing, just looking.

Here I am walking into the kitchen, looking at my mother's body standing over the stove, stirring the food cooking in the sauce pan, tasting the food, smelling good, making me want to eat.

Here I am walking through the dining-room, carrying the bucket in my hand, walking past my father, watching his face looking into the big, big book.

Here I am walking up the stairs, wondering in my mind, wondering about the book my father is looking at.

Here I am inside the bath-room, returning the bucket down on the floor under the sink where it belongs.

Here I am wondering in my mind, thinking; where did daddy get the big book from; wondering what the big book is saying.

Here I am thinking in my mind, walking down the stairs, walking past my father, watching his eyes moving across the page inside the big book.

Here I am wandering what is the book name, the book with the white cloth like cover.

Here I am standing in the presence of my father and brothers and sister; listening to my mother's voice humming a song.

Here I am inside the dining-room, looking at my father, watching his head leaning forward looking into the open book.

Here I am; wanting to know what the book is name, wanting to ask my father what the book is name.

Here I am. Daddy; daddy; what is that book you have in your hand daddy?

Here I am looking at my father, wondering in my mind, looking at my father's face looking into the book, wondering if my father can hear the body that I am speaking to him.

Here I am. Daddy; daddy. I am speaking. Yes, I did hear you the first time, just one minute. I am reading something.

IAM®

Here I am watching wondering what my father is reading about; watching his eyes moving across the page, smiling to himself reading in his mind. I am speaking. Yes Hazel. This is the Bible. This book is a Bible like the one your mother carry with her when she go to church.

Here I am. Thank you daddy.

Here I am now of the understanding that the book is name Bible. The book name Bible comes in many shape and size, and colour.

Here I am walking into the kitchen, thinking in my mind, wanting to read, wanting to understand, wanting to know the meaning of every word inside the book name Bible.

Here I am standing inside the kitchen, looking at my mother's body standing over the kitchen sink, washing her hands.

Here I am watching my mother, wondering in my mind, wondering about the book name the Bible.

Here I am wondering who gave the book its name the Bible. Why is the book name Bible?

Here I am mummy. I am speaking. Hazel you work hard today. Put those in the cupboard for me. Then we can go and sit down. Wash up those few things in the sink.

Here I am listening to my mother praising my body.

Here I am putting the things away inside the kitchen cupboard where they belong.

Here I am listening to my mother speaking to herself; watching her hands mixing the flour and water together inside the big mixing bowl.

Here I am collecting the dirty things off the worktop, putting them into the washing-up bowl inside the sink, lifting the chair over to the sink.

Here I am standing on the chair, turning on the hot water tap, putting washing-up liquid into the bowl, washing the cooking things clean, resting them down on the draining-board.

Here I am lifting the chair over to the worktop, standing on the chair, wiping the worktop clean, wiping the things dry on the tea-towel in my hand, putting them away where they belong. I am speaking. You are going to school with your brothers on Monday. Your father believe that I can do everything myself.

IAM®

Here I am making the kitchen look clean, listening to my mother speaking to herself.

Here I am inside the kitchen, returning the cooking things where they belong, listening to my mother, wondering why mummy always talk to herself whenever she and daddy have words with each other.

Here I am. Mummy, I will finish cleaning everything, you should go and sit down now. I am speaking. Thank you. I have almost finished. Only you one know how hard I am working in this house.

Here I am watching my mother's hand folding the dishcloth small inside her hands, wiping the outside of the saucepan of food cooking on top of the stove, wiping the stove top all over, making the stove and everything upon it look clean, looking good to the body that I am, watching everything I can see my mother is doing inside the kitchen where I am.

Here I am watching my mother's hands working; listening to my mother speaking to herself, watching her body; feeling hurt for my mother, understanding every word that I can hear her speaking as if she is lone by herself.

Here I am inside the kitchen; smelling the food cooking, smelling the food smelling good, tasting the food in the air surrounding the body that I am. I am speaking. Hazel, I am going to sit down now. My leg is hurting me. Just wash the bowl out for me.

Here I am standing on the chair, standing over the kitchen sink, washing the bowl inside clean, wringing out the dishcloth, thinking in my mind; thinking about my mother.

Here I am standing inside the dining-room.

Here I am looking at my father looking inside the Bible, reading to himself.

Here I am looking at my mother, watching her body resting her head on her hand leaning on the dining-table.

Here I am looking at Ruel and George and Mavis; all looking at the television. Delroy is sleeping in his pram.

Here I am standing by the fire, looking at the television picture. I can hear the music and the sounds coming from the television box, but I do not understand all that I can hear.

Here I am wondering in my mind, looking at the television picture, thinking in my mind; wondering what is this film show about.

IAM®

Here I am; wanting to understand all that I can see. I am speaking. Ruel, George. Why won't you keep your bed-room clean? If your mother; have to tell me your room is dirty again, watch out.

Here I am listening to my father, watching his face change. I can see Ruel eyes looking at George's body. I can see my father's face looking without expression, looking at Ruel, looking at George. Ruel and George look like they do not know what to do with them self, not wanting to look at daddies face, just looking at them. I am speaking. Ruel and George need to be under some control. All they do is break up everything they put their hands on. You want to see all the food me clear from under the bed in their room. Gee; you beta put them under control before rat start coming into the house. I am speaking. Are you listening to your mother?

Here I am hearing my mother and father talking about Ruel and George.

Here I am thinking in my mind, thinking. Good, it's about time mummy tell daddy about you two.

Here I am sitting down on the floor, resting the exercise book on my lap, copywriting the day names that Ruel write on the page for me.

Here I am hand-writing, remembering the days, remembering the names that make one week. I can remember the word sounding the day name Sunday. The day Sunday is the time when we all put on our good clothes and go to the building name church. The next morning is name Monday, the time I am going to the school with Ruel and George. The next morning time is name Tuesday, and the next morning is Wednesday, and this day time is name Thursday. This is the day mummy go out shopping when she is looking to buy special things like the nice clothes Mavis wear, and the things she use to do her hand-sewing, and do some shopping for food. The next morning time is name Friday. Friday is the day when mummy buys the food to last until the next Friday time comes around again. Mummy likes to buy the fish flesh to cook for dinner on Fridays. The next morning time is name Saturday, the last day that mummy go out to the shops to buy food for us to eat. We always have soup for our dinner on Saturdays and daddy always watch the wrestling show on the television, and make sure he marks the pool score draw coupon paper. Then all our favourite day is the next morning time name Sunday. Mummy likes to put on the television on Sunday morning, to hear the Sunday church music and we sometimes go to the church building, and we have our favourite breakfast on Sundays. On Sundays we have eggs, and bacon, and bake beans and sometimes with fried dumpling instead of bread. Mummy makes punch or carrot juice to drink with our dinner, and we always have rice and peas and chicken and jelly with fruit and ice-cream. Mummy's cooking taste nice.

Here I am writing, remembering the names of every day that make one week.

Here I am feeling good inside myself, thinking in my mind.

Here I am writing the letters sounding the name of the alphabet, writing, wanting to remember the big letters of the alphabet, wanting to remember the little letters of the alphabet.

Here I am feeling good with myself, wanting to read good, knowing that I can write.

Here I am looking at the words I am writing, thinking in my mind, wanting to read.

Here I am looking inside the once upon a time book.

Here I am looking at the words on the page, looking on the pictures and colours all over the page.

Here I am; wanting to sound the words that I can see inside the book.

Here I am; wanting to read good like George can read the words to sound good. I am speaking. How come Hazel always has a book in her hand? What you two doing? The two of you go and get a book. I want to see what you know. Turn off the television, now.

Here I am hearing my father raising his voice making me jump. My father is going to do some writing with us. I am speaking. Hazel, go and look at the food on the fire and turn off the pot with the meat.

Here I am walking fast into the kitchen, lifting the chair to the front part of the stove.

Here I am standing on the chair, holding the tea-towel and fork in my hand, taking the cover off the big saucepan.

Here I am pushing the fork into a piece of potato, blowing the steam off the potato, tasting the potato, turning the fire down low, returning the cover on the pan, wanting the potato to cook just right, the way mummy like the potatoes to taste.

Here I am standing on the kitchen ground, lifting the chair over by the dutch-pot, smelling the meat inside the air.

IAM®

Here I am standing on the chair, standing over the stove, winding the tea-towel around my hand, lifting the cover of the pot, pushing the fork into a piece of meat. The meat; is smelling; good; feeling hot on my tongue, tasting good.

Here I am standing on the kitchen ground, lifting the chair over to the sink, standing on the chair holding the kettle in my hand, holding the kettle under the cold water-tap, watching the water falling into the kettle.

Here I am holding a matchstick in the flame, watching the fire burning into the matchstick, lighting the stick flaming with fire.

Here I am lighting the gas under the kettle, turning the flame down low.

Here I am standing inside the dining-room, listening to my father's voice speaking.

Here I am. The food is nearly ready mummy; the potato is still a little hard. I am speaking. You turn off the fire from under the meat?

Here I am. Yes mummy. I am speaking. Who can tell me how many days make one week?

Here I am listening to my father.

Here I am feeling good inside, knowing that I know the answer to my father's question. I am speaking. I know daddy. I am speaking. Speak it let me hear. I am speaking. Seven days make one week. Monday, Tuesday Wednesday Thursday Friday Saturday and Sunday. I am speaking. Good George. Now; who can tell me, how many weeks make one month?

Here I am listening to every word that my father is speaking, but I am not understanding what the word month mean. I can see George is holding up his hands again. George is looking at daddy and smiling all over his face. I bet George know. I am speaking. What is the answer Ruel? I am speaking. I don't know daddy. I am speaking. Didn't you go to school in Jamaica? Okay George. I am speaking. Four weeks make one month. I am speaking. Yes, you are right. Tell me then; how many days in one month?

Here I am listening to every word that my father is speaking, listening to the words coming out of George's mouth, understanding in my mind, realizing the meaning of the word name month.

Here I am listening to my brother speaking, learning the meaning of the word month, the word that I am hearing for the one time. I am speaking. Go on George. I am speaking. Twenty-eight days make one month. I am speaking.

IAM®

Them teach you good back home in Jamaica, didn't they George? Good; now who can tell me; how many months make one year? I am speaking. I know, I know. I am speaking. Ruel; how many months make one year?

Here I am looking at Ruel's face. Ruel's face is changing. Ruel look like he is thinking, looking like he is wondering what he must say. I am speaking. Seven months; I think. I can see George's face looking pleased with him self. I am speaking. Twelve month make one year. I am speaking. Yes George, twelve month make one year. Write down the names of the twelve month if you can.

Here I am hearing every question my father asked, listening to Ruel and George speaking.

Here I am not feeling good with myself, wishing that I can write what daddy wants us to write.

Here I am realizing that there is more to life than learning how to wash and cook.

Here I am; wanting to understand.

Here I am; wanting to understand all that one can understand about writing.

Here I am not feeling good with myself, knowing that I do not know anything about all that George and daddy know inside their heads.

Here I am; wanting to write like my father can write, wanting to understand.

Here I am; wanting daddy to write the names of the twelve month that make one year, so I can understand what my father knows.

Here I am; wanting to learn.

Here I am. Daddy; will you write the names of the months for me? I want to write them. I am speaking. Come.

Here I am feeling good, standing at my father's side.

Here I am watching my father's hand with the pencil, writing on the paper. I am speaking. Say it after me now.

Here I am speaking as I am hearing the sounds coming out of my father's mouth, watching his mouth forming the sounds of the words my father has written on the paper, watching his finger pointing on each word, speaking each word so I can understand the look of the name of the twelve months that I am hearing. Now I know that twelve months make one year.

IAM®

Here I am learning the meaning of time; thinking in my mind; wanting to know when the girl body that I am came into being.

Here I am learning from my father the meaning of time.

Here I am; understanding that I am from time.

Here I am; knowing that my father does not realize that I understand what he is teaching me.

Here I am seeing in my mind eye can see. I can see every word in my mind I can see the sounds that I can hear my father is speaking.

Here I am feeling what my mind want me to understand, feeling my inside moving around, hearing the words of my father making me see the meaning of time. I am speaking. And again.

Here I am. Twelve months make one year. January, February, March, April, May, June, July, August, September, October, November, December. Twelve months make one year.

Here I am speaking the sounds, forming the names of the months.

Here I am speaking every word as I can hear my father is speaking, wondering in my mind, feeling in my mind, understanding in my mind; the meaning of the words that I am speaking.

Here I am; understanding that time is divided into day and night, into week, into month, into year.

Here I am wondering about time; wondering about the time before the body that I am came into being the girl body form that I am.

Here I am looking at my father's eyes looking down on the piece of paper that George write on; watching my father moving his eyes up and down the paper, looking at George's hand-writing, raising his head looking up at George, looking with a big smile upon his face. I am speaking. Good George. Let me see what you write Ruel.

Here I am watching my father looking at Ruel's body, not wanting to give daddy his piece of paper; watching daddy looking on Ruel's piece of paper; hearing daddy make sounds to himself. I am speaking. Ruel; didn't you go to school back home? I am speaking. Yes daddy. I am speaking. Then how come you write like this?

Here I am looking at Ruel's body not wanting to look-up on daddy's face, hearing daddy talking to Ruel; speaking without any expression on his face;

IAM®

looking at Ruel's face looking down on the ground before him. I am speaking. Write it all out again so that I can read what you write, understand.

Here I am in the presence of my father, in the presence of my mother, in the presence of my brothers Ruel and George and Delroy, in the presence of my sister Mavis; all present inside the dining-room inside my father's house, the building that surround the body that I am on the ground name England.

Here I am understanding myself, learning about my brothers, realizing that there is more to know about one another, knowing that George's mind know a lot more than I know; knowing that Ruel does not know as much reading and writing as George's body; even though Ruel's body is older than George and mine.

Here I am realizing that there are different ways one can learn.

Here I am; knowing that I know how to do a lot of things with my two hands that make me understand the girl body that I am.

Here I am realizing that George know a different kind of learning. George knows how to write down what he is thinking in his mind, and George know how to read what others have written out of their minds.

Here I am; wanting to understand, wanting to learn all that George and my father know in their minds.

Here I am; wanting to go to school like George went to school back home on the ground name Jamaica.

Here I am realizing that I can know what George knows; realizing that all I have to do is learn the alphabet, and learn to write and read words like George and daddy can write and read words; then I can write what is in my mind.

Here I am; knowing, that every body mind knows something different and if I want to know what is in another bodies mind; all I have to do is ask that body what I want to know.

Here I am; knowing, that every person knows, something different.

Here I am; understanding that when I open my mouth, my body makes a sound for every other body to hear.

Here I am; understanding myself, learning about myself; thinking; realizing the presence inside the body that I am teaching me about myself, making my body understand myself and everyone outside the body that I am.

I AM®

Here I am, just one.

Here I am thinking, wanting to know all there is inside George's mind.

Here I am; wanting to know all there is inside Ruel's mind.

Here I am; wanting to know all there is inside my father's mind, wanting to know every-thing about my father.

Here I am knowing that I belong to myself, as my father belong to himself, as my mother belong to herself, but here I am wanting to know my mother and father.

Here I am; knowing that I am learning all that I can from everyone. I know that I can see all there is to see through the eyes I am. I can hear all there is to hear through the ears I am.

Here I am; wanting to do something, wondering in my mind thinking; not knowing what I want to do.

Here I am; wanting to do something for myself. I want to do something. What can I do?

Here I am wondering in my mind, thinking. I am speaking. Turn on the television please George.

Here I am thinking in my mind, watching my hand writing the word that I am thinking in my mind, watching my hand writing, realizing in my mind; my mind is my teacher.

Here I am; knowing that I can know anything I want to know about anything; or anyone because my mind is teaching me.

Here I am sounding the words in my mind. I can read, I can read; I can read.

Here I am. I am reading, I am reading; I am reading.

Here I am looking on the words inside the once upon a time story book on my lap.

Here I am speaking the words, listening to the sounds coming out of my mouth.

Here I am reading. I can read, I can read.

Here I am speaking the words, listening to the sounds that I am making, forming the words that I can see, wanting to read, knowing that I can. I can read, I can read, I can read.

IAM®

Here I am. George; will you read the beginning of the story book? I want to read like you. Please George; please. I am speaking. O-n-c-e; says once. Once upon a time there were three bears.

Here I am looking at the words George's finger is pointing on, listening to George speaking the sounds, forming each word. I can see in my mind the picture is in my mind.

Here I am; understanding that words are sounds we make when speaking.

Here I am listening to the sounds George is making, hearing the words making pictures in my mind eye can see.

Here I am feeling good knowing that I can read, understanding every sound George is speaking for me to hear.

Here I am listening to George reading the words inside the once upon a time story book. I am speaking. Hazel, light the fire under the food please. I am speaking. Hazel, you carry on with what you doing. Ruel; go and do what your mother says. I am speaking. What did you say mummy? I am speaking. Light the fire under the food.

Here I am feeling good hearing my father tell Ruel to do something instead of mummy always telling me to do everything that she wants doing.

Here I am speaking the sounds, listening to George speaking the words that I can see George's hand point on the words that I can hear him speaking the words, making the picture in my mind.

Here I am feeling good with myself, listening to myself speaking the words that I am reading in time with George. I can read, I am reading, I can read, I am reading. Now I understand, I can read because I am reading; I am reading; I am. I am speaking. Someone set the table.

Here I am hearing my mother's voice.

Here I am looking at each one present inside the dining-room; wondering who is going to move first to do what mummy wants. I am speaking. I want to watch the television now Hazel.

Here I am. Thank you George.

Here I am on my knees, returning the story book under the television table, thinking in my mind, wondering if Ruel or George is going to do what mummy wants.

Here I am. Excuse me please mummy.

IAM®

Here I am folding out the dining-table, spreading the table-cloth over the top, making the table ready for mummy and daddy to have their dinner.

Here I am thinking in my mind; why didn't Ruel or George move to do what mummy want; thinking in my mind; didn't they hear mummy speak, or are they just pretending again, pretending not to hear.

Here I am. Mummy.

I am speaking. What you want.

Here I am. What are you having, to drink with your dinner? I am speaking. Ask your daddy. I am speaking. I want tea please.

Here I am walking into the kitchen carrying mummy and daddy's dinner plates, placing them down on the kitchen worktop.

Here I am standing inside the kitchen, standing on the chair, leaning on the sink, watching the cold water running into the kettle.

Here I am; smelling the food in the air, making my body feel hunger inside.

Here I am lighting the fire under the kettle, turning the flame up high, wanting the water to boil quick.

Here I am lifting the chair over by the stove, standing on the chair winding the tea-towel around my hand, lifting the cover off the saucepan, feeling the air hot on my face.

Here I am looking at the vegetables inside the pot, looking right, smelling good.

Here I am standing on the kitchen ground, getting the tea-pot from the cupboard, putting two tea-bags inside, resting the pot down on the kitchen worktop, making ready to make the tea.

Here I am thinking in my mind, wondering in my mind, thinking about myself, knowing that I can read, thinking about the words inside the story book, remembering the big book like the preacher man read when we go to church.

Here I am the presence present, feeling good inside myself.

Here I am standing on the chair over the stove, holding the tea-cloth in my hand, pouring the hot water out of the kettle into the tea-pot.

Here I am walking into the dining-room, carrying the tea-pot resting on the towel in my hand, putting it down on top of the tea-pot stand on the dining-table.

IAM®

Here I am looking inside the fridge, getting the can of milk, resting it down on the dining-table, remembering the sugar.

Here I am looking across the dining-table, making sure the table is set with everything mummy and daddy need to eat their dinner.

Here I am. Mummy; the dinner is ready. I am speaking. Yes, I am coming.

Here I am looking at my mother raise her body up off the chair. I can see my mother's face is looking tired, wanting sleep, watching her body moving slow, dragging her feet, walking towards the kitchen. I am speaking. Bring a little side plate for Delroy and Mavis.

Here I am looking inside the cabinet, getting two little plates. One for Mavis and one for Delroy's dinner.

Here I am taking the knife and fork out the drawer, placing them down on the table, setting a place for Mavis to have her dinner with mummy and daddy.

Here I am putting the cup down on the table for Mavis, thinking in my mind.

Here I am walking into the kitchen, carrying the plates in my hand, resting them down on the kitchen worktop for mummy to see.

Here I am standing on the chair over the kitchen sink, washing Delroy's bottle, brushing the insides clean with washing-up liquid.

Here I am inside the kitchen, watching my mother's body; her face is looking tired, wanting sleep.

Here I am inside the dining-room, looking inside the cabinet, getting the bottle of juice.

Here I am inside the kitchen, standing on the chair over the sink, pouring the juice into Delroy's feeding bottle, making Delroy a drink with his dinner.

Here I am inside the dining-room, returning the bottle of juice inside the cabinet cupboard where it belongs.

Here I am standing by the fire, looking around the dining-room, looking at everyone with their eyes fixed on the television screen. I am speaking. Hazel; come and give me a hand.

Here I am standing inside the kitchen, watching my mother's hand holding the two little plate of food down before me.

I AM®

Here I am walking slow, carrying Mavis and Delroy's dinner, taking my time, smelling the food, resting the plate down before Mavis's body sitting at the dinner-table.

Here I am standing before Delroy; holding Delroy's plate of food, watching Delroy's eyes fixed on the plate in my hand.

Here I am watching Delroy holding out his hands, making up noise, wanting to eat.

Here I am putting Delroy's food into his mouth, watching Delroy swallow down the food, eating the food quick.

Here I am thinking, thinking in my mind, wondering about Mavis.

Here I am thinking; how come mummy always serves Mavis her food the same time she and daddy is having their food. How come mummy never serves Ruel or George's food first?

Here I am thinking; Mavis is mummy and daddies favourite of all their children.

Here I am with the little spoon in my hand mixing the potato and cabbage together in the meat gravy, feeding Delroy his food.

The food smells good, making my body want to eat now.

Here I am feeding Delroy his food, thinking in my mind, wondering about myself; thinking about the school where I am going with Ruel and George on Monday.

Here I am watching Delroy licking his lips, looking on the empty plate in my hand.

Here I am. Here is your bottle Delroy. There is no more food. Have your juice.

Here I am on my way into the kitchen, carrying Delroy's empty dinner plate in my hand.

Here I am collecting the dirty things together, putting them inside the washing-up bowl inside the sink.

Here I am standing on the chair over the sink, pouring the washing-up liquid over the plates.

Here I am wiping the plates clean, resting them down on the draining-board.

I AM®

Here I am wringing the water out of the dishcloth, wiping the work-top clean, wanting the kitchen to look clean, just the way mummy make the kitchen look good inside.

Here I am standing on the chair over the work-top, wiping all the cooking things dry, putting them down on the work-top before me.

Here I am standing on the kitchen ground, putting everything away inside the kitchen cupboard where they belong.

Here I am remembering the clothes outside drying on the clothes-line.

Here I am inside the pantry, getting the clothes basket.

Here I am walking across the dining-room, on my way outside.

Here I am outside the house, walking along the garden footpath, feeling the air blowing up inside my dress, making my body shake.

Here I am standing under the clothes-line, pulling the stick down from its stance.

Here I am on my toes, pulling the big sheet across the line, pulling it off the line, pulling it down into the basket before me on the ground.

Here I am collecting the pieces of clothes off the line, feeling my body hurting inside my neck.

Here I am pulling the basket full with clean clothes, pulling it along the ground, walking towards the kitchen doorway.

Here I am. Ruel; will you help me lift the basket inside? It is heavy now. I am speaking. Where do you want it Hazel?

Here I am. <u>Inside</u> the back bed-room. Thank you Ruel.

Here I am standing at the dining-room entrance, holding the door open, watching Ruel holding the basket of washing against his belly, carrying it to the back bed-room. I am speaking. Thank you Hazel. I clean forgot that the clothes were out there. I can see mummy and daddy have finished eating there food. I am speaking. Hazel; light the fire under the food for you lot and share it out for me. George; run up stairs and get the bowl and Delroy night clothes, bring them come; quick.

Here I am walking into the kitchen, carrying the empty dinner plates, placing them down in the bowl inside the sink.

IAM®

Here I am standing before the stove, holding the matchbox and matches in my hand, lighting the fire under the pots of food, turning the flames up high, wanting the food to get hot quick; I am hungry.

Here I am standing inside the dining-room, clearing the table, making it ready for Ruel and George and me to have our dinner.

Here I am putting all the dirty things inside the sink I can hear the water boiling up inside the big saucepan. The food is smelling good; making my body want to eat.

Here I am turning the fire down low, not wanting the food to burn.

Here I am inside the dining-room, getting a plate for Ruel and George and me to have our dinner.

Here I am putting the orange squash into the big glass jug.

Here I am inside the kitchen, standing on the chair over the kitchen sink, feeling the water falling from the cold water tap, watching the water mixing the squash, filling up inside the jug.

Here I am walking into the dining-room, carrying the jug full of squash, placing it down on the table.

Here I am inside the kitchen, lifting the chair over to the stove.

Here I am standing on the chair, holding the tea-towel, lifting the cover off the saucepan, placing it down on top of the stove.

Here I am standing on the floor, placing the tea-towel around the pot handle, lifting the pot down off the stove, onto the work top.

Here I am lifting the dutch-pot off the stove, resting it down on the work-top.

Here I am lifting the chair over by the work-top, standing on the chair, sharing the potato out on the plates, sharing the meat out onto the plates, feeling my insides going round, feeling hunger.

Here I am. Ruel, George; your dinner is ready. I am speaking. Which one is mine Hazel?

Here I am. This is yours Ruel.

Here I am walking into the dining-room, carrying my plate of food, placing it down on the table.

IAM®

Here I am sitting at the dining-table, eating my food, tasting good, thinking in my mind, wondering, looking around the space where I am, watching everyone, thinking in my mind.

Here I am eating, watching my father leaving the dining-room.

Here I am eating, watching my mother taking off Delroy's clothes, getting Delroy's body ready for night-time.

Here I am eating my food, looking at my mother's face, wondering in my mind, wondering; what are you thinking about.

Here I am watching my mother, thinking about her body having a baby, wondering how mummy is going to manage by herself.

Here I am eating, thinking about myself, looking at my mother, wanting to understand her expression, watching her face, watching her hands putting on Delroy's pyjama top. I am speaking. Hazel; make sure the kitchen is clean and tidy the dining-room when you done. Keep the noise down your daddy gone to his bed.

Here I am. Yes mummy.

Here I am eating, watching my mother, her body walking into the hall-way carrying Delroy on her arm, watching Mavis following after her.

Here I am the presence present.

Here I am inside the dining-room, looking at Ruel, looking at George.

Here I am walking into the kitchen, carrying the plates, resting them down inside the bowl.

Here I am standing on the chair over the sink, watching the hot water coming into the bowl.

Here I am washing the dirty plates, turning them down on the draining-board.

Here I am thinking, wondering in my mind, thinking, listening to Ruel and George talking to each other, laughing out loud.

Here I am. Will one of you bring the dirty cups and things come? I am speaking. Hazel; where do you want the things?

Here I am. Leave them over there please. George; will you and Ruel tidy up the dining-room please? I am tired. Have any one empty the bowl of water mummy use to wash Delroy? I am speaking. No; I am going to empty it now.

Here I am. Thanks George.

IAM®

Here I am standing on the kitchen floor, lifting the chair over to the work-top.

Here I am standing on the chair, wiping dry the plates, placing them down on the work-top.

Here I am standing on the kitchen floor, putting the big sauce-pan away inside the kitchen cupboard where it belongs.

Here I am putting washing-up liquid into the bowl, watching the hot water coming into the bowl, washing the cups clean, making sure everything is clean.

Here I am walking into the dining-room, carrying the pile of plate, resting them down on the table.

Here I am. Put these away for me please Ruel.

Here I am standing on the chair over the sink, wringing the water from the dishcloth.

Here I am lifting the chair over to the stove.

Here I am wiping the stove top, making the stove look clean, just like my mother make everything she touch look good.

Here I am putting all the big cooking knife and fork and spoon away inside the kitchen cupboard draw where they belong.

Here I am walking into the dining-room, carrying the cups, resting them down on the table.

Here I am putting the cups and plates away inside the cabinet where they belong.

Here I am standing inside the kitchen, looking around the space, feeling good inside myself, knowing that the kitchen is clean again.

Here I am with the broom, sweeping the kitchen ground, sweeping all the food pieces over to the kitchen doorway, sweeping the rubbish into the little dustpan, emptying the rubbish into the dustbin. The kitchen is looking clean now.

Here I am feeling good with myself, knowing that I am my mother's helper.

Here I am lifting the chair over by the stove where it belongs.

Here I am standing on the chair, turning the light switch off, thinking in my mind.

IAM®

Here I am inside the dining-room, standing by the fire, looking at the television picture. I can see all that is happening that I am not; understanding. I can see the body of a man and a woman. The man and the woman is sitting down on the grass on the ground under the sky. The man is holding the woman's hand down on the ground with his body pressing down on top of the woman, resting his body between the woman's legs. I can see the man's hand pulling the woman's dress high up her leg so I can see the colour of her skin like ice-cream. I can see everything that the man is doing, looking like he is loosing his breath; rushing to take off his clothes quick.

Here I am looking at the television, watching the man's body with his mouth open, pressing onto the woman's mouth, lying between the woman's open legs, moving his hands all over the woman's body, making my inside change, feel different. I can see the woman moving her body in time with the man's body lying between her legs, watching the man's hands moving over her breast, holding her breast tight inside his hands, making the woman sound like a baby playing.

Here I am feeling my inside moving around fast, watching the man's bottom moving up and down on top of the woman's body. I am speaking. Turn the television off and go and get yourselves ready to go to your bed, now.

Here I am walking up the stair, thinking in my mind, thinking about the television picture show, wondering why mummy just come down and turn the television off like that.

Here I am inside the girl's bed-room, thinking in my mind, wondering about the television picture, wondering; is that how mummy and daddy play with each other?

Here I am standing inside the bath-room.

Here I am thinking in my mind, watching the water coming into the bath. I can feel my mother's presence coming to where I am. I am speaking. Who say you can have a bath.

Here I am listening to my mother, wondering what to say.

Here I am looking down at my mother's two foot, wondering in my mind, thinking; what has mummy ask me that for. I am speaking. Hurry up and get to bed.

Here I am on my knees, kneeling inside the water, feeling good with myself, wondering about my mother.

IAM®

Here I am lying down inside the bath, feeling the water all over my body, making my body feel good.

Here I am wiping the water off myself, watching the water going down the hole, draining out the bath.

Here I am wiping the inside of the bath, shaking the cleaning powder on the cloth, rubbing the bath inside clean, making sure it is looking just the way mummy like it to look clean.

Here I am walking along the landing; realizing mummy's bed-room light is off.

Here I am standing inside the girl's bed-room, looking around into the night light, realizing that mummy is in the room, lying with Mavis inside Mavis's bed.

Here I am feeling my inside moving around, changing, moving quick; spreading my clothes over my bed-railing.

Here I am lying still inside my bed, wondering in my mind, wondering; why is mummy not sleeping with daddy inside their bed? Why is mummy sleeping in mine and Mavis's room?

Here I am thinking, wondering in my mind, thinking about mummy.

IAM®

CHAPTER 18

Here I am asleep inside my bed; hearing my mother calling my name Hazel. I am speaking. Hazel; get up, Hazel.

Here I am. Yes mummy. I am speaking. Get yourself dressed and come down stairs.

Here I am; wanting to sleep, looking up on my mother's body, looking at her face looking down on me.

Here I am thinking. How come mummy gets up at this time? The time is not day light yet. Mavis is still sleeping in her bed. Why must I get up now?

Here I am standing inside the bath-room, standing by the sink, wiping the sleep from my eyes, wiping my face, feeling my body trembling.

Here I am sitting down on the toilet, doing a wee-wee; thinking in my mind, wondering about my mother.

Here I am standing on the toilet seat, pulling the chain down, feeling the air on my body, making me tremble.

Here I am standing on the toilet seat, leaning over into the hot water tank, getting my clean knickers off the water tank.

Here I am feeling wide awake, standing inside the girl's bed-room, putting on my dress, thinking in my mind.

Here I am making up my bed, wanting it to look good, putting my night dress under my pillowcase where it belongs.

Here I am walking down the stairs, on my way to the dining-room.

Here I am standing inside the dining-room, feeling the air surrounding my body feeling good, smelling good. I can see the new pieces of cloth set out along the dining-table.

Here I am wondering where mummy is; thinking in my mind, thinking; mummy must have got up a long time. I can smell the food mummy is cooking.

Here I am standing at the open kitchen door-way, feeling the air coming up inside my dress, raising my dress up into the air, making my body tremble. I can see my mother down at the back gate entrance of the garden; watching my mother's hand throwing corn grain into the chicken house.

IAM®

Here I am standing inside the dining-room, looking at the different pieces of cloth set-out along the table.

Here I am thinking in my mind, wondering; what is mummy making. I am speaking. Good; you ready. Come go and get the iron-board and iron.

Here I am standing inside the pantry-room, lifting the iron-board off the wall, lifting it to the door-way, lifting it over by the dining-room doorway.

Here I am inside the dining-room, resting the chair by the door, wanting the door to stay open.

Here I am lifting the iron-board down the step into the dining-room, resting it on the wall.

Here I am. Where do you want the iron-board mummy? I am speaking. Put it up by the television.

Here I am inside the pantry; lifting the iron off the shelf.

Here I am. Do you want the iron turned on now mummy? I am speaking. Go and fetch me the basket of clothes.

Here I am on my way to the back bed-room.

Here I am pulling the basket full with clothes; dragging the basket along the floor, dragging it along the hall way, around the corner, down the step, on my way to the dining-room.

Here I am lifting the basket down the step into the dining-room.

Here I am standing inside the dining-room, watching my mother's hand cutting the cloth with the big cutting scissors. I am speaking. Sort out the socks and pants and fold Delroy cot blanket.

Here I am listening to my mother, looking down on the basket of clothes, wondering in my mind, thinking; how am going to fold all the blankets. I am speaking. Here; hold that end and do like this.

Here I am holding up the blanket, watching my mother's hand holding up the corner parts so I can understand. I am speaking. Fold it in half first, fold it in half again. Come with your end, pass me another, quick.

Here I am with my mother folding the blankets, watching my mother's hand, listening to the words my mother is speaking so I will remember; understanding the difference now between a blanket and a sheet. I am speaking. Put them down on the chair by where you are standing. Plug the iron in now.

IAM®

Here I am on my knee, reaching under the television table, holding the iron cord-plug in my hand, pushing the plug into the socket on the wall, pushing the electric switch down to make the iron work.

Here I am watching my mother's hand, rolling up the pieces of cloth together; then tying the bundle firm together with a long length string piece of the same colour cloth; watching my mother making use of all the pieces of the cloth she cut. I am speaking. This is how you iron the sheet. Watch what I am doing.

Here I am watching my mother's hand inside the bowl of water, watching her put her finger on the metal part of the iron, and lift it off quick, testing to see if the iron is hot, ready for her to use.

Here I am watching my mother's hand hang the white cotton sheet spread over the iron-board, watching the iron in her hand pressing down hard on the sheet, watching the steam rising up off the damp sheet, watching the creases disappear from the sheet my mother is pressing, resting the iron down on its face down on the hard board on the end of the ironing-board, watching my mother's hand lift the sheet up off the board, flattening the sheet down over the board with her hand, pushing down with the iron, pressing the sheet, demonstrating her words so I will understand. Now my mother is opening up the sheet, folding the inside outside, placing the sheet over the ironing-board, watching her keep doing the same action; pressing the sheet, watching the creases disappear every time my mother press the iron down hard on the sheet.

Here I am watching my mother folding the sheet in half length way and in half again, and again in half, pressing each fold down. I can see the sheet is looking good like new. I am speaking. Carry on sorting the clothes.

Here I am putting the trousers together, hearing my mother inside the kitchen preparing the food for our breakfast.

Here I am sorting through the clothes, taking out all the under-pants and knickers, putting them in order, ready to carry them up stairs.

Here I am watching my mother entering the dining-room; carrying bowls of porridge, one in each hand, resting them down on the dining-table. I am speaking. Spread the table cloth out quick.

Here I am looking inside the television table drawer, getting the tablecloth, spreading it out over half the dining-table.

Here I am standing on the chair, taking two spoons from the cabinet safe drawer, placing one next to each bowl of porridge.

IAM®

Here I am watching my mother entering the dining-room, holding a plate of bread and butter, placing it down on the table. I am speaking. Turn the iron off Hazel and come and have your breakfast.

Here I am on my hands and knees; reaching under the television table, pushing the electric switch, up to off.

Here I am sitting at the table, watching my mother holding her hands together, watching her eyes close; listening to her saying her prayer.

Here I am eating my porridge, thinking in my mind, wondering what mummy is making, wanting to ask my mother what she is making out of the pieces of cloth she cut. I am speaking. The porridge tastes good mummy. I am speaking. Come move quick Hazel. I am cutting out your school dress today. How do you want me to make it?

Here I am listening to my mother asking me how I want her to make me a dress.

Here I am thinking, thinking in my mind, wondering; what do you mean. I am speaking. How you want me to make your dress Hazel?

Here I am. Can I have one with pleats in like my green one upstairs? I am speaking. You want one with pleats?

Here I am. Yes please mummy. I am speaking. Right; switch the iron back on, let me iron out the big sheet.

Here I am on my hands and knee, pushing the electric switch down to on.

Here I am walking into the kitchen, carrying the empty bowls in my hand, placing them down inside the washing-up bowl.

Here I am feeling good inside, knowing that my mother is going to make a new dress for me to wear to school.

Here I am standing inside the dining-room, looking at my mother's body standing over the ironing-board, watching her face smiling, watching her hand holding the iron, pressing the sheet.

Here I am thinking; all the clothes mummy press always look good like new.

Here I am watching my mother pressing the sheet, watching her hand rest the iron down on the dining-table; watching her lift the iron-board up and drop it down low level to my body. I am speaking. Hazel; you finish off the balance now so I can make a start on your dress. Leave your daddy's clothes and mine and your sister's in the basket. I will iron them.

IAM®

Here I am standing over the iron-board holding the iron in my hand, pressing down on the pillow case, wanting it to press good like my mother's ironing looks good.

Here I am doing the ironing, looking up at my mother's hand holding the big scissors, cutting the cloth to make me a dress. I can hear Ruel and George moving about up stairs in their room on top of the dining room. I am speaking. Come; let me see how this look.

Here I am standing by my mother; feeling her hand on my shoulders; holding the newspaper dress shape on my back. I am speaking. Good; hold out your hand.

Here I am standing with my hands raised, feeling my mother's hand on my shoulder, holding the measuring tape in place, moving the tape across my body, taking measurements of my body to make my school dress. I am speaking. Turn around. Now my mother is holding down one end of the measuring tape on my neck; feeling her hands moving down my body to the top of my foot; balancing the tape in place; writing down some words on the piece of paper; feeling my inside go round; feeling the touch of my mother's hands. I am speaking. Turn around.

Here I am watching my mother's hand holding the pencil, writing down some more words. Now my mother is holding the measuring tape around my centre, resting her hand against my navel, holding the tape firm in place, holding the pencil, watching her hand writing down some more words. I am speaking. Where do you want the pleats?

Here I am. All the way around please mummy. I am speaking. I have to see how far the cloth will go. Good; you can carry on with what you were doing.

Here I am holding up one of my brother's trousers, wondering in my mind, thinking; which part of the pants to start. I am speaking. Hazel; ride the top of the pants over the end of the ironing-board and press the inside first.

Here I am turning the trousers inside out, pulling the waist end over the round end of the ironing-board, pressing the pocket shaping, feeling the steam coming hot from under the iron burn hot on my finger, making water come into my eyes, making water come out all over my face, feeling my body hurting, pressing the trouser.

Here I am doing the ironing, watching my mother's hand shaking out the cloth, folding it out on the dining-table.

IAM®

Here I am feeling the iron mark making my finger burn, ironing the pants, watching my mother placing the measuring tape onto the cloth, moving the tape around, measuring the cloth. I can see my mother is feeling good with herself, smiling all over her face.

Here I am ironing Delroy's cotton all in one body suit, watching my mother's hand folding up the piece of newspaper, clearing the table of all the bits of cloth and paper, throwing them on the fire.

Here I am ironing my house-dress, feeling the inside of my legs hurting, wanting to finish the ironing now.

Here I am on my hands and knee, under the television table, pushing the electric switch down, pulling the plug out the wall, resting the iron down under the table to cool.

Here I am placing the chair by the door, wanting to keep it open.

Here I am lifting the ironing-board up, wanting to make it lie flat, lifting it up the dining-room step into the hall way, resting it against the pantry room, opening the pantry door, lifting the board inside the pantry, resting it against the wall.

Here I am standing inside the dining-room, sorting the clothes into room order, watching my mother holding the pile of sheets and clothes she iron, walking into the hall way.

Here I am following my mother walking up the stairs, on my way to the girl's bed-room, placing the clothes down on my bed, putting them away where they belong inside the dressing-table drawer.

Here I am standing out-side the boys bed-room, wanting to go inside.

Here I am. Ruel; can I come in? I am speaking. Come Hazel.

Here I am entering my brother's bed-room, smelling the air smelling like they have wet their bed again.

Here I am holding my breath, putting the clothes away where they belong.

Here I am running from the bed-room, running down the stairs into the dining-room, getting the blankets, walking slow up the stairs, carrying the blankets to the girls bed-room, resting them down on my bed, opening the wardrobe door, placing the blankets down on the wardrobe bottom where they belong.

Here I am walking along the hall way, thinking in my mind, wondering. I am speaking. Hazel.

IAM®

Here I am. Yes mummy. I am speaking. Put the kettle on while you down there.

Here I am. Yes mummy.

Here I am walking down the stairs, walking into the dining-room, on my way to the kitchen.

Here I am standing inside the kitchen, lifting the chair over to the sink.

Here I am standing on the chair, holding the kettle in my hand, watching the cold water falling into the kettle feeling heavy in my hand.

Here I am lighting the fire under the kettle, turning the flame up high.

Here I am standing inside the dining-room, putting the socks and pants and knickers together on the towel.

Here I am walking into the hall, carrying the towel and socks and pants and knickers up the stairs, on my way to the boy's bed-room.

Here I am inside my brother's bed-room, putting Ruel and George socks and under-pants inside the drawer where they belong.

Here I am standing inside the girl's bed-room standing at the doorway, looking around the bed-room. I can see Mavis bed is made up looking good.

Here I am sorting Mavis's socks and knickers, putting them away inside her dressing-table drawer where they belong.

Here I am putting my knickers and pants and socks inside my dressing-table drawer where they belong with my other good pair of socks and knickers, putting them down in line, wanting my things to look good, the same as my sister Mavis's clothes look good inside her dressing-table drawer.

Here I am walking down the stairs, hearing the different sounds inside the house.

Here I am walking down the stairs, thinking in my mind, realizing that everyone is wide awake now, making noise, making the house sound alive.

Here I am standing at the dining-room entrance, looking at Mavis's body looking good.

Here I am thinking in my mind, thinking; mummy dress Mavis up to look good. Everything Mavis has on her body looks good and her hair is comb, making Mavis's body look good from her head down to her shoes.

I AM®

Here I am looking at my sister, thinking about myself, thinking in my mind, wondering; wanting my body to look good, just like my Mavis body is looking good.

Here I am on my way up the stairs, running into the girls bed-room, standing before my dressing-table, looking at my face, looking into the mirror glass, looking at the body that I am; looking; pulling out the plaits in my hair.

Here I am; wanting my body to look good, wanting my hair to look good, just like Mavis's hair always look good.

Here I am brushing my hair, brushing all the blanket bits away.

Here I am rubbing the hair oil into the palm of my two hands, rubbing my hands into my hair, just like my mother do when she is combing Mavis hair.

Here I am resting my hand, thinking in my mind, wondering about the body that I am hurting inside.

Here I am wondering in my mind thinking; wondering why mummy never makes my body look good the same as she always make Mavis's body looks good?

Here I am wondering in my mind thinking; what is special about Mavis? Why does mummy treat Mavis like she is better than me and Ruel and George?

Here I am parting my hair, holding my hair down, pushing the comb into my hair, wanting it to stay down.

Here I am plaiting my hair, feeling my fingers hurting, plaiting my hair, wanting my body to look good; looking at my hair plait sticking up in different direction off my head, making my face look funny.

Here I am; wanting mummy to plait my hair; wanting my hair to look good like Mavis hair look good. I am speaking. Hazel; mummy want you down stairs.

Here I am putting the cover on top of the hair oil, thinking in my mind, wondering; what does mummy want me for now?

Here I am walking down the stairs, thinking in my mind, walking to the dining-room; thinking about my mother.

Here I am standing inside the dining-room, standing looking at my mother's body sitting down by the window, holding the cloth inside her hand, sewing the pieces of cloth together with the needle and thread.

Here I am. Here I am mummy. I am speaking. What are you doing?

IAM®

Here I am. I was just plaiting my hair mummy. I am speaking. Go and get the comb and come.

Here I am running up the stairs, running into the girl's bed-room, getting the comb off the mantle, wanting mummy to comb my hair.

Here I am walking running down the stairs, running to the dining-room, standing at the dining-room entrance, hearing my body breathing quick; looking at my mother.

Here I am. Here I am mummy. I am speaking. Pull out your hair.

Here I am standing by the fire surround, feeling the air on the back of my feet feeling hot.

Here I am pulling the plaits out my hair, watching my mother's hand holding the pieces of cloth together, watching her hand pushing the needle down into the cloths, sewing the two pieces together.

Here I am. I have finished mummy. I am speaking. Come with the comb.

Here I am on my knee, kneeling down on the ground before my mother's body.

Here I am holding my head still, feeling my mother's hand inside my hair, plaiting my hair. I am speaking. Turn your head around.

Here I am holding my head to one side, feeling my hair inside my mother's hand hurting my head, feeling my mother's hand holding my hair tight, pulling the skin on my head, making my head hurt.

Here I am thinking, thinking about the dress my mother is making for me, wondering in my mind, feeling the water falling from my eyes, falling on my hands, feeling my body hurting inside.

Here I am thinking, thinking about myself, thinking about going to the school; thinking about the dress mummy is making for my body; thinking about myself, thinking in my mind, wondering. I am speaking. Here is the comb.

Here I am. Thank you mummy.

Here I am walking into the kitchen, pulling the hair bits from the comb; putting the hair into the kitchen dustbin.

Here I am walking up the stairs, walking to the girl's bed-room, returning the comb on top of the mantle where it belongs.

IAM®

Here I am standing before the dressing-table mirror, looking out from the body that I am, just looking at myself.

Here I am standing inside the dining-room, looking at my mother's hand, holding up the pieces of cloth holding them up to the window light.

Here I am inside my father's house, looking at each one present, thinking in my mind, thinking; what can I do? I am speaking. Ruel, George, haven't you two got anything to do. Stop making the noise or get out of my sight.

Here I am hearing my mother raise her voice at Ruel and George, making my body not want to be in here presence.

Here I am standing on the chair over the sink, turning the hot water tap on, putting some washing-up liquid into the water, placing the dirty breakfast things inside the bowl.

Here I am standing over the sink, washing the things clean, wanting the kitchen to look good.

Here I am on my knees, kneeling on the chair before the kitchen sink, washing clean all the dirty food things we use to have our breakfast from.

Here I am washing the big saucepan, scraping the burn porridge off the bottom around the inside; rubbing the scouring pad all over the inside and outside; making the saucepan shine.

Here I am wringing the water from the dishcloth, wiping the big saucepan dry, putting it away inside the kitchen cupboard where it belongs.

Here I am lifting the chair over by the work-top, standing on the chair wiping the work-top clean, reaching over the work-top, wiping everywhere clean, feeling good with myself, knowing that I am my mother's helper.

Here I am standing on the chair over the work-top, wiping dry all the food bowls and things, placing them down on the work-top.

Here I am standing on the ground, holding the dish-cloth in my hand, lifting the chair over by the stove.

Here I am wiping the stove top clean, wiping away the porridge marks, rubbing the cloth hard on the stove, wanting the stove to look good.

Here I am lifting the chair over to the kitchen sink, standing on the chair, washing the dish cloth clean inside the warm soapy water inside the washing-up bowl, emptying the water into the sink.

IAM®

Here I am wiping the draining-board dry, wiping the hot and cold water tap dry, wiping the inside and outside part of the sink, making sure everywhere is looking good.

Here I am with the big sweeping brush inside my hand, sweeping the kitchen ground, sweeping all the dust away from the corner of the room, sweeping the dirt towards the kitchen doorway.

Here I am with the dustpan and little hand-brush in my hand, sweeping all the dust into the dustpan. I can see the kitchen is looking clean, looking good to the body that I am.

Here I am inside the kitchen, getting the cups, carrying them into the dining-room, standing on the chair, putting the cups away inside the cabinet where they belong.

Here I am inside the kitchen getting the pile of spoons off the work-top, carrying them into the dining-room, putting them away inside the cabinet drawer where they belong.

Here I am putting the bowls down inside the cabinet where they belong with all the other food bowls and plates.

Here I am feeling the body that I am feeling good inside, standing in the presence of my mother.

Here I am looking across the room, looking at my mother's hand holding up the pieces of cloth. I can see the shape of the cloth my mother is holding up into the air. The pieces of cloth mummy sew together is looking like the top part of my dress.

Here I am watching my mother's hand putting the pieces of cloth together, making my body feel good, thinking about my mother; watching her making the dress for me to wear to school.

Here I am watching my mother's hand pushing the thread into the needle, winding the thread around and around, and around her finger, rolling the thread end together, pulling on the thread, making a knot at the end of the thread. Now my mother is placing the two pieces of cloth together, holding them together with her one hand, pushing the needle down through the two pieces of cloth, sewing them together.

Here I am watching my mother looking like she is smiling, watching her hand sticking the needle and white cotton thread into the cloth inside her hands.

IAM®

Here I am looking at my mother's face, thinking in my mind, wondering at my mother, watching her expression, watching her hands working; wondering what my mother is thinking in her mind.

IAM®

CHAPTER 19

Here I am; wanting to do some hand sewing like what I can see my mother's hand is doing.

Here I am. Can I do some sewing mummy? I am speaking. You want to sew?

Here I am. Yes mummy. I am speaking. If you can find a needle, you can, yes.

Here I am thinking, wondering where to look for a needle; thinking I want a needle. I want to sew.

Here I am. Mummy; do you have a needle that I can have? I am speaking. Go and look in the sewing table drawer in the back bed-room. Look in the right hand drawer.

Here I am on my way to the back bed-room, thinking in my mind wondering; what does mummy mean? What is the right-hand drawer?

Here I am inside the back bed-room, standing before my mother's sewing table.

Here I am looking at the drawers; one at each side of me.

Here I am holding the two drawer handles, pulling them open. I can see lots of things inside the drawers, lots of colour cotton and ribbons and elastic on card paper.

Here I am turning the things over inside the one drawer, feeling good with myself seeing a piece of round card paper with some needles sticking around the side.

Here I am looking at the many different shape needles with different size holes.

Here I am; understanding the meaning of the right-hand drawer that is on my right-hand side.

Here I am looking into the right-hand drawer of my mother's sewing table, looking at all the things that I can see; all the things my mother use to make the clothes she makes.

Here I am looking at the things inside the drawer, wondering in my mind, wondering.

Here I am walking along the hall-way, on my way to the dining-room, holding the needle in my hand.

I AM®

Here I am standing before my mother.

Here I am. I have got the needle mummy. I am speaking. Pass me that bag over there.

Here I am looking at my mother's eyes looking down into the bag on the floor.

Here I am looking at my mother's hand taking a handful of different little pieces of cloth out of the bag. I am speaking. You can have these.

Here I am taking the pieces of cloth from my mother's hand, feeling pleased with myself. I am speaking. Here is some cotton.

Here I am. Thank you mummy.

Here I am sorting through the pieces of cloth, spreading each piece out on the floor before me.

Here I am wondering in my mind, thinking; what can I make?; thinking in my mind; looking at the pieces of cloth; feeling the touch of the pieces of cloth feeling different in my hands.

Here I am winding the cotton thread around my finger, wanting to break a length of thread off the cotton reel in my hand. The cotton string is strong, making marks in my skin around my finger. I am speaking. Hazel; use your teeth. That is why you have them for you to use.

Here I am holding the cotton string between my teeth, pulling the cotton to break.

Here I am feeling good with myself, breaking the thread with my teeth.

Here I am looking down on the floor before me, wondering where the needle is.

Here I am holding the needle in one hand, and the cotton thread in the other hand, wanting the cotton to go through the eye hole of the needle.

Here I am missing the eye hole, feeling my hands hurting, feeling the needle falling out my finger, feeling my body feeling wet, wanting the thread to go through into the eye hole of the needle.

Here I am; wanting to do some sewing, wanting to ask mummy to thread the cotton through the eye hole of the needle so that I can do some sewing.

Here I am. Mummy; mummy will you put the cotton in the needle for me please? I am speaking. I beg you pardon. Thread the needle yourself. You cannot sew anything if you cannot thread the needle.

IAM®

Here I am hearing my mother; feeling water come into my eyes; wanting to sew.

Here I am on my knees, holding the needle and thread in my hand, wanting the thread to go into the eye hole of the needle; watching the thread miss the eye hole, making my body not know what to do with itself, wanting the thread to go into the eye hole of the needle now.

Here I am feeling hurt, wondering why my mother won't help me.

Here I am; wanting to sew, watching the thread hanging through the needle eye hole.

Here I am staying still, pulling the thread through the needle eye hole, wanting the thread to stop inside the needle, knowing the long time it took me to threading the needle; wanting to do some sewing like my mother's hand can sew.

Here I am feeling good now, holding up two piece of the same colour cloth in my hand. I am speaking. You see. You can do it. Come; give me the cloth with the needle.

Here I am looking at my mother holding the needle in her hand, winding the end of the thread around and around her one finger. I am speaking. Are you watching Hazel? This is how you make the knot to stop the cotton from coming through the cloth when you start to sew, understand.

Here I am watching what my mother's hands are doing, understanding every word that I can hear my mother is speaking, watching my mother's hand push the needle under the thread she have around her finger, watching her wet the thread with her mouth water, watching my mother rolling the wet thread between her finger and thumb together, rolling the thread off her finger, watching her pull down on the thread, making a little round ball at the end of the thread so I can see. I am speaking. You see what I mean. Give me the pieces of cloth.

Here I am watching my mother's hand holding the two pieces of cloth together in one hand, pushing the needle down through the two pieces of cloth, and up through the two pieces of cloth so I can understand. I am speaking. This is called a straight stitch. Do the straight stitches till you reach to the end then let me see.

Here I am taking the needle thread and cloth from my mother's hand.

Here I am looking down at the piece of cloth, looking at what my mother has done.

IAM®

Here I am pushing the needle down through the cloth, pulling the needle through on the other side.

Here I am pushing the needle down through the cloth, wanting to sew good like my mother can sew in a straight line; ouch; looking at the needle inside my finger, hurting my body, making water come into my eyes. I am speaking. What is the matter with you?

Here I am. The needle went into my finger mummy. I am speaking. Put your finger in your mouth. It is your blood. Keep your finger inside your mouth until it stops bleeding. Let me see what you have done.

Here I am standing before my mother, feeling hurt inside, watching my mother's eyes looking down on my sewing. I am speaking. Look; this is how you stop the cotton from coming out when you finish your sewing.

Here I am watching my mother's hand holding the needle, pushing the needle down and up through the cloth, and pushing the needle down and up through the cloth on the same part, winding the thread around her finger, breaking the thread from the cloth so I will understand. I am speaking. This is good Hazel. Let me show you another sewing stitch.

Here I am watching my mother demonstrate another stitch; watching her hand sewing, pushing the needle down into the cloth, watching her hand move under the cloth, watching the needle point come up through the cloth at the middle of the stitch, making the cotton stitch line look different on the other side of the cloth.

Here I am watching my mother's hand making the sewing stitch joining the two pieces of cloth together.

Here I am thinking, watching my mother's hand sewing, thinking in my mind.

Here I am wanting to sew like my mother can, wanting my sewing to look good like all my mother's sewing look good to the body that I am. I am speaking. Sew this one now. Let me see your finger. Good; carry on with that one. Your finger will get better.

Here I am on my knees, kneeling down on the floor, holding the cloth still, pushing the needle into the cloth, remembering the way my mother make the stitch, wanting my sewing to look good.

Here I am pushing the needle down into the two piece of cloth, moving my finger away from the needle, not wanting to stick my fingers again.

Here I am learning to sew, thinking in my mind, thinking about my mother.

IAM®

Here I am wondering about my mother, thinking; mummy can do everything she does to look good.

Here I am wondering about my mother, thinking; I am learning from my mother. I am learning to do all the things my mother can do with her hands.

Here I am sewing, wondering about my mother, thinking in my mind, thinking; mummy can wash and make the clothes and things look clean like new. Mummy can cook the food and make it taste good. Mummy can dress up everyone to look good. Mummy can even make our clothes.

Here I am thinking; I want my hands to do good things, just like my mother's hands can make everything look good.

Here I am thinking about myself, thinking; I can wash the clothes and things, just like my mother can. I can clean the house to look good. I can make up the fire to warm the house. I can do everything I see my mother's hand do and now I am sewing just like my mother can.

Here I am thinking in my mind, thinking; what can I sew. I am speaking. Come let me try this on you.

Here I am looking at the dress my mother is holding up in her hand.

Here I am standing before my mother, feeling good inside myself; looking down at the dress front my mother is holding on my body. I am speaking. Hold your hands up so I can see what I am doing.

Here I am standing before my mother, feeling her hand on my skin. I am speaking. It looks good Hazel.

Here I am. Yes mummy. I am speaking. I have finish with you now. Put the needle down safe where you can put your hands on it again and go and bring me a glass of water please.

Here I am pushing the needle inside my sewing, placing my sewing down on the dining-table.

Here I am standing on the chair by the cabinet, getting a glass and saucer. I am speaking. Hazel; let the cold water run a while before you fill the glass.

Here I am inside the kitchen, standing on the chair over the sink, turning the cold water tap on, watching the water falling into the sink.

Here I am reaching over the sink, holding my two hands together, catching the water, drinking, feeling the water filling up my inside. The water taste good; making my body want more, drinking down the water fast.

IAM®

Here I am holding the glass under the water, watching the water filling up inside the glass.

Here I am walking into the dining-room, carrying the glass of water on the saucer.

Here I am inside the dining-room, resting the glass of water on the table by my mother's body, watching her hand still sewing my dress.

Here I am. Here is the water mummy. I am speaking. Thank you. Go and see if anything is at the front door for me.

Here I am on my way towards the front doorway; looking to see what I can see; wondering at the thing on the ground by the front door.

Here I am standing by the front door, picking up two flat pieces of paper packet. Here I am walking towards the dining-room, thinking in my mind, wondering what the paper packet is. I can see writings on the packets.

Here I am wondering what the words say, recognizing the word Grant and the sign 17, the number of my father's house.

Here I am walking along the hall way, looking at the words on the packet, realizing that I can read the number on my father's house.

Here I am feeling good inside, feeling good with my mother for showing me how to write so I can understand.

Here I am walking into the dining-room, thinking in my mind, wondering what is inside the paper packets in my hand.

Here I am standing before my mother, watching her hand sewing my dress.

Here I am. These were at the front door on the floor mummy. I am speaking. Thank you. Put them down on the table. I was waiting for this letter to come.

Here I am hearing my mother speak, wondering in my mind, wondering; where did the letters come from.

Here I am on my knee, kneeling down on the dining-room floor, holding my two piece of cloth together, watching my mother's hand tearing the brown paper packet into pieces.

Here I am watching my mother's face, looking down on the book that was in the paper packet.

Here I am watching my mother making up her face talking to herself.

IAM®

Here I am looking at the piece of cloth in my hand, pushing the needle into the cloth, sewing the stitch like my mother show me how to sew the stitch to hold the two pieces of cloth together.

Here I am sewing, thinking in my mind, wondering about going to school, thinking; I am going to look good when I go to school. Mummy is making a new dress for my body to wear to school with my new cardigan and a new coat, and my new pair of shoes and socks and knickers and vest and slip.

Here I am thinking, wondering about school, feeling good knowing that I am going to wear my new clothes.

Here I am. I have done it mummy. I am speaking. You are good at sewing Hazel. What you want to do now.

Here I am. I want to make something mummy. I am speaking. I haven't got anything for you to make. Wait a minute. You can make a pin-cushion like that one on the table.

Here I am feeling good inside myself, listening to my mother say that I can make the thing like her pin-cushion.

Here I am understanding every word my mother is speaking, learning all that I can from my mother. My mother knows how to do a lot of things. My mother can make all kind of things with her hands. Here I am watching my mother's hands sewing over and over the same stitch at the end of the piece of cloth in her hands. I am speaking. Pass me the big scissors under the cloth over on the table.

Here I am holding the big scissors my mother use to cut the cloth. The scissors feel heavy in my hand.

Here I am watching my mother taking the pieces of cloth from the cloth bag full of all kind of pieces of cloth, of all kind of shape and colour and size and feel. I am speaking. Hazel; turn the scissors around. Hold the pointed end in your hand when you are giving the scissors to anyone.

Here I am holding the scissor blade in my hand, holding the scissor handle towards my mother, understanding her every word.

Here I am watching my mother's hand, holding the two pieces of cloth together inside her one hand, holding the pieces of cloth, one on top of the other down on the dining-table, turning them around, looking like she is making up her mind what to do.

IAM®

Here I am watching my mother's hand holding the scissors, watching her cutting the cloth round like a circle. I am speaking. Here; sew these together with the back stitch you just sew and leave about half an inch space opening.

Here I am watching my mother hold up her finger and thumb demonstrating half an inch space opening so I will understand.

Here I am taking the two pieces of cloth from my mother's hand, wondering in my mind, thinking; which one of these stitches does mummy mean?

Here I am looking down at my sewing cloth, wondering in my mind, thinking; which one is the back-stitch?

Here I am holding my sewing cloth up to my mother, wanting my mother to show me the stitch name back-stitch.

Here I am. Which one is call back-stitch mummy? I am speaking. The one you last sew is the back-stitch.

Here I am, understanding that my sewing stitches have different names. I am speaking. The back-stitch will hold the cloth together firm. Look, I am making these tacking stitches to hold the cloth in one place; then I am going to back-stitch it together.

Here I am watching my mother's hand sewing, understanding her every word.

Here I am putting the thread through the needle eye hole, wanting to sew the cloth together, wanting to make the pin-cushion for my mother to use.

Here I am winding one end of the thread around my finger, pushing the needle under the cotton thread, and again and again, just like my mother make the knot at the end of the thread.

Here I am hand-sewing the two piece of cloth together, sewing the back-stitch around the edge of the cloth. I am speaking. Let me see what you are doing.

Here I am looking up at my mother looking down at the cloth that I am sewing; seeing my mother's eyes looking and looking at my sewing; watching the smile appear on my mothers face. I am speaking. Just make the stitch a little shorter and it will be perfect and keep the sewing line about quarter inch from the edge. Look at my finger. About this much, understand.

Here I am watching my mother demonstrate her meaning so I will understand.

IAM®

Here I am sewing the pin-cushion, feeling good inside myself.

Here I am looking at my mother's hand sewing, thinking in my mind, thinking about myself, thinking about my brothers and sister.

Here I am the presence, thinking in my mind, realizing that my mother and I are doing something with our hands.

Here I am looking at my mother's body, watching her sewing, thinking; I am my mother's helper.

Here I am realizing in my mind, understanding how my father come by the many things he have inside his house.

Here I am realizing that my mother is the cause why my father has lots of things inside his house <u>is because</u> mummy makes the clothes to put on hers and Mavis and Delroy's body and mummy made all the things to dress-up the furniture things inside the house.

Here I am knowing that it is my father that go out to work for the money, but my father do not understand that the money he work did not buy the many things I see inside his house.

Here I am understanding that one dress in the shop is price one price, but because my mother buy the cloth instead, I can have two dresses for the one price because my mother can sew with her hands, and I am learning all the time how to use my hands to make, watching my mother making the clothes and things she makes out of her mind.

Here I am feeling good inside myself, understanding myself, knowing that I can make like my mother can make things with her one two hands.

Here I am thinking in my mind, wondering what daddy does in the factory building.

Here I am thinking. Ruel and George should do the things that mummy and I am doing.

Here I am thinking; if mummy and I did not get up each day to clean the house, and make the fire, and wash the dirty clothes and things, and prepare the food, then daddy would not have anything good to come home to.

Here I am thinking; my father spends all his time in the factory building. My father is always working at the factory, or eating, or sleeping when he is at home.

I AM®

Here I am sitting down on the dining-room floor, sewing the two round pieces of cloth together, wondering in my mind; thinking.

Here I am thinking, wondering if my father gets a lot of money when he goes to work.

Here I am thinking; daddy must work for some more money now; mummy is having a baby.

Here I am. I have done it mummy. I am speaking. Good; thread the needle with a long piece of thread.

Here I am breaking off a long piece of thread, wanting to thread the needle, feeling good inside myself knowing that I can do anything if I put my mind to it.

Here I am winding the thread around and around my finger, wetting the thread inside my mouth-water, rolling the thread to the end of my finger, making it knot.

Here I am. Here is the needle and thread mummy. I am speaking. I am sewing the raw edge of the cloth together to stop the cloth from coming apart. This is call blanket-stitch.

Here I am standing by my mother, watching her hands sewing, making the different stitch, sewing the two edge of the cloth together; making her sewing look good. I am speaking. You understand.

Here I am. Yes mummy.

Here I am taking the needle and cloth from my mother's hand, remembering in my mind, thinking, wanting to remember the way mummy sew the blanket-stitch.

Here I am sewing, wanting my sewing stitches to look good like mummies sewing stitches looks good. The stitch does not look like the ones mummy sews.

Here I am, feeling my inside go round, wanting to sew the blanket-stitch like the ones mummy sew.

Here I am sewing, wanting the stitch to look like my mother's sewing. The blanket-stitch is making me spend time on it, wanting it to look like my mother's sewing.

IAM®

Here I am sewing, making the stitch look the same as my mother's sewing; making the blanket-stitch, sewing it around the edge of the pin cushion I am making.

Here I am sewing; feeling good, wondering in my mind, wondering what Ruel and George are doing upstairs in their bed-room.

Here I am looking up; looking through the dining-room window, looking into the air outside my father's house, wondering in my mind, wondering what time daddy going to come home.

IAM®

CHAPTER 20

Here I am thinking about my father at work inside the factory building.

Here I am wondering what is going on outside my father's house.

Here I am sewing, thinking in my mind.

Here I am looking down at my hand making the blanket-stitch around the cloth edge, making a knot about half an inch before the beginning of my first blanket-stitch.

Here I am. I have done it mummy. I am speaking. Gather up the pieces of cloth now Hazel. Pick up the bits off the floor for me. Your daddy will be home soon.

Here I am putting my pieces of cloth into my paper bag, putting the bag under the television table where I keep all my things.

Here I am standing inside the dining-room, looking down on the floor where I am standing, looking at all the little pieces of cloth and different colour threads on the floor around my mother's body sitting on the chair sewing my school dress.

Here I am on my hands and knee, picking the pieces of cloth off the floor, putting them onto the piece of newspaper.

Here I am. Here is a pin mummy. I am speaking. Thank you Hazel. Have a good look if any more has fallen on the floor.

Here I am on my hands and knees, picking the pieces of cloth off the floor; making the dining-room floor look clean, watching my mother's body stand up, brushing the bits of cloth and threads down off her clothes.

Here I am watching my mother holding up the dress she is making for me. The dress is looking good. My mother's hands can sew quick.

Here I am collecting the bits of cloth off the table, and off the chair, picking up every little bit of cloth I can see, wanting the dining-room to look clean again.

Here I am standing inside the kitchen, putting the newspaper of cloth into the kitchen dustbin.

Here I am standing on the dining-kitchen door step, looking at my mother's hand folding flat the dress; looking at the dress shape looking good with all the pleats around it. I can see Delroy's body is moving in his pram, looking like he is waking up now. I am speaking. Hazel; make Delroy a drink.

IAM®

Here I am inside the kitchen, lifting the chair over to the sink.

Here I am standing on the chair with the kettle in my hand, turning on the cold water tap, watching the water falling into the kettle, feeling the kettle getting heavy in my hands.

Here I am standing on the kitchen floor, lifting the kettle up onto the stove, lighting the stove with the burning match in my hand, turning the flame up high.

Here I am standing inside the dining-room, taking the bottle half-full of milk out of the fridge, carrying it into the kitchen.

Here I am standing on the chair, reaching across the kitchen work-top, getting Delroy's feeding bottle. I am speaking. Hazel; put the kettle on after and make the big tea-pot full of tea for you lot.

Here I am taking the tea bag from the box, putting it into the little saucepan, putting it down on the stove near the kettle.

Here I am standing on the chair over the stove, holding the tea towel around my hand, turning the fire down to low, pouring the hot water into the saucepan, watching the water soaking into the tea-bag.

Here I am standing on the floor, getting the big tea-pot from the kitchen cupboard, placing it down on the work-top.

Here I am lifting the little saucepan off the stove, lifting it up down on the draining-board, lifting the chair over to the sink.

Here I am standing on the chair, putting cold water into the big plastic jug, resting it down on the work-top.

Here I am lifting the chair over to the stove, standing on the chair, holding the jug of water, pouring the water into the kettle, watching the kettle filling up.

Here I am turning up the fire under the kettle, wanting the water to boil. I can hear my mother's voice singing to her self, hearing the sound of the cabinet bang shut.

Here I am standing on the chair over the draining-board, taking the tea bag out the little saucepan, putting it into the teapot.

Here I am pouring the milk out the bottle into the saucepan, mixing it into the tea.

Here I am walking into the dining-room, carrying the bottle of milk, returning it to the fridge where it belongs.

IAM®

Here I am getting the sugar packet from the cabinet. I can see my mother is standing over the table, holding the margarine and the corn-beef can and the packet of bread before her.

Here I am inside the kitchen, standing on the chair, taking one tea-spoon full of sugar out the packet, putting it into the saucepan, mixing the milk-tea drink for Delroy.

Here I am pouring the tea into the bottle, screwing the top on tight, putting the bottle inside the saucepan, turning the cold water tap on, watching the water filling up the saucepan, wanting the drink to cool quick for Delroy.

Here I am feeling my mother's presence coming into the kitchen, watching her put the things down on the work-top.

Here I am thinking in my mind, wondering; what is mummy going to make?

Here I am kneeling down on the chair over the sink, watching my mother take the big frying pan from the kitchen cupboard, resting it down on top of the stove, watching her peel the skin off the big onion. I am speaking. Go and get me the lard and two tomatoes from the fridge please.

Here I am inside the dining-room, taking the piece of lard packet from the fridge and two tomatoes from the bowl, carrying them to my mother.

Here I am standing on the chair, washing the tomatoes under the cold water, wiping them dry on the tea-towel, getting them ready for my mother to use.

Here I am pouring the drink from Delroy's bottle onto my hand, testing it, feeling just right, ready for Delroy to drink.

Here I am walking into the dining-room, carrying Delroy's bottle, watching Delroy's face smiling at one.

Here Iam. Here you are Delroy.

Here I am looking at Delroy. I can see Delroy wants his drink; feeling the way he grab the bottle from my hand; swallowing the milk tea; watching his cheeks going in and out, quick.

Here I am standing inside the kitchen watching my mother light the fire under the frying pan.

Here I am watching my mother's hand holding the knife, slicing the onion into the frying pan, watching her stirring the onions I am smelling in the air surrounding my body. Now my mother is slicing the tomatoes into the frying pan, mixing the onions and tomato together. Now my mother is opening the

IAM®

can of corn-beef, holding the tin can key with the corner of her apron, watching her face wanting the can to open.

Here I am watching my mother mashing the corn-beef into the frying pan. Now my mother is taking a little margarine out of its tub, putting the margarine into the frying-pan, and a little black pepper powder, mixing everything together. My mother's cooking smells good. I am speaking. Butter the bread on the big plate.

Here I am lifting the chair over to the work-top.

Here I am on my knee kneeling on the chair, holding the knife, scraping the knife inside the margarine.

Here I am spreading the margarine onto the bread; listening to my mothers voice singing to herself, preparing the food for our lunch.

Here I am. Is that enough mummy? I am speaking. Hazel; scrape some of the margarine off the bread. Do about ten slices.

Here I am spreading the margarine all over the bread, thinking in my mind, wondering, how many slices of bread is ten.

Here I am spreading the margarine over the bread, thinking in my mind, wondering; how many ones make ten? One, two for Ruel, two for George, two for Mavis, two for me, one for Delroy, thinking in my mind wondering if that is enough.

Here I am. Is this right mummy? I am speaking. Do another one to make ten and three slice extra.

Here I am, now knowing how many ones make ten.

Here I am standing on the chair over the stove, holding the tea-towel around my hand, lifting the kettle of boiling water off the stove, pouring the hot water into the big tea-pot.

Here I am inside the dining-room, taking the milk can out of the fridge, hearing Delroy making a happy sound, playing by himself inside the pram.

Here I am inside the kitchen pouring the milk into the tea-pot, mixing the milk into the tea, watching the colour change. Now I am putting the sugar into the tea. One, two, three big spoon full of sugar into the tea, sweetening the tea for us to drink.

Here I am inside the dining-room, returning the milk can inside the fridge, returning the sugar packet inside the cabinet where it belongs.

IAM®

Here I am looking inside the television table drawer, taking out the table-cloth, spreading the cloth out over the table, making the table ready for lunch.

Here I am looking inside the cabinet, taking out the little side-plates. One for Ruel and George and me and Mavis and mummy and Delroy. I am speaking. Where is mummy Hazel?

Here I am. Mummy is cooking lunch.

Here I am taking the cups from the cabinet, setting them out on the table next to the tea-pot stand.

Here I am setting the table, thinking in my mind, wondering; how come everyone only knows to come down here when food is ready.

Here I am. Sit over there please Mavis. You are in the way there.

Here I am inside the kitchen, standing on the kitchen door mat, looking up at my mother standing over the kitchen work-top. I can see my mother has made the corn-beef sandwiches. I am speaking. Now; pour me a glass of milk please.

Here I am winding the tea-towel around my hand, lifting the tea-pot of tea down off the stove, balancing the pot on the cloth in my hand, walking slow into the dining-room, placing it down on the tea-pot stand on the table.

Here I am standing on the chair by the cabinet, taking the glass and a little cup-saucer from the cabinet, placing them down on the table.

Here I am taking the bottle of milk from the fridge, pouring it out into the glass, watching the milk filling up the inside of the glass, returning the balance of milk inside the fridge where it belong. I am speaking. Hazel; call your brothers come.

Here I am walking into the hall way, on my way up the stairs.

Here I am. Ruel, George; Ruel its lunch time.

Here I am walking up the stairs listening for Ruel, listening for George's voice to answer me. I am speaking. What do you want Hazel?

Here I am. Lunch is ready. Tell Ruel it is ready on the table now.

Here I am walking into the dining-room, hearing Ruel and George's foot-steps running down the stairs.

Here I am looking at my mother's hand, sharing the sandwiches out on each plate. Two for Ruel and two for George. One and half slice of bread for me

IAM®

and one and a half slice of bread for Mavis. I can see Delroy's mouth looking like he is already eating. I am speaking. Here Hazel. This is yours.

Here I am. Thank you mummy.

Here I am sitting down at the dining-table, looking around at everyone. I am speaking. Put the food down let me grace the table.

Here I am listening to my mother's voice speaking, praying, thanking God for the food we are going to eat.

Here I am watching my mother make the cross sign across her chest. I am speaking. Amen. You can eat now.

Here I am eating the corn-beef sandwich. The sandwich taste nice. I am speaking. Pass the tea-pot please Hazel.

Here I am pouring the tea into the cups.

Here I am eating, watching Ruel's mouth eating his sandwich quick, thinking in my mind, wondering; what does mummy mean by the word grace? My mother is always speaking new words expecting us to understand what she means.

Here I am eating, watching my mother taking the bowl with the meat out of the fridge.

Here I am thinking in my mind, wondering; what is mummy going to cook for our dinner today, watching her walking into the kitchen with the bowl of meat in her hand.

Here I am collecting the empty plates, carrying them into the kitchen, placing them down on the work-top. I can see my mother standing over the draining-board, holding the big cooking knife, cutting into the piece of flesh in her hand. The flesh looks different from all the other flesh meat.

Here I am looking at the flesh my mother is preparing for our dinner.

Here I am wondering what the meat flesh name is.

Here I am. Mummy; what is that flesh meat name? I am speaking. This is kidney meat.

Here I am, understanding in my mind, understanding that the flesh meat has many different names.

Here I am in the presence of my mother, watching my mother preparing the kidney flesh, thinking in my mind, realizing the meaning of the word meat.

IAM®

Here I am, understanding that the word meat means flesh; and the flesh comes form the animals that people kill and cut-up into pieces; and call the pieces different names like kidney and liver and neck of lamb and sausage and bacon and chicken and fish.

Here I am feeling my inside go round, understanding in my mind the meaning of the word meat.

Here I am, smelling the kidney flesh, not wanting to stay in the kitchen, smelling the kidney flesh in the air surrounding my body.

Here I am walking into the dining-room, collecting the cups off the dining-table, carrying them into the kitchen, thinking in my mind, placing the cups down on the work-top.

Here I am thinking in my mind, folding up the table cloth, returning it inside the television table drawer where it belongs.

Here I am. Fold down the table please someone.

Here I am standing inside the kitchen, pushing all the dirty cups and plates together on the work-top. I am speaking. Leave the frying pan. There is some food in there for your daddy when he comes.

Here I am inside the kitchen, watching my mother's hand preparing the kidney flesh that looks different from all the other flesh meat. My mother is putting the salt and black pepper powder over the kidney flesh inside the mixing bowl. Now my mother is slicing the onion rings on top of the kidney flesh, and the garlic's, and a little bit of herb thyme, mixing everything together with her hands.

Here I am watching my mother washing her hands inside the bowl of water, wiping her hands dry on the dish-cloth.

Here I am watching my mother cutting the big cabbage into two half pieces, cutting one half into two half pieces, cutting the two little pieces into little pieces into the middle-size saucepan on the draining-board. Now my mother is washing the cabbage under the cold water falling onto the cabbage into the saucepan.

Here I am watching my mother, wondering in my mind, thinking, looking around the space where I am watching my mother preparing the food for dinner.

Here I am wondering in my mind, wanting to do something.

IAM®

Here I am. Do you want anything doing mummy. I am speaking. Yes; you can wash some potatoes please.

Here I am reaching down into the big brown paper bag on the ground against the kitchen wall.

Here I am picking the potatoes out of the bag, putting them into the sink. Two big ones for daddy, two big ones for mummy; a big one for Ruel and a big one for George; one for me, one for Mavis, one for Delroy and another one more big one.

Here I am standing on the chair over the sink, turning on the cold water tap, washing the dirt off the potato skin, putting the potatoes inside the washing-up bowl, ready for my mother to peel.

Here I am looking under the kitchen sink, looking for the old newspaper, opening the newspaper out on the draining-board, making ready to peel the potato skin on.

Here I am putting cold water into the middle-size saucepan, resting it down on the draining-board ready to put the peeled potatoes in.

Here I am standing on the chair over the draining-board, wanting to peel the potato with the little cooking knife, hearing my mother put the dutch-pot on the stove, hearing the gas light the fire on the stove.

Here I am holding the little knife and potato in my hands, watching my mother putting half of the half of lard into the dutch-pot.

Here I am peeling the skin off the potato, thinking in my mind; I like helping you mummy.

Here I am peeling the skin off the potato, thinking about my mother, watching her prepare the food for dinner. I am speaking. Hazel; run and get me the parcel of plain flour.

Here I am walking into the dining-room, standing by the cabinet, looking for the plain flour, the packet with the red colour writings on it, looking to see if there is a packet already open.

Here I am walking past Ruel and George sitting at the dining-table playing the game name snakes and ladder with each other, making up noise, not paying my body any attention.

Here I am walking into the kitchen, carrying the parcel of nearly empty plain flour and the new packet, placing them down on the work-top.

IAM®

Here I am standing on the chair peeling the skin off the potato, thinking in my mind, feeling the potato slipping in my hand, making me spend time peeling the potato feeling heavy in my hand. I am speaking. Excuse me a minute. Turn on the cold water please.

Here I am watching my mother's hand holding the big saucepan under the cold water tap, watching the water falling into the pan, listening to the water splashing up the inside. I am speaking. Turn the water off now please.

Here I am holding the potato, watching my mother lighting the gas under the saucepan, watching her hand turn the flame up high. Now my mother is putting a piece of the kidney meat flesh into the oil. I can hear the oil making the frying noise, hearing the hot oil bubbles burst, splashing up hot oil frying the kidney meat flesh. My mother always fry the meat flesh until it changes into a different colour brown, and goes soft and easy to chew. The kidney meat flesh is scenting the air.

Here I am watching my mother scraping the onion rings and the garlic and thyme off the kidney meat flesh, quickly putting the pieces into the hot oil, using the big metal spoon turning the kidney meat flesh over inside the hot oil; looking at my mother's face making water; feeling the air surrounding my body hot, scenting of cooked kidney meat flesh.

Here I am peeling the potato, watching my mother empty the packet of plain flour into the big mixing bowl, and the salt, binding everything together with the cold water, mixing the dumpling dough. I can see everything my mother is doing from where I am standing on the chair over the draining-board peeling the potato in my hand, feeling good with myself, wanting to know everything my mother is doing, smiling all over her face, watching her turning the kidney meat flesh over with the big metal spoon inside her hand.

Here I am peeling a potato, watching my mother scraping everything from the meat-bowl onto the kidney meat flesh cooking inside the dutch-pot. Now my mother is cutting, slicing the tomato onto the kidney meat flesh, pouring some hot water from the kettle onto the kidney meat flesh, and a little vinegar, and now a little of the corner part of the margarine.

Here I am watching everything my mother's hands are doing, understanding in my mind, knowing why my mother's food is always tasty nice. I am speaking. Good.

Here I am peeling the potato, looking at my mother's hand pressing down on the dough inside the mixing bowl, kneading the dough mix ready to make the dumpling. I can see my mother is pushing down all her body weight onto her

IAM®

hand kneading the dough inside the mixing bowl. My mother is rolling the dough long between the palms of her two hands rubbing together fast.

Here I am watching my mother cutting the long piece of dough into all the same size, watching her hand kneading a piece into a round inside her palm, returning the round dough mix down inside the mixing bowl.

Here I am spending time peeling the potato helping my mother to prepare our dinner, wanting to see everything my mother is doing with her hands.

Here I am in the presence of my mother, feeling good; hearing the water boiling inside the dutch-pot; changing the kidney meat flesh smell in the air; thinking in my mind; wondering what the kidney meat flesh cooking look like; watching my mother's hand turning the fire down low under the dutch-pot, wiping the stove top clean, wiping the dutch-pot outside clean, making everything on top of the stove look clean.

Here I am watching my mother put a little salt over the cabbage inside the saucepan, and a little of the margarine, placing the cover on top, lifting the saucepan over onto the stove on the back burner. I am speaking. Come Hazel. Move over a bit let me help you peel the potatoes.

Here I am with my mother peeling the skin off the potatoes. My mother's hand is peeling the skin fast, making me want to peel the potato quick.

Here I am rolling the newspaper up with all the potato skin inside, putting it into the kitchen dustbin.

Here I am looking up at my mother's body standing over the kitchen sink, moving her hands quick, slicing the potatoes into half under the cold water falling from the tap, washing the potato pieces clean.

Here I am watching my mother putting the potatoes into the big saucepan of boiling water. Now my mother is wiping her hands dry on the tea-towel, placing the dumpling rounds inside the pan on top of the potatoes, and one teaspoon half-full with salt into the pan, turning the fire up high, placing the cover on top. I can see my mother is nearly finish now, watching her hands wiping the big saucepan clean all over, wiping the stove surrounding clean, making everywhere the food is cooking look good.

Here I am feeling good inside, watching everything my mother's hands are doing inside the kitchen. I am speaking. Good Hazel; you can finish clearing up the kitchen for me and let me go and carry on with your dress. Only God knows what I would do without you in this house to help me.

Here Iam thinking; I am my mother's helper.

I AM®

Here I am watching my mother's body walking into the dining-room.

Here I am inside the kitchen, standing on the chair over the sink, tuning on the hot water tap, watching the hot water falling into the washing-up bowl.

Here I am putting a little washing-up liquid into the water, washing the things clean, placing them down on the draining-board.

Here I am emptying the dirty water, watching the clean water coming into the bowl, washing the soap suds away, watching the water falling into the bowl, rinsing the suds off the plates, turning them down on the draining-board.

Here I am wringing the water out of the dishcloth, standing on the ground, lifting the chair over to the work-top.

Here I am standing on the chair wiping the work-top clean, feeling myself hurting inside my neck.

Here I am wiping everything dry, placing them down the work-top.

Here I am doing, thinking, wondering in my mind; thinking about the body that I am.

Here I am putting all the cooking things away inside the kitchen cupboard where they belong. I am speaking. Hazel; turn the fire off from under the meat and light the fire under the cabbage.

Here I am. Yes mummy.

Here I am lifting the chair over to the stove, standing on the chair, wrapping the dishcloth around my hand, pushing the dutch-pot to the back burner of the stove, feeling my hands getting hot, feeling the heat from the dutch-pot coming through the cloth onto my hands.

Here I am lifting the saucepan with cabbage over to the front burner of the stove, turning the fire up high to boil the water quick.

Here I am turning the fire down under the big saucepan of food, watching the hot water boiling up high, lifting the cover up and down on top of the pan, boiling hot water over the sides.

Here I am standing inside the kitchen watching my father walking past the kitchen window.

Here I am feeling good inside, knowing that daddy is home.

IAM®

Here I am looking up at my father's body standing on the kitchen door-mat, looking at my body, smiling all over his face, making my body not know what to do with myself.

Here I am. Hello daddy. I am speaking. Everything all right?

Here I am. Yes daddy, I am.

Here I am standing on the kitchen ground; watching my mother standing at the dining kitchen doorway; smiling at my father.

Here I am looking up at my father's body, watching his hands around mummy's waist, looking down on her face, smiling up at him, bowing down his head kissing her face, making my body feel good, watching my mother and father acting up to each other, looking pleased with each other. I am speaking. Here Hazel; take my bag.

Here I am holding my father's work bag, watching my father holding my mother's hand, leading her into the dining-room. I am speaking. I work hard today.

Here I am with my father's work bag, pulling the string loose, wanting to see what daddy bring home for us today. I am speaking. Put the kettle on Hazel please.

Here I am hearing my mother.

Here I am lifting the chair over to the sink, standing on the chair holding the kettle under the cold water tap, watching the water falling into the kettle, feeling the kettle getting heavy, feeling good inside, thinking about my mother and father looking pleased with each other.

Here I am standing by the stove, lighting the match, lighting the back stove burner, pushing the cabbage saucepan onto the back burner, lifting the kettle up down on the front of the stove, wanting the water to boil the water quick, knowing that daddy wants a cup of tea now.

Here I am walking into the dining-room, carrying the cups, placing them down on the dining-table.

Here I am inside the kitchen, picking the pile of plates off the work-top, carrying them into the dining-room, placing them down on the dining-table. I can see my mother is holding the dress piece in her hand, looking at my father, smiling at each other, talking to each other.

Here I am. Do you want anything to eat daddy? I am speaking. I could do with something yes. What do you have to give me? I am speaking. Some

IAM®

corn-beef is in the oven. Make your daddy some sandwich. Use four slice of bread.

Here I am inside the kitchen, lifting the frying-pan out of the oven. I can see the corn-beef looks hard on the bottom of the pan.

Here I am lifting the dutch-pot off the stove onto the work-top, pushing it over to the wall.

Here I am placing the frying-pan of corn-beef down on the stove, lighting the fire, turning the flame down low.

Here I am standing on the chair over the stove, stirring the corn-beef warming in the pan, smelling good.

Here I am standing on the kitchen floor, taking the little tea-pot out the cupboard, resting it down on the stove, taking two tea-bags out the box, putting them into the tea-pot, making ready to make my father a pot of tea. I am speaking. Hazel; hurry your father is going out.

Here I am standing on the chair inside the dining-room, putting everything away inside the cabinet safe; taking two cup and two saucers out for mummy and daddy to have a cup of tea and a plate for daddy's sandwiches.

Here I am spreading the table-cloth over the dining-table, half-way, setting the table ready for daddy to have his lunch.

Here I am looking inside the fridge, getting the can of milk, carrying it into the kitchen, feeling good inside, thinking about my mother and father.

Here I am inside the kitchen standing on the chair over the stove, winding the tea-towel around my hand, lifting the kettle of hot water off the fire, resting it down on the draining-board, standing on the chair, pouring the boiling water into the tea-pot.

Here I am scenting the smell of cabbage, smelling like it is burning.

Here I am standing on the ground, lifting the chair over to the stove, standing on the chair, winding the tea-towel around my hand, lifting the cover off the pan of cabbage. I can see the cabbage looks just the way mummy like it.

Here I am returning the cover to the saucepan, turning the fire off from under the saucepan of cabbage.

Here I am lifting the chair over to the draining-board, standing on the chair pouring the milk into the tea-pot, mixing the milk into the tea looking just right, just like my father likes the colour of his tea to look.

IAM®

Here I am inside the dining-room, returning the milk inside the fridge, remembering the bread, and the margarine.

Here I am carrying everything into the kitchen, placing them down on the work-top, lifting the chair over to the work-top, getting the knife from the kitchen draw, standing on the chair, spreading the margarine over the bread.

Here I am standing by the stove, lifting the frying-pan down off the stove, resting it down on the work-top.

Here I am putting the corn-beef onto the pieces of bread, making sandwiches for my father.

Here I am cutting into the bread, smelling the corn-beef, making my body feel hunger, wanting to eat.

Here I am walking into the dining-room, carrying the plate of sandwiches for my father, resting it down on the dining-table, wondering in my mind, thinking; where has daddy gone.

Here I am standing by the work-top, winding the tea-towel around my hand, lifting the tea-pot down off the work-top, walking slow into the dining-room, resting the tea-pot down on the stand on the dining-table; looking at my father coming into the dining-room.

Here I am. Your lunch is ready for you now daddy.

Here I am standing inside the dining-room, looking up on my father's face smiling down on the body that I am watching my father sitting down at the dining-table.

Here I am remembering daddy's work bag, wondering in my mind, wanting to see what daddy bring home for us.

Here I am inside the kitchen, taking my father's work bag down off the hook; looking inside; taking the paper brown bag out the bag, returning the bag on the hook; thinking about my father; thinking daddy always bring home some of his sandwich food he carry with him to the factory; feeling good; knowing that daddy always brings home some of his work food for us to share. I can see daddy had cheese on his sandwiches today.

Here I am on my knees kneeling on the chair over the work-top, scraping the balance of corn-beef out of the frying-pan onto the bread, making myself a corn-beef cheese sandwich; cutting the sandwich into two half, and two half for Ruel and George and Mavis.

IAM®

Here I am standing at the kitchen dining-room entrance, looking at Ruel and George and Mavis watching the television.

Here I am. Do you want some of daddy's work sandwich Ruel; George? I am speaking. Yes please. Where is it?

Here I am. Come and get it, it's in the kitchen. Where do you think? Do you want some Mavis? I am speaking. No.

Here I am walking fast into the kitchen, wanting Mavis's piece of sandwich.

Here I am. I am having Mavis's piece of sandwich.

Here I am eating inside the kitchen, watching Ruel and George eating quick, smiling at each other. I am speaking. Any more Hazel?

Here I am. No, daddy only bring home one sandwich today. Leave the bread Ruel. I am speaking. You're getting to sound like mummy you are.

Here I am. Are you looking forward to going to school Ruel? I am speaking. Course I am. I am speaking. Are you Hazel?

Here I am. Yes I am Are you George? I am speaking. I can't wait. There is nothing to do in this house. I am speaking. We can't even go outside and play like all the other kids can. I am bored I am. I am speaking. We can't even play inside the house without mummy keep shouting at us all the time. I wish I was back in Jamaica I do.

Here I am listening to Ruel talking; thinking in my mind, looking at Ruel and George's body, thinking about my brothers wanting to go to school for something to do.

Here I am thinking in my mind, wondering about my father, wondering; where is daddy going?

Here I am. We only have three more days and three more night times to go to go to school. I am speaking. No it's not. It's two days; I am counting them. The days seem to get longer and longer in this place.

Here I am standing on the chair over the sink, washing everything clean, listening to Ruel and George talking.

Here I am getting to understand how Ruel and George's mind think, listening to the words they are saying, talking to each other.

Here I am. Ruel; you and George can keep talking about being bored. The days only seem long because you and George never do anything good with your time inside the house. You and George just sit around the house and play games and dirty-up the house all the time. Why don't you go and do some drawing or help me dry up these plates. I am speaking. I want to do what other kids are doing but. I am speaking. What you two doing? I am speaking. Nothing daddy.

Here I am washing-up the dirty food plates, watching my father, put his empty cup and plate inside the water, thinking in my mind, wondering if daddy did hear what Ruel was saying. I am speaking. What have you done today Ruel? I am speaking. Nothing daddy. I am speaking. What you mean nothing. Do you thing I go to work every day to come home and hear you say you sit on your backside and do nothing all day?

Here I am listening to my father speaking, raising his voice, looking down on Ruel and George's body not wanting to look up at daddy, not wanting to move; feeling my father's presence making the air surrounding my body change.

Here I am watching my father walking into the dining-room, watching his head moving from side to side. I am speaking. I want to get out of this house now. He is picking on me now.

Here I am washing the frying-pan, listening to Ruel speaking his mind, listening to his voice sounding hurt.

Here I am thinking in my mind, thinking; daddy is right. Ruel and George don't do anything with any of their time. All I see Ruel and George do is eat and play games and sit and watch the television. I am speaking. I am going back to my room.

Here I am wiping the things dry, putting them away inside the cupboard, remembering the big sauce-pan on the fire.

Here I am lifting the chair over to the stove, standing on the chair, winding the tea-towel around my hand, lifting the cover off the saucepan, feeling the steam hot on my body, feeling Ruel and George's presence leave the kitchen.

Here I am looking down into the saucepan of potatoes and dumpling, looking like everything is overcooked. I can see the water is nearly gone out of the pan.

Here I am turning the fire off, winding the tea-towel around my hand, pouring hot water inside the pan, wondering if the food is stuck onto the bottom.

Here I am standing on the ground, lifting the chair over to the work-top, standing on the chair wiping the cups and things dry, feeling my inside

IAM®

hurting, feeling my body feeling tired, thinking about myself, wondering in my mind.

Here I am walking into the dining-room, carrying the plates, resting them down on the table. I can see my mother is still doing her sewing, making my dress and Delroy is sitting up in his pram, looking at the television, looking with his eyes and mouth wide open.

Here I am walking into the kitchen with the tea-pot in my hand, removing the tea-bag, throwing it away inside the kitchen dust-bin.

Here I am carrying the bread packet and margarine tub into the dining-room, returning them were they belong.

Here I am inside the kitchen, standing on the chair over the sink, wringing the water from the dishcloth, wiping the draining-board dry, standing on the ground, lifting the chair over by the work-top, wiping the work-top clean, reaching over to the wall, wiping all over the work-top, wanting the kitchen to look clean. I am speaking. Come here one minute Hazel.

Here I am inside the dining-room, standing before my mother holding the dress on her lap, resting her hands on the table, watching her eyes looking at the television.

Here I am. Here I am mummy. I am speaking. The foods cooking all right?

Here I am. Yes mummy. It is all ready now. I am speaking. Try this on let me see what I am doing.

Here I am walking behind my mother's chair. I am speaking. Where are you going?

Here I am. To put on the dress mummy. I am speaking. You stand before me and put it on so I can see you. Anyone would believe you have something you want to hide, a little thing like you.

Here I am standing before my mother; taking off my dress, feeling my insides go round, not wanting Ruel and George to come into the dining-room and see me just wearing my knickers.

Here I am putting on the dress mummy is making; pulling it down over my head, pulling it over my body, wanting to see what it looks like. I am speaking. Come closer. Turn around.

Here I am turning my back before my mother; feeling my mother's hand resting heavy on my shoulder. I am speaking. Hold up your head.

IAM®

Here I am standing with my back turn to my mother, holding my hands up; feeling my mother's hands fixing the dress shape under my arm feeling her hand resting on my shoulder, feeling her hand pulling on the edge of the dress, pulling it down in the direction of the floor. I am speaking. Turn around.

Here I am turned to face my mother; watching her face smiling looking at my body. I am speaking. It is making alright Hazel. Turn around again let me see.

Here I am turned with my back facing my mother; feeling my mother's hand pushing the pin into the cloth, pulling the cloth together at the centre at the top, in the middle at the back of my neck. I am speaking. Turn around. Stand still.

Here I am standing facing my mother, feeling her hands pulling the dress down, making the dress length shorter, turning the edge up at my knee joint; putting the pins into the cloth, holding the cloth in place. I am speaking. Turn and hold your head straight. Walk over by the door let me look at you.

Here I am standing by the dining-room door, looking at my mother looking at me, watching her face smiling, smiling to her self, looking at my body.

Here I am, wanting to see the dress on my body, wanting to see what my mother can see. I am speaking. Come let me take the pin them out.

Here I am standing close to my mother, feeling her hands on my body feeling her hands taking the pins out of the cloth.

Here I am putting on my house dress, thinking in my mind, wondering how the dress looks on my body, wanting it to look good.

Here I am watching my mother's hand sewing the dress, watching her smiling all over her face.

Here I am looking at my mother's face, wondering in my mind wondering; what is mummy smiling at? What is mummy thinking in her mind?

Here I am remembering what I was doing.

Here I am inside the kitchen, sweeping the kitchen floor, sweeping the food up off the floor, wanting the kitchen to look clean.

Here I am sweeping the rubbish into the dust-pan, emptying the dust-pan into the kitchen dust-bin.

Here I am standing inside the kitchen, looking around the space where I am, looking up; looking around the room, making sure the kitchen inside is clean.

Here I am inside the dining-room.

I AM®

Here I am feeling good inside myself looking under the television table, looking for my sewing bag, wanting to do my sewing, wanting to finish the pin-cushion I am making for my mother.

Here I am holding my sewing, looking at the stitches I am sewing, looking for the needle.

Here I am making the blanket stitches, thinking in my mind, wondering about my father; thinking about my father gone outside his house.

Here I am thinking, wondering what my father is doing away from home, wishing daddy will take me with him the next time he goes out.

Here I am making the blanket stitches, wanting to sew quick, wanting to finish making the pin cushion, feeling good with myself sewing the last stitch, leaving about half an inch space open.

Here I am looking at my sewing, looking at the stitches, looking at George's body coming into the dining-room, looking like he just wake up, watching his hands rubbing his eyes.

Here I am. I have finish sewing mummy. I am speaking. Yes, I will be with you in a minute.

Here I am standing by the fire surround, looking around the dining-room, looking at everyone.

Here I am looking at Ruel's body sitting at the dining-table, looking at the television picture; looking at George sitting on the chair next to Ruel at the dining-table, looking at the television.

Here I am looking at Delroy's body sitting in his pram looking at the television picture; looking at Mavis looking at the television, sucking her finger.

Here I am looking at my mother's eyes looking at the dress she is making for my body.

Here I am thinking in my mind, wondering; what would everyone do with them self if the television was not here in the house?

The television picture seem more important to each one than each other.

Here I am thinking, wondering in my mind, realizing that Ruel and George and Delroy and Mavis spend all their time watching the television.

Here I am thinking; mummy and daddy should turn the television off; thinking in my mind; Ruel and George do not understand the meaning of the picture showing on the television.

IAM®

Here I am, knowing that we cannot talk to the television, knowing that the television picture show is like the once upon a time story book with people pretending about what is happening all the time.

Here I am, knowing that Ruel and George and Delroy and Mavis and daddy think that what they see on the television is real.

Here I am looking at Ruel's mouth wide open, looking at the food picture on the television; thinking in my mind; Ruel and George and Delroy, Mavis and daddy seem lost in what they can see on the television; like the television has taken control over their mind; thinking in my mind; the people that come on the television are fooling everyone into believing that what they see on the television screen is real; but I know it is only pretending to make people do what they want; thinking in my mind; Ruel and George and Delroy and Mavis and daddy get lost in the television show because when mummy call their names; Ruel and George and Delroy and Mavis and daddy seem like they do not hear because they never answer mummy unless she raise her voice and shout at them; then they hear.

Here I am, understanding to myself, the television show is only good if you know what you are watching it for.

Here I am thinking, understanding in my mind, wondering about myself, wondering in my mind. I am speaking. Let me see what you have Hazel.

Here I am standing before my mother, watching my mother's eyes looking at my sewing, listening to her body making sounds to herself. I am speaking. You learn quick Hazel.

Here I am listening to my mother's words making my body feel good inside, watching my mother's hands pushing the cloth edge through the little hole opening, turning the bright side of the cloth outwards so I can see what I have done, understanding all that I can see, looking at the round pin-cushion that I am sewing. I am speaking. You want some stuffing inside it now before you sew up this hole. Pass me my bag with the scrap pieces of cloth.

Here I am watching my mother's hand inside the cloth-bag, picking out all the little pieces of cloth, watching her hands sorting out the bigger pieces, dropping the little bits and pieces onto the floor before me. I am speaking. Use that little scissors and cut them up into little pieces, then you can stuff out the cushion.

Here I am feeling good inside myself, kneeling down on the floor, gathering the bits of cloth together in a pile, placing the scissors on my finger, making to cut the cloth, wanting the cloth to cut, feeling the scissors not working, not

IAM®

cutting into the cloth like mummy's scissors cut into the cloth properly. The scissors keep sticking, not opening

Here I am, wanting the scissors to cut, feeling the scissors stick, holding the cloth between its blades, making my body not know what to do with myself, wanting the scissors to cut the cloth now.

Here I am wondering if mummy will let me use her big cutting scissors, knowing in my mind that mummy's scissors always cut through everything mummy use it on.

Here I am. Mummy; can I use your big scissors please mummy? This one keeps sticking together and won't cut the cloth. I am speaking. If you can manage it yes you can. Be careful, the point is sharp.

Here I am with the scissors in my hand, feeling the scissors weighing down my hand, making my fingers hurt trying to open the scissors to cut the piece of cloth. I can't work the big scissors, my hand is two small.

Here I am returning the big scissors onto the table by my mother, thinking in my mind, thinking, wanting the cloth to cut, feeling my body wanting to cry, feeling water falling on my hands, feeling my inside hurting, wanting to make the scissors work and cut the cloth, wanting to finish making the pin-cushion.

Here I am holding a different piece of cloth, holding the scissors tight, closing it, watching the scissors cutting into the cloth, making my body feel good, realizing that different cloths are easier to cut than others.

Here I am cutting the bits of cloth that feel like cotton.

Here I am thinking in my mind, thinking about all the cloth my mother have, thinking about all the things that I can make, wanting to make things, just like my mother can.

Here I am cutting the cloths into pieces, feeling good with myself, working the scissors, making it cut, realizing that the cloth pieces are different, and the colours and patterns are different, and the feel and weight are different, and all of the cloth look different, and the different cloth cuts quicker, depending on what the cloth is made from or the way the cloth is made.

Here I am wondering in my mind, thinking, where does the different cloths come from?

IAM®

Here I am. Is that enough mummy? I am speaking. Put them into the opening of the pin cushion you're making and see for yourself. It must look puffed out and firm like this one when you finish it.

Here I am, understanding every word my mother said, now I can see what I am making.

Here I am pushing the bits of cloth into my pin-cushion, stuffing the insides, watching the circle filling out, wanting it to look round like the one mummy make.

Here I am pushing more pieces of cloth into the opening of my pin-cushion, watching it puffing out on the dining-table, looking just like my mother's pin-cushion.

Here I am feeling good with myself, watching my mother's face, wanting my mother to see what I have done.

Here I am. I have done it mummy. I am speaking. Good; now thread the needle with a long piece of thread and come.

Here I am looking inside my mother's sewing tin, looking at the many different colour cotton threads.

Here I am pulling the cotton off its reel; making the thread long breaking the thread between my teeth, holding my needle up, pushing the thread to go into the eye hole, wanting the thread to go into the eye hole, thinking about the pin-cushion that I am making, wanting to see it finished.

Here I am standing at my mother's side, holding the thread and needle out before one, watching my mother's hand-sewing the dress for my body to wear.

Here I am. I have done it mummy. I am speaking. Knot the two end of the thread together.

Here I am pulling the thread lengths together, winding the thread around my finger, wetting my finger inside my mouth water, rubbing my fingers and thumb together.

Here I am watching my mother's hand pushing the pin through the two piece of cloth, sewing up the opening of the pin-cushion I am making. I can see my mother's hand sticking the needle through the cloths, making the blanket stitch around the opening, making my pin-cushion look good. I am speaking. You can finish it off now.

Here I am. Thank you mummy.

IAM®

Here I am feeling good inside myself, taking the pin-cushion I am making from my mother's hands.

Here I am, watching my hand sewing the blanket-stitch, wanting to sew quick, wanting to see the pin-cushion finish now.

Here I am feeling good with myself, knowing that I have made a pin-cushion. I am speaking. Let me see.

Here I am watching my mother looking down at the pin-cushion, smiling all over her face. I am speaking. You are good Hazel. You learn quick. Now you can decorate it if you want. You can sew some embroidery stitches like the picture on Delroy play suit. This is good Hazel.

Here I am listening to my mother praising the body that I am, making my body feel good; thinking about myself, watching my mother turning my pin-cushion over, turning it around inside her hands. I am speaking. Thread the needle with a bright colour thread and let me show you what I mean.

Here I am looking inside my mother's sewing tin, looking at the many different colour threads, wanting to choose one, not knowing which thread to use.

Here I am winding the thread around my hand, breaking it with my teeth, wondering in my mind, wanting to know the colour of the thread in my hand.

Here I am pushing the thread into the needle eye hole, wondering what to do next.

Here I am. Shall I put a knot in it mummy? I am speaking. No; not this time.

Here I am watching my mother's hand make the stitch at the edge of the pin-cushion. The stitch look good, look different, making the pin-cushion look new. I am speaking. This stitch is name zigzag stitch. Come closer and see what I am doing.

Here I am looking down on my mother's hand sewing, listening to her words, watching her hand sewing making my pin-cushion look like new. I am speaking. Take this quick Hazel. Your father is trying to get in.

IAM®

CHAPTER 21

Here I am watching my mother's body jump up off the chair, moving fast into the kitchen.

Here I am standing on the kitchen door-step, watching my mother's body walking fast towards the back gate-way.

Here I am standing on the kitchen door-step, wondering in my mind, watching my mother open the back door gate, thinking in my mind, wondering; where does the back door gate entrance path way go?

Here I am watching my father's body entering his land; looking at my father's face looking tired, walking towards the house, carrying the big brown paper bag sack on his shoulder back.

Here I am thinking in my mind, thinking; daddy is strong carrying a big bag like that on his back.

Here I am watching my father's body leaning forward, watching the bag fall down off his shoulder, falling heavy onto the kitchen door-mat.

Here I am watching my father's body looking tired, lifting the bag of potatoes across the kitchen ground, dropping it down by the kitchen wall where it belong.

Here I am thinking in my mind, thinking; daddy could do with a cup of tea now.

Here I am putting my sewing cloth and things together inside my sewing bag, returning it down under the television table.

Here I am inside the kitchen, lighting the fire under the kettle, turning the flame up high, thinking in my mind wondering; is it dinner time yet?

Here I am inside the dining-room, wondering in my mind, looking at my mother's hand still sewing, watching my father's body sitting down at the dining-table, looking tired all over his face.

Here I am. Mummy, shall I put the food on to warm up now. I am speaking. Are you ready for your dinner Ge? I am speaking. Yes if it is ready. The bag of potato is heavy. It is a good job me only had to walk from down the road.

Here I am standing inside the kitchen, lighting the fire under the sauce-pans, turning the fire down low.

I AM®

Here I am feeling good inside, taking the little tea-pot out the cupboard, wondering in my mind, thinking about all the different things that I can do with my hands.

Here I am putting two tea-bags into the tea-pot, resting it down on the work-top, feeling my body smiling all over my face, feeling good inside, thinking about myself.

Here I am the presence wondering in my mind, thinking about my body, feeling pleased with myself, knowing that I am live, I am living.

Here I am inside the dining-room, gathering the pieces of cloth together, returning the cloth into my mother's sewing bag, clearing the table, making it ready for my mother and father to eat their dinner.

Here I am spreading the clean table cloth over the table, looking at Mavis's body on the other side of the table, watching her sucking her finger, just looking at one.

Here I am. Do you want your dinner with mummy and daddy Mavis? I am speaking. Yes please.

Here I am standing by the cabinet, taking the dinner plate down off the shelf, and the cups and saucer, resting them down on the table with the knife and fork and teaspoon, and the sugar bowl and the tea-pot stand, and the bottle of sauce that Mavis like.

Here I am looking inside the fridge, getting the can of milk, carrying it to the kitchen, resting it down on the work-top. I can smell the food is warming hot.

Here I am standing on the chair over the stove, winding the tea-towel around my hand, lifting the cover off the dutch-pot.

Here I am with the spoon in my hand, taking the meat out the pot, scenting the meat, feeling it hot, burning my tong, tasting just right.

Here I am thinking; mummy can cook good.

Here I am returning the cover on top of the sauce-pan, hearing the kettle making the whistling noise.

Here I am standing by the stove, winding the tea-towel around my hands, lifting the kettle down off the stove onto the work-top.

Here I am lifting the chair over to the draining-board, standing on the chair, pouring the water into the tea-pot.

IAM®

Here I am standing on the chair over the kitchen sink, watching cold water falling into the kettle getting heavy with water, carrying it over to the stove, resting the kettle down on top of the fire, turning the flames down to low.

Here I am standing on the chair over the work-top, mixing the milk into the tea, watching the tea change colour.

Here I am standing on the ground, winding the tea-towel around my hand, lifting the tea-pot down off the work-top, walking slow towards the dining-room, walking into the dining-room, feeling the heat coming from the tea-pot, warming my hand resting the tea-pot down on its stand on the table

Here I am looking around the dining-table, thinking in my mind, making sure I have put everything in the right place, ready for mummy and daddy to have their dinner.

Here I am. Do you want tea or squash with your dinner Mavis. I am speaking. Squash please Hazel.

Here I am looking inside the cabinet, getting the squash bottle, carrying it into the kitchen.

Here I am standing on the chair over the sink, pouring the squash into the cup, watching the cold water falling into the sink, thinking in my mind, wondering about Mavis.

Here I am thinking; how come Mavis is speaking so nice to me.

Here I am watching the water rising up inside the cup, thinking about my sister.

Here I am remembering Delroy, thinking in my mind, thinking about making Delroy some squash.

Here I am walking into the dining-room, carrying the squash for Mavis and Delroy, placing the cups down on the dining-table. I can feel Delroy's presence looking at my body, watching every move I am making with his cup.

Here I am. The food is hot now mummy. I am speaking. Yes I am coming.

Here I am standing at the dining-room doorway, looking at my mother, watching her put her sewing away into her sewing bag, placing it down on the side of the television-table, watching her body walking into the kitchen.

Here I am looking around the space, watching everyone present in my presence.

IAM®

Here I am looking at my father with his hands in each other, resting them down on the table, watching his eyes looking at the television screen, smiling all over his face, watching the Tom and Jerry picture show.

Here I am thinking in my mind; daddy likes Tom and Jerry.

Here I am looking at Ruel's body looking at George's body, looking at Mavis and Delroy's eyes all looking in one direction, watching the cat running after the mice on the carton picture showing on the television screen. Everyone is having a good time laughing out loud, watching Tom and Jerry.

Here I am watching everyone, listening to the sounds coming from everyone, listening to father's laugh sounding loud.

Here I am listening to my father's laugh, wondering; what does daddy find so funny?

Here I am looking at the cartoon picture, thinking in my mind, wondering if my father realize that the time he spend watching the television is the same time he could spend making something, doing something with his hands and become the example to Ruel and George and Delroy, just like mummy is always making something with her two hands, so I can see how I can use my body two hands to make my body work, so that I can see that I can do anything if I want.

Here I am realizing that Ruel and George and Delroy will never understand themselves because all they see daddy do is watch television instead of showing them how to use their hands to make or do something.

Here I am, understanding that Ruel and George behave like daddy, copying everything daddy does when he is at home.

Here I am knowing that if daddy clean-up the house like mummy does, or wash his dirty clothes or prepare the food he eat, or even sew a button on his shirt, then Ruel and George would understand how to use their two hands to help themselves and help each other.

Here I am watching everyone just watching the television.

Here I am my mother and father's helper, understanding that my father does not realize that he is responsible for Ruel and George and Delroy's behaviour, because Ruel and George is watching him and copying his behaviour. My father does not understand that his body is the example of man to his children and if Ruel and George do not see him using his two hands to make something, then Ruel and George will not know what to do with their two hands inside the house. Ruel and George do not do anything of themselves because daddy does not do anything of himself for us to see and learn from his doing. I am speaking. Hazel; Come and help me here.

Here I am hearing my mother's voice calling me.

Here I am inside the kitchen, looking at the food on the plate on the work-top. I am speaking. Carry your sister and brother' dinner plate in please.

Here I am walking into the dining-room, carrying Mavis and Delroy's dinner plate full with food, placing Mavis plate down on the table before her body looking at my body and smiling.

Here I am standing by the pram, holding the spoon in my hand, making ready to give Delroy his dinner. Delroy's mouth is wide open, making noises at my body looking at Delroy, watching his mouth wide open ready to eat.

Here I am giving Delroy his feed, looking at Delroy's face eating down his food quick, realizing that Delroy is not chewing the food. Delroy is making to cry, looking like he is choking on the food, acting as if he wants to take the spoon from my hand, looking like he wants to feed himself.

Here I am understanding in my mind, realizing that Delroy and Ruel and George, and Mavis pretend that they cannot help themselves because mummy believe that they do not understand, but here I am knowing that Ruel and George and Delroy and Mavis each have two hands that can feed themselves, so they can learn to do other things, but all they do is sit and wait for mummy and I to serve them.

Here I am, knowing that my brothers and sister can do something to help themselves, but they prefer to pretend that they cannot.

Here I am thinking; Ruel and George and Delroy and Mavis can fool mummy and daddy, but they cannot fool me; I am their sister.

Here I am, knowing that I am the life that is living because I am helping my mother to do her work, because I want to.

Here I am scraping the food off the plate so Delroy can see that it is all gone.

Here I am. Delroy; here is your drink, there is no more food.

Here I am holding Delroy's cup, watching Delroy's eyes looking into the eyes I am looking into Delroy's eyes, wanting Delroy to understand that I understand the way he is acting, pretending for mummy to give him attention.

Here I am walking into the kitchen, carrying Delroy's dinner plate, placing it down inside the sink.

I AM®

Here I am on the chair, kneeling down over the sink, washing the dirty food things; thinking in my mind; Ruel and George and Mavis and Delroy can pretend they know nothing with mummy and to daddy, and pretend to themselves, but I know the truth. The truth is; Ruel and George and Delroy and Mavis are all lazy. Not one wants to do anything for themselves. The truth is; each one will never know each other if they carry on pretending like they cannot do anything.

Here I am standing inside the dining-room, looking at Ruel, looking at George pretending to watch the television, looking at mummy, looking at daddy eating their food.

Here I am wondering in my mind thinking; if Ruel and George could see how they look, looking like dogs waiting to grab the food off mummy and daddies plate. Ruel and George are standing around mummy and daddy, waiting to grab the plate off daddy; not giving daddy time to put down his knife and fork.

Here I am looking at daddy's face looking hurt; realising Ruel and George's behaviour. I am speaking. Put the plate down; put it down. I am going to show you that I am not putting up with you lot behaviour no longer. Anyone would believe that I am bringing up a pack of animals. Are you an animal? Give me the fork. Pearl; eat all your food. Do not leave any on the plate for them. The boys them act like them is animal. Anyone would believe they haven't eaten from morning. Don't leave anything on your plate.

Here I am feeling my inside go round, hearing my father raise his voice, making the air around my body change, watching Ruel and George's face drop, not smiling, watching their heads bowing away from daddy.

Here I am listening to my father, watching George and Ruel, looking at mummy and daddy eating every last bit of food off their plate.

Here I am watching my father turning his head to Ruel, looking down at Ruel's face not wanting to look up at daddy looking with no expression looking at George's face, just looking, looking making sure Ruel and George understand the reason why he has done what he has done.

Here I am collecting together the dinner plates, carrying them into the kitchen, putting them into the washing up bowl inside the sink.

Here I am lighting the fire under the saucepans, wanting to eat my food now, feeling hunger inside my body.

IAM®

Here I am inside the dining-room, looking around the space from where I am standing before the dining-table, collecting the cups and saucers, carrying them into the kitchen; hearing daddy talking about Ruel and George.

Here I am standing on the chair by the cabinet taking out the plates for Ruel and George and me, resting them down on the table.

Here I am inside the kitchen, standing on the chair by the stove, winding the tea-towel around my hand, lifting the cover off the big saucepan, looking into the pot, feeling the hot air rising out of the pot making my body jump-up inside.

Here I am stirring the meat inside the dutch-pot, smelling the scent tasting good.

Here I am standing inside the dining-room, looking at Ruel, looking at George's body not doing a thing, watching the television picture show.

Here I am. Ruel; can you or George set the table ready for our dinner?

Here I am inside the kitchen, standing on the chair over the stove, winding the tea-towel around my hand, lifting the covers off the saucepans, resting them down on the draining-board.

Here I am looking into the big sauce-pan, looking at the food, counting three dumplings in the pan.

Here I am standing on the floor, lifting the sauce-pan down off the stove, lifting it up onto the work-top, standing on the chair, sharing the food onto the plates. A dumpling for Ruel; one for George and one for me.

Here I am standing on the ground, lifting the pan with cabbage off the stove, lifting it up onto the work-top, lifting the dutch-pot of meat down off the stove, resting it down upon the work-top.

Here I am with the big spoon with holes, sharing the cabbage onto the plates. I am speaking. What are we having to drink Hazel?

Here I am. Orange squash drink. I haven't made any tea.

Here I am sharing the meat onto the plates, just like mummy share out the food for us.

Here I am carrying the plates of food into the dining-room, resting them down before Ruel and George sitting at the dining-table ready to eat. I can see mummy and daddy have gone upstairs with Mavis and Delroy.

IAM®

Here I am inside the kitchen getting my plate of food, carrying it into the dining-room.

Here I am sitting at the dining-table, sitting with Ruel and George, watching them eating their food, quick.

Here I am eating, thinking in my mind; the dinner taste nice.

Here I am pouring the squash into the cup, watching my mother's body entering the dining-room, walking through into the kitchen, smiling all over her face, looking at my body, making my body feel good inside.

Here I am eating my dinner, thinking in my mind, thinking of myself, thinking about going to school, thinking of my mother making my school dress. I am speaking. Hazel; bring me the kettle of water up stairs when it boils.

Here I am listening to my mother, watching her lifting the sheets off Delroy's pram, carrying them up stairs.

Here I am thinking in my mind, looking at Ruel, looking at Georg's body eating, listening to Ruel saying he is still hungry, wanting some more food.

Here I am. If you didn't eat so fast Ruel, you would still be eating now. There are some pieces of potato inside the saucepan if you want.

Here I am watching Ruel's body jump down quick off the chair, walking fast into the kitchen, holding his plate tight, watching George's body following after him, wanting some of any food left inside the saucepan.

Here I am inside the kitchen, standing on the chair over the sink, turning on the hot water tap, watching the water running into the washing-up bowl, feeling the water feeling cold on my hands, listening to Ruel and George's body arguing over the food in the saucepan.

Here I am hearing the water boiling-up inside the kettle, making the whistling noise, remembering that mummy is waiting for the hot water.

Here I am holding the saucepan under the hot water tap, watching the water rising up inside the pan.

Here I am standing on the floor, lifting the sauce-pan with water down off the draining-board, resting it up, down on the stove, winding the tea-towel around my hand, standing on the chair lifting the kettle off the fire, resting it down on the back burner, lifting the saucepan of water on top of the fire, turning the flames up high, wanting the water inside the pan to boil quick.

IAM®

Here I am standing on the ground, lifting the kettle down off the stove, walking slow, walking across the dining-room, on my way up stairs, feeling the water splashing out the kettle onto the stairs, splashing on my foot; feeling the hot water burning my skin.

Here I am standing at the top of the stairs, wondering in my mind wondering; where does mummy want the kettle of water?

Here I am carrying the kettle into the bath-room, lifting the kettle up, down into the bath, feeling my hands feeling tired, hurting inside.

Here I am standing outside my mother's bed-room, knocking on the door, listening to the sounds like Mavis's voice sounding like she and Delroy is playing. I am speaking. Come.

Here I am standing inside my mother's bed-room, looking at my father's body wearing his pyjamas, looking ready to go to bed.

Here I am watching my father looking into the big Bible, reading to him self.

Here I am. The water is ready mummy. The kettle is inside the bath-room inside the bath.

Here I am talking to my mother, watching her hands sewing the dress for my body to wear to go to school. I can see my dress is looking good, looking like mummy has nearly finished making it. Mavis is lying on the bed and Delroy is playing with his foot, laughing at Mavis making up faces at him. I am speaking. What are you doing now?

Here I am. I am going to wash the dirty things in the kitchen mummy. I am speaking. Go and put some of the water into the face bowl and bring Delroy's flannel and bed-clothes come before you go.

Here I am looking at Mavis playing on mummy's bed, listening to mummy speaking, thinking in my mind, walking into the hall way, wondering in my mind thinking; how come Mavis and Delroy is the only ones that can play inside mummy and daddies presence? What about me? I never get to play. What is so special about them?

Here I am inside the bath-room, standing on the toilet seat, reaching into the hot water tank cupboard, looking for Delroy's bed clothes, carrying them into the boy's bed-room, getting the big bath towel off Delroy's cot rail, carrying everything to my mother's bed-room.

Here I am standing outside my mother's bed-room, knocking on the door, listening to mummy and daddy laughing with each other.

I AM®

Here I am inside the bed-room, placing everything down on the bed beside my mother's body still sewing, making my dress.

Here I am walking along the hall way, walking into the bath-room, standing over the bath turning on the cold water tap, watching the water falling into the bowl, pouring the hot water from the kettle, mixing the water, making it feel warm on my hand.

Here I am lifting the bowl of water out of the bath, walking slow along the hall way, walking towards my mother's bed-room, feeling the water splashing up outside the bowl, splashing onto my tummy, making my body feel wet; walking slow, carrying the bowl into my mother's bed-room, resting it down on the floor beside my mother's body still sewing making my dress.

Here I am running along the hall way, walking fast into the bath-room, getting Delroy's flannel and the soap in the soap-dish, carrying them into my mother's bed-room, putting the cloth inside the bowl of water, resting the soap dish down on the floor, near to my mother's body.

Here I am. Do you want the balance of the water in the kettle mummy? I am speaking. Yes thank you. Leave it in the bath-room.

Here I am. Is there anything more you want me to do mummy. I am speaking. No; that is all thank you. Tell Ruel and George to keep the noise down and keep the place clean for me, please do.

Here I am listening to every word that my mother is saying as I am leaving her presence, walking down the stairs, running into the dining-room, hearing the television sound sounding loud.

Here I am inside the dining-room, turning the television sound down, remembering what mummy said.

Here I am. Ruel and George, mummy said you must keep the noise down and keep the place clean. Ruel; Ruel. Did you hear what I said?

Here I am standing in the presence of Ruel and George's body, speaking to them, watching them looking at the television, watching them not paying me any attention.

Here I am calling Ruel's name, wandering why Ruel is not answering my body; wondering if Ruel is pretending not to hear me calling him.

Here I am. Ruel; Ruel. I am speaking. What you want?

Here I am. Can you come and lift the saucepan off the fire for me. I am speaking. Wait a minute. I am coming. I am coming Hazel.

I AM®

Here I am standing inside the kitchen, watching Ruel lifting the sauce-pan down off the stove, watching Ruel lifting the pan up, down onto the draining-board.

Here I am standing on the chair over the sink, holding the little saucepan, taking the hot water out the saucepan, pouring the water into the washing-up bowl inside the sink, turning the cold water tap on, mixing the water, making it hand-hot, ready to wash the dirty cups and plates clean.

Here I am washing the cups and plates clean, placing everything down on the draining-board, pouring the cup full of cold water over everything, rinsing the soap suds away; making everything look clean and bright.

Here I am wringing the water out of the dishcloth.

Here I am standing on the ground, lifting the chair over to the work-top, standing on the chair wiping the work-top clean.

Here I am standing on the floor, wiping the saucepans dry, placing them inside the other, returning them inside the cupboard where they belong.

Here I am carrying the plates into the dining-room, resting them down on the table.

Here I am inside the kitchen, hanging a cup on each finger, carrying them into the dining-room, resting them down on the table.

Here I am inside the kitchen, collecting the knives and forks and spoons, carrying them into the dining-room, resting them down on the table.

Here I am inside the kitchen, collecting the two glasses off the work-top, walking slow into the dining-room, placing them down on the table.

Here I am standing on the chair by the cabinet, putting everything away where they belong, putting the knives and forks and spoons into the drawer.

Here I am inside the kitchen, standing on the chair by the stove, wiping the stove top clean, wiping the stove sides clean, wanting the stove to look good, just the way my mother leave the stove looking good.

Here I am lifting the chair over to the sink, standing on the chair washing the food out of the big saucepan, resting it down on the draining-board.

Here I am feeling my body hurting, resting my body against the sink, watching the dirty food water going down the plug-hole.

Here I am watching the water falling into the saucepan, rising up the side.

IAM®

Here I am standing on the ground, lifting the pan down of the draining-board, lifting it up onto the stove, lighting the match, lighting the gas under the saucepan, turning the flame up high, wanting the water to boil up quick.

Here I am standing on the chair, holding the scouring pad, scrubbing the saucepan inside, scrubbing the outside parts, making the saucepan look clean, washing the saucepan clean; turning it down on the draining-board.

Here I am standing on the ground, lifting the saucepan of hot water down off the fire, walking slow to the sink, resting it down on the draining-board.

Here I am standing on the chair over the sink, pouring the water into the washing up bowl.

Here I am turning the water tap on, putting some washing-up liquid into the water, washing the sauce-pan clean, turning them down on the draining-board.

Here I am wringing the water out of the dishcloth, wiping the big sauce-pan inside dry, resting it on my tummy, wiping the outside dry, putting it away inside the cupboard where it belong.

Here I am standing on the kitchen ground, looking around the space where I am, feeling good inside myself, feeling tired all over, thinking in my mind, walking into the dining-room, carrying the little hand-brush, pushing the chairs under the dining-table, making the room look tidy.

Here I am on my hands and knees by the hall way entrance, sweeping the floor, sweeping around the cabinet, around the television table, hearing Ruel and George laughing at the television picture.

Here I am sweeping, feeling my body hurting inside my neck at the back of my neck is hurting.

Here I am sweeping the floor around the fire surround, feeling my body hurting, wanting to stop working.

Here I am kneeling on the floor, looking at the television picture, wondering what the picture is about, looking at George, looking at Ruel; looking at their eyes fixed on the television.

Here I am. What is the show about please Ruel? I am speaking. You have to watch it if you want to know.

Here I am. George. What is the film about please George? I am speaking. It is a ghost film.

IAM®

Here I am listening to George, wondering about the ghost film.

Here I am sweeping the dining-room floor, sweeping the dust together at the kitchen doorway, sweeping the dust into the dust-pan.

Here I am inside the kitchen, holding the big broom, sweeping the kitchen ground, sweeping the dirt towards the kitchen outside doorway, sweeping the dirt into the dust-pan, emptying the pan into the kitchen dust-bin.

Here I am walking outside the house, carrying the dust-bin on my tummy, placing it down beside the big rubbish bin on the wall by the back gate.

Here I am taking the rubbish bin-cover off, placing it down on the ground, lifting the kitchen bin onto the side of the rubbish bin, leaning it forward into the rubbish bin, feeling the air blowing the scent of the rubbish, smelling all around my body, holding my breath, not wanting to taste what I can smell.

Here I am standing on the kitchen doorstep, looking into the air, looking up into the heaven, looking at all the different shades of colour in the heaven, making my body feel good inside, looking at the sky, shining all over the heaven on the ground of the land where I am standing inside my father's house, looking into heaven, thinking in my mind, wondering at all that I can see.

Here I am closing shut the kitchen door, turning the key around inside the key-hole, making the catch click lock.

Here I am returning the kitchen dust-bin on the ground in the corner where it belongs.

Here I am lifting the broom-cloth bucket over to the sink, emptying the bowl of water into the bucket.

Here I am rubbing the broom-cloth handle inside the palms of my hands, making the broom-cloth swish around inside the water, feeling the broom-cloth weighing heavy in my hands lifting the broom-cloth onto the bucket drain.

Here I am pressing down with my body weight, pressing down on the broom-cloth, pressing the water out, rubbing the broom-cloth along the kitchen ground, mopping around the stove, and the cupboard door bottom, and the sink, mopping over by the kitchen doorway, making the kitchen ground look shine with water.

Here I am standing on the kitchen doormat, rubbing the broom-cloth handle inside the palms of my hand, making the broom-cloth swish around inside the

IAM®

water, making suds appear, washing the broom-cloth, looking clean inside the water.

Here I am feeling myself feeling good inside, knowing that I have finished cleaning-up the kitchen.

Here I am standing inside the kitchen, looking around the room, feeling pleased with myself making the kitchen room look good, just like my mother make the kitchen room look clean.

Here I am lifting the broom-cloth bucket by the stove, lifting the chair by the stove, standing on the chair turning off the kitchen room light.

Here I am standing inside the dining-room, standing by the fire surround, looking around the dining-room, looking at Ruel watching the television, looking at George's body watching the television.

Here I am looking at the television, wanting to understand what I can see.

Here I am standing by the dining-room window, looking through the glass, looking into the air, watching the sky moving, just moving in one direction; thinking in my mind; looking at the moon shining, watching the sky moving across the moon in the heavens.

Here I am thinking in my mind, wondering about my mother.

Here I am walking into the hall way, walking into the grey light, feeling my way walking up the stairs.

Here I am standing inside the girl's bed-room, thinking about Mavis, wondering; is Mavis going to sleep with mummy and daddy again?

Here I am walking along the hall way, walking inside the boys bed-room, pushing the door open wide so I can see inside. I can hear Delroy's sleeping noise.

Here I am walking towards my mother's bed-room, thinking in my mind, wondering what mummy is doing.

Here I am standing outside my mother's bed-room, listing, knocking on the door, wanting, waiting, wanting to go inside. I am speaking. Come.

Here I am opening the bed-room door, walking into the room, watching my mother sitting on her ottoman box, sewing a different piece of cloth. I can see my mother is dressed ready for her bed, and daddy and Mavis are sleeping in mummies and daddies bed.

IAM®

Here I am. I come to see if you want anything doing mummy. I am speaking. No thank you. Is everything alright down stairs?

Here I am. Yes mummy. I am speaking. What are your brother's doing.

Here I am. Ruel and George are watching the television mummy. I am speaking. Bring the kettle down with you. It is in the bath-room, and tell Ruel and George to come on up to their bed.

Here I am. Good night mummy.

Here I am walking along the hall way, walking into the bath-room; thinking in my mind; collecting the kettle off the floor, walking down the stairs, walking into the dining-room, thinking about my mother, wondering; what is mummy making now.

Here I am standing on the chair over the kitchen sink, putting cold water into the kettle, lifting the kettle up, down onto the stove, lighting a match from the match-box, lighting the gas under the kettle, turning the flame up high, wanting the water to boil quick so I can have a wash.

Here I am inside the dining-room, sitting down on the chair, feeling my body hurting, feeling tired, wanting to sleep.

Here I am thinking in my mind, wondering about myself, looking down at my two hands, not understanding why my hands look the way they look cold, without colour.

Here I am looking into the palm of my hands, thinking in my mind, thinking about myself, wondering; how come my hands look different to Ruel and George and Mavis and Delroy's hands?

Here I am looking into the palm of my two hands, thinking about the body that I am, wondering in my mind; thinking. I am speaking. Hazel, didn't I tell you to tell Ruel and George to turn off the television?

Here I am listening to my mother's voice shouting, watching her body stamping her foot towards the television, feeling her presence making the air change.

Here I am standing inside the kitchen, turning the fire off from under the kettle, winding the tea-towel around my hand, lifting the kettle down off the stove, listening to my mother talking to herself, banging the furniture about inside the dining-room.

Here I am walking across the dining-room, carrying the kettle of hot water, walking past my mother, feeling her presence surrounding my being, making my body not know what to do with itself. I am speaking. You hurry up out the bath-room and get to your bed, quick.

Here I am on my way up the stairs, walking into the grey light; thinking in my mind, walking slow not wanting the water to splash out the kettle, walking into the bath-room, thinking in my mind, thinking about my mother's change of behaving.

Here I am wondering in my mind wondering; why does mummy call my body different names?

Here I am pouring the hot water from the kettle into the bowl inside the bath, turning on the cold water tap, watching the water falling into the bowl, listening to my mother's footstep stamping coming up the stairs. I can feel her presence coming closer to where I am unable to move from where I am, feeling my body shaking, wanting my mother to leave my body alone and stop shouting at my body. I am speaking. What are you doing?

Here I am listening to my mother, watching her face looking down at my body; thinking in my mind wondering; why are you asking me that for when you can see what I am doing?

Here I am. I am getting ready to have a wash mummy, thinking in my mind, watching my mother's body turn and walk away from the bath-room doorway, listening to my mother's body talking to her self.

Here I am walking along the hall way, walking into the girl's bed-room, getting my night-dress from under my pillow, carrying it to the bath-room.

Here I am inside the bath-room, taking off my clothes, thinking in my mind; Ruel and George have gone to their bed again without washing any part of their body, but I didn't hear mummy raising her voice at them.

Here I am standing inside the bath leaning over the bowl of water, rubbing the soap on my flannel, wiping my face, rubbing soap on the cloth washing my neck and inside my armpit, and inside my belly-button, and my bottom, wanting my body to be clean.

Here I am bent down squatting over the bowl, splashing the water all over my body, feeling my body trembling in the air, wanting my body to be clean.

Here I am standing inside the bath, rubbing soap all over my knickers, scrubbing it, wanting it to look clean; wringing out the water hanging it down on the side of the bath.

IAM®

Here I am wringing the water out my flannel, wiping my body dry, climbing out the bath, putting my night-dress over my head, feeling my body trembling in the air, wanting to get warm.

Here I am emptying the dirty water into the bath, watching the water going down the plug hole.

Here I am retuning the bowl down on the floor under the sink where it belongs.

Here I am standing on the toilet seat, reaching into the hot water tank cupboard, spreading my knickers over the tank, wanting it to dry for the next day; tomorrow.

Here I am standing on the side of the bath, pulling the light switch to off; walking to the girl's bed-room; looking at mummy's bed-room light's still on, shining at the bottom of the door.

Here I am inside the girl's bed-room, standing over my bed, spreading my dress over my bed-railing, feeling my body wanting to sleep; getting into my bed, lying down under the sheets, feeling my eyes wanting to shut, not wanting to stay open, wanting to sleep; feeling my body sinking into the bed, tired, wanting sleep, sleeping.

IAM®

CHAPTER 22

Here I am; the time is daylight and I am feeling wide awake, feeling good, in my bed, looking over on Mavis's empty bed; looking like Mavis has gone into mummy's bed-room again.

Here I am getting out of my bed, feeling the sunshine warm on my face, feeling the light shining through the curtain window. My body is feeling good, thinking about myself, wondering if any one gets up yet.

Here I am standing by the window, parting the curtains to open, feeling the morning light all over the body that I am hearing the sounds of the birds talking to each other, making my body want to get dressed now.

Here I am looking through the window, looking out over my father's land, looking up into the air, looking at the sky clear blue standing still; feeling my insides change; thinking; I am feeling good today.

Here I am making up my bed to look neat, wondering if Mavis potty is clean.

Here I am on my knees, looking under Mavis's bed, smelling something under the bed, smelling like Mavis has done a do-do in the potty, smelling stink in the air, smelling inside my body carrying the potty along the hall way, walking to the bath-room, thinking in my mind.

Here I am wondering how many times I will have to keep emptying Mavis do-do.

Here I am standing inside the bath-room, emptying the potty into the toilet.

Here I am turning on the cold water tap inside the bath, watching the water falling into the potty, turning off the water, placing the potty on the floor, sprinkling the scouring powder into the potty, scrubbing the potty inside with the toile brush, feeling the body that I am not wanting to do what I am doing, smelling the rank potty smells inside my body.

Here I am sitting down on the toilet, doing a wee-wee, listening to someone walking up the stairs, coming along the hall way, realising the sounds of my brothers footstep walking past the bath-room, listening to the bed-room door open and shut.

Here I am. Is that you George; George? I am speaking. It is me Hazel.

Here I am. Is mummy down stairs Ruel? I am speaking. No.

Here I am wiping my wee-wee dry, wondering in my mind, thinking; how come Ruel get up at this time.

IAM®

Here I am standing on the toilet seat, pulling on the chain, listening to the water flushing the toilet bowl clean, wondering in my mind, thinking; what was Ruel doing down stairs?

Here I am standing over the sink, turning the hot water tap on, feeling the water feeling cold inside my hands, rubbing the soap over my flannel, wiping my face quick, putting the tooth paste on my brush, brushing my teeth, washing my mouth inside clean.

Here I am rubbing soap over the cloth, wiping my wee-wee, wiping my bottom clean, wanting my body to smell good.

Here I am wringing the water out my cloth, spreading it over the pipe railing under the sink, wiping the sink surrounding clean, making sure the bath-room is looking clean for when mummy get up.

Here I am standing on the toilet seat, reaching into the hot water tank, getting my knickers off the tank, feeling my knickers looking wrinkled, putting my foot inside the legs, pulling the knickers over my bottom, feeling it hard on my skin.

Here I am coming out the bath-room, hearing Ruel and George's voice laughing with each other.

Here I am standing outside my brother's bed-room, knocking on the door, wanting to go inside. I am speaking. What do you want?

Here I am standing outside my brother's bed-room, listening to the sounds like biscuit paper packet.

Here I am inside the bed-room, looking at Ruel's body looking at the food crumbs on the side of his face, looking at George's body moving his hand as if hiding something under the blanket.

Here I am watching Ruel and George looking at each other, not knowing what to do with them-selves, looking at each other with their mouth full of food.

Here I am. There is no point in you trying to hide the biscuit packet George. I can hear you know and there are biscuit crumbs on yours and Ruel mouth; look. I am speaking. It doesn't matter anyway. You can tell mummy if you want.

Here I am looking at Delroy holding his piece of biscuit as if copying Ruel and George trying to hide it away from me.

IAM®

Here I am. You better clean up the biscuit crumbs out of Delroy's cot before mummy come and see it.

Here I am walking along the hall way, carrying Mavis's potty, realizing in my mind, understanding now, why Ruel and George never come out of their bedroom in the daytime. Ruel and George get up before everyone and go down stairs and help them-self to all the food they want to eat.

Here I am on my knee; returning Mavis's potty under her bed.

Here I am standing by my bed, putting on my house dress, folding up my night-dress, returning it under my pillow.

Here I am walking down the stairs on my way to the dining-room.

Here I am looking around the room, thinking in my mind, walking into the kitchen, lifting the chair over by the sink, standing on the chair with the kettle in my hand, watching the water filling up the kettle weighing heavy in my hand.

Here I am with the match in my hand, lighting the gas under the kettle, realizing in my mind; daddy has gone to the factory. I can see daddy's work bag is not on the kitchen wall hook where it belongs.

Here I am getting the coal bucket and shovel from under the cupboard corner shelf, and the newspaper from under the sink, carrying everything into the dining-room.

Here I am kneeling before the fire surround, opening up the big Sunday newspaper, spreading it out on the floor before the fire surround.

Here I am with my hand inside the fire-hole, moving the ashes down into the ashtray, pulling the ashtray out onto the newspaper, scraping the ashes away from the fire, cleaning out the grid, emptying the ashes into the coal bucket, returning the fire tray back under the grid where it belong.

Here I am standing on the kitchen door-mat, turning the lock inside the door, pulling the door open wide, lifting the bucket full of ashes off the mat, carrying it outside, carrying the bucket along the ground walking towards the end of our garden, emptying the ashes by the chicken-house, feeling the air blowing up under my dress, blowing the ashes into my face.

Here I am standing on the land, looking inside the chicken-house, looking at the chicken body eyes looking into the eyes I am; thinking in my mind, wondering to myself.

IAM®

Here I am wondering if the chicken body understand my body, the way I am looking into their eyes, watching the chicken eyes looking into the eyes I am.

Here I am inside the coal-house, shovelling the coal into the bucket, gathering some pieces of fire wood off the coal-house floor, putting them on top of the coal inside the bucket.

Here I am closing the coal-house door shut, holding the bucket handle with my two hands, lifting the bucket up off the ground, carrying it towards the house, feeling the bucket weighing my body down, making my shoulder and hands hurt.

Here I am inside the house, lifting the bucket of coal into the dining-room, resting it down on the newspaper before the fire surround.

Here I am inside the kitchen, looking under the kitchen shelf, looking for the coal light box to build the fire.

Here I am standing on the chair by the stove, getting the match box down from the top part of the stove grill, carrying everything into the dining-room.

Here I am on my knees before the fire-hole, rolling the pieces of newspaper tight, placing it inside the fire-hole, putting the coal on top of the grate, and some sticks of wood, and more coal pieces, filling the fire-hole half full, building up the fire, smelling the paraffin scent in the coal light blocks I am putting between everything inside the fire-hole; striking the match to light, lighting the role of newspaper in my hand, watching the flames burning high, lighting the wood, watching the paper and wood burning, smoking into the air.

Here I am watching the fire burning, lighting the blocks of coal light, burning the wood, making the fire look good, feeling the heat getting warm on my face, feeling good with myself knowing that I can make the fire.

Here I am putting the big metal sheet over the fire face, listening to the blazing sounds coming from the fire-hole, smelling the coal and wood burning, making the snapping sound, sparking light, burning the flames of fire inside the fire-hole.

Here I am emptying the coal bucket into the fire, feeling the hot air rising off the fire, making the air surrounding my body feel hot.

Here I am rolling up the newspaper off the floor, sweeping the ashes into the shovel, emptying it out onto the burning fire.

Here I am walking into the kitchen, with the coal bucket and shovel and things, returning everything where it belongs.

I AM®

Here I am standing on the chair over the sink, washing the coal marks off my hands, pouring the washing-up liquid into my hands, rubbing my hands together hard, wanting to make my hands look clean.

Here I am walking into the dining-room, feeling the air smelling good, listening to the sounds of the fire crackling snap, burning just like my mother build the fire to burn just right.

Here I am standing by the fire, feeling the heat feeling hot on my legs; thinking in my mind, wondering; what must I do now?

Here I am inside the kitchen, getting the big broom and dustpan, walking across the dining-room, on my way to the front doorway, wondering in my mind thinking; the water is going to get hot now the fire is made.

Here I am standing at the front door, standing on my tip toes, turning the door lock open, walking outside onto the front garden, standing on the land, looking into the air, smelling the morning air, breathing in the air, feeling good with myself.

Here I am standing inside our garden fence, sweeping the dirt off the front door-step, sweeping around the big front window wall along the footpath, sweeping forward towards the gateway.

Here I am sweeping the garden path clean, sweeping the dirt together inside the fence, listening to the foot-steps coming close to where I am standing still, watching to see who it is coming.

Here I am. Good morning. I am speaking. Good morning.

Here I am sweeping the dirt into the dustpan, thinking in my mind thinking; it is a good day today.

Here I am picking up the milk bottles off the ground, placing them down on floor by the front door inside the house. The milk-man has left us two more bottles of milk today.

Here I am resting the broom and dust-pan on the floor inside the house, closing the door shut, turning the lock off, making the door shut tight.

Here I am on my way to the kitchen, carrying the milk bottles, one in each hand.

Here I am walking into the dining-room, feeling the air feeling warm on my face, making my body feel good.

IAM®

Here I am resting the milk bottles down on the floor, opening the fridge door, placing the bottles down on the shelf inside the fridge where it belongs.

Here I am standing at the front doorway, sweeping the floor, sweeping along the hall way, sweeping towards the stairway, sweeping the dirt and dust around the corner, down into the next hall way, sweeping past the coat-room, past the pantry-room, sweeping towards the dining-room, sweeping the dust into a heap outside the dining-room entrance.

Here I am running to the front doorway, picking up the dustpan and hand-brush, running to the dining-room doorway, sweeping the dirt into the dust-pan.

Here I am inside the kitchen, emptying the dustpan into the kitchen dustbin. I can hear the kettle making the whistling noise, making me wonder what to do, thinking in my mind, wondering if mummy is awake.

Here I am inside the kitchen, looking inside the cupboard, getting the tea-pot, putting the tea-bag inside, placing it down on the draining-board.

Here I am standing on the chair over the stove, winding the tea-towel around my hand, lifting the kettle off the stove, pouring the water into the tea-pot; hearing someone entering the dining-room.

Here I am looking inside the cupboard, getting the little saucepan, resting it down on the draining-board.

Here I am inside the dining-room, standing in the presence of my mother standing before my body, looking at one, wondering in my mind, thinking about my mother, wondering; what is mummy thinking, standing there without expression, just looking at one.

Here I am. Good morning mummy. Would you like a cup of tea? I am speaking. Who build the fire?

Here I am. I did it mummy. Do you want a cup of tea? I am speaking. Yes please.

Here I am looking inside the fridge, getting the bottle of milk, placing it down on the table.

Here I am looking inside the cabinet, getting one cup and a saucer, and the teaspoon out the drawer, placing them down on the table beside the tea-pot stand.

IAM®

Here I am looking inside the television table, getting the table-cloth, spreading it over a portion of the table where my mother is sitting, resting her hands on her lap, leaning her face forward, looking into the burning fire.

Here I am walking into the kitchen, carrying the milk bottle, thinking about my mother.

Here I am standing on the chair over the draining-board, pouring the milk into the saucepan, watching the milk rising halfway up the side.

Here I am standing on the floor lifting the pan down off the draining-board, lifting the pan up onto the stove, resting it down on the fire, turning the flame up high.

Here I am inside the dining-room, taking the packet of sugar and the sugar-bowl out the cabinet, placing them down on the table, with the tea-pot stand.

Here I am walking past my mother, watching her face smiling at one, making my body inside feel good.

Here I am looking inside the fridge, getting the can of milk, placing it down on the table, thinking in my mind, wondering about my mother, thinking about her expression, smiling at one.

Here I am carrying the packet of sugar into the kitchen, resting it down on the work-top, hearing the milk boiling up the sides of the pan, making my body move quick to turn the fire off.

Here I am winding the tea-towel around my hands, lifting the saucepan down off the stove, lifting it up onto the draining-board, lifting the chair over to the draining-board, standing on the chair pouring the tea into the milk, watching the tea mixing into the milk changing colour.

Here I am remembering mummy's cup of tea.

Here I am carrying the tea-pot, walking slow into the dining-room, resting the tea-pot down on its stand on the table near my mother.

Here I am standing in the presence of my mother, thinking in my mind, wondering about my mother, looking at her body looking different, looking like she is thinking inside, looking without expression; just looking into the fire.

Here I am inside the kitchen, standing on the chair over the draining-board, spooning the sugar into the saucepan, mixing the milk-tea ready for Delroy's morning feed.

IAM®

Here I am placing the funnel into Delroy's bottle; pouring the milk-tea into Delroy's bottle, wiping the bottle sides dry on the dishcloth, placing the bottle down on the work-top, leaving it to cool down by itself.

Here I am placing the cover on top of the saucepan, lifting the pan down off the draining-board, lifting it up, down on the stove back burner.

Here I am walking into the dining-room, carrying the packet of sugar, returning it inside the cabinet where it belongs.

Here I am standing in the presence of my mother, watching her body sitting by the table, shuffling her body about on the chair, just looking into the fire.

Here I am. Are you feeling right mummy. I am speaking. I am not feeling well; my body is sick.

Here I am. The tea is ready mummy. Do you want me to do anything? I am speaking. Yes; go and look see if Delroy wake.

Here I am walking up the stairs, thinking in my mind, walking along the hall way, wondering about my mother, wanting her body to feel good, wondering about the baby making her body change, making her body feel sick, making her body not know what to do with itself.

Here I am standing outside my brother's bed-room, knocking on the door. I am speaking. Hazel; you can come in Hazel.

Here I am standing in the presence of my brothers, looking at Ruel's face smiling at George, looking at Delroy's face smiling, making my body feel good. I am speaking. Has mummy get up yet Hazel?

Here I am. Yes, mummy is down stairs but she is not feel good. Come on Delroy. Your bottle is ready for you down stairs.

Here I am watching Delroy's hand reaching out to me, smiling all over his face, looking like he understands every word I said.

Here I am. Are you coming down? I am going to do the breakfast now. I am speaking. What are you going to do for us Hazel?

Here I am listening to George, thinking in my mind wondering; what am I going to cook for breakfast?

Here I am. Depending on what we have. Why don't you and Ruel clean up your room; it smells you know.

Here I am watching Delroy's body crawling out the bed-room, moving fast, crawling backwards down the stairs.

IAM®

Here I am down stairs, holding the dining-room door open, watching Delroy's body crawling backwards down the step into the dining-room.

Here I am looking at my mother, wanting to understand her expression, wondering what my mother is thinking.

Here I am inside the kitchen, standing on the chair by the work-top, getting Delroy's bottle.

Here I am standing on the ground, lifting the chair over by the sink, standing on the chair, turning on the cold water, holding Delroy's bottle in the water, watching the water running over the bottle, cooling the milk-tea inside.

Here I am, tasting the milk feeling just right for Delroy to drink now.

Here I am wiping the bottle dry, carrying it into the dining-room, watching Delroy's face smiling up at my body, holding out his hands, reaching for his bottle. I can see Delroy cheeks sucking hard on his bottle, breathing quick, watching the milk inside his bottle disappearing fast.

Here I am looking at my mother, wondering in my mind, thinking what to do for our breakfast.

Here I am. What do you want for your breakfast mummy? I am speaking. Nothing for me, thank you. Put some milk on for you lot to have some cereals.

Here I am taking the milk bottle out of the fridge, carrying it into the kitchen, placing it down on the work-top, feeling my inside go round, moving around fast inside the body that I am, wondering to myself, thinking about my body changing, feeling the feeling making my body not know what to do with myself.

Here I am with the match-box in my hand, lighting the match, watching it burning, lighting the gas at the front of the stove.

Here I am taking the saucepan out the cupboard, resting it down on the stove.

Here I am lifting the chair over by the stove, standing on the chair with the bottle of milk in my hand, pouring the milk into the saucepan, turning the fire flames up high.

Here I am inside the dining-room, taking the bowls out the cabinet, placing them out on the table, getting the spoons out the drawer, making the table ready for our breakfast.

IAM®

Here I am lifting up the table-flap, making the table longer, realizing that mummy's tea-cup is still full of tea.

Here I am moving the tea-pot stand and tea-pot off the tablecloth, resting them down on the other side, arranging the tablecloth over the whole table.

Here I am looking down at Delroy's body, wondering where Delroy's bottle is; looking under the table, looking for Delroy's bottle; remembering the milk on the fire.

Here I am inside the kitchen, just in time; hearing the milk boiling up the sides of the pan, rising to the top, making my body run to turn the fire off quick before the milk boils over the top.

Here I am inside the dining-room, looking at Delroy's body just sitting on the floor, looking like he don't know what to do just sitting on the floor looking up at one.

Here I am. Delroy; where is your bottle? Delroy; I am speaking to you. Where did you fling your bottle? Show me.

Here I am looking at Delroy looking into the eyes I am; realizing in my mind, understanding that Delroy understand every word I am saying to him, watching his head turn to find his bottle, watching his body crawling over to the television table, reaching his hands under, crawling over to my body, holding up his bottle before one, looking into the eyes I am, smiling all over his face, looking pleased with himself.

Here I am. Thank you. In future you give me your bottle when you're finish and don't, throw it on the floor again, understand.

Here I am inside the kitchen, standing on the chair by the stove, spooning the sugar into the milk, counting each spoon full. One, two, three and one more big spoonful of sugar into the pan, mixing it into the milk.

Here I am standing on the ground, winding the tea-towel around my hand, lifting the saucepan of milk down off the stove, walking slow, carrying it into the dining-room, feeling the saucepan weighting down my hands, making water come out of on my skin, feeling the heat of the pan burning through the cloth onto my hand; putting the pan down quick onto the table.

Here I am feeling the water coming out my skin onto my face, feeling my body itching all over, feeling my hand inside my thumb feeling hot, burning with heat from the pan.

I AM®

Here I am looking at my mother's eye, watching her hand holding the pencil upright on the piece of paper, watching her expression looking like she is thinking in her mind, watching her hand write a number sign on the paper before her on the table.

Here I am looking inside the cabinet, taking out the little jug and saucer to pour the milk from the saucepan.

Here I am inside the kitchen, getting the saucepan cover out the cupboard, carrying it into the dining-room, kneeling on the chair, placing the cover over the milk inside the saucepan.

Here I am looking on Delroy's body sitting on the floor, playing with his fingers.

Here I am thinking in my mind, thinking about Derloy's bottom, realizing that he is still wearing his nappy from last night.

Here I am. Come on Delroy, let's go and change your nappy. Come on up stairs with me.

Here I am holding the dining-hall way door open, watching Delroy's body crawling up the step into the hall way, crawling quick up the stairs.

Here I am standing at the bath-room entrance, watching Delroy's body crawling down the step, crawling onto the bath-room floor, sitting down looking up at one, smiling all over his face.

Here I am laying Delroy down on his back, taking off his rubber pants, smelling the rank wee-wee rising off the nappy on Delroy's bottom. The nappy is soaking wet, smelling like it is full of do-do, making me hold my breath, not wanting to taste the smell of Delroy's dirty nappy.

Here I am. Keep still Delroy. Your nappy is full of do-do. Hold your legs up. You should sit on the potty now; I know you understand what I am saying. Do you hear me Delroy? Mummy and daddy think you are two small to understand what they are saying, but I know you understand, don't you. Now stay there let me put this into the bucket. Stay still Delroy.

Here I am standing over the toilet bowl, shaking the do-do off the dirty nappy, putting the nappy into the nappy bucket; leaning over the bath, watching the cold water falling onto the nappy, filling up halfway inside the bucket, turning the water off, leaning over the bath, lifting the dirty nappy up and down into the water, wanting to wash the do-do off the nappy, wanting to wash away the dirty smells, wanting the nappy to be clean.

IAM®

Here I am wringing the water out the nappy, putting it into the bucket under the sink with all Delroy's other dirty nappies soaking inside the soap water, listening to Delroy making the happy sounds, playing by himself.

Here I am lifting the bucket of dirty do-do water out the bath, emptying it into the toilet bowl, leaning over the bath, turning on the cold water tap, watching the water falling into the bucket, turning off the water, washing away the dirty do-do marks off the inside of the bucket, emptying the water into the toilet, returning the bucket under the sink where it belong.

Here I am standing over the sink, turning on the cold water, rubbing soap all over my hands, rubbing my hands together, wanting to wash away all the do-do smell.

Here I am standing over the sink, pushing the plug into the plug hole, turning the hot water tap on, feeling the water getting hot on my hands, turning off the water, wetting Delroy's flannel, rubbing the soap over the flannel, wringing it out to wipe Delroy's bottom clean.

Here I am on the floor, kneeling before Delroy's body, wiping Delroy's wee-wee, wiping his bottom, rinsing out the flannel, kneeling before Delroy's body wiping his bottom, making sure all the do-do and wee-wee smells go away, making Delroy's body look clean.

Here I am standing on the toilet seat, pulling the chain down; leaning into the hot water tank, getting a clean nappy and rubber pants for Delroy.

Here I am. Delroy; stay there. I am going to get the powder and vaseline.

Here I am standing in the hall way, watching Mavis coming out of mummy's bed-room, watching her body coming along the landing, feeling my inside go round, just looking at my sister.

Here I am. Good morning Mavis; breakfast is ready. I am speaking. Where is mummy Hazel?

Here I am. Mummy is inside the dining-room.

Here I am standing outside the boy's bed-room, knocking on the door, wanting to go inside. I am speaking. Come in Hazel.

Here I am standing inside my brother's bed-room, looking at Ruel, looking at George's body stretched out on their bed, reading the book name magazine.

Here I am. Breakfast is ready.

Here I am remembering Delroy is inside the bath-room.

IAM®

Here I am looking inside Delroy's cupboard drawer, getting a nappy and baby powder and vaseline and clean vest and rubber pants and house clothes.

Here I am moving quick, walking fast into the bath-room, remembering Delroy, wondering what he is doing.

Here I am inside the bath-room, looking down on Delroy's body playing with his toes, making the happy sound, making my body feel good inside.

Here I am on my knees, kneeling before Delroy's body, folding the nappy into half, pushing it under Delroy's bottom, lifting Delroy's bottom on top, spreading the vaseline over his bottom, sprinkling the powder on top, pulling the nappy edge together, pushing the pin through the nappy, holding the nappy up at Delroy's side.

Here I am putting Delroy's foot into the rubber pants, pulling the pants up over his nappy, watching Delroy's face smiling up at one, making my body feel good inside thinking about Delroy's body, thinking about the baby mummy is having.

Here I am putting the cover on the vaseline bottle, hearing Ruel and George's footstep coming out of their bed-room, on their way down stairs.

Here I am standing at the bath-room entrance, watching Delroy's body crawling into the hall way, sitting on the floor, looking up at one.

Here I am inside the boy's bed-room, returning the vaseline and powder bottle on top of Delroy's drawer.

Here I am. Come on Delroy, we can go down stairs now.

Here I am standing on the stairs watching Delroy's body sliding down, coming backwards down the steps; hearing the front door letter box bang, making my inside jump.

Here I am running to the front door, picking up the letter paper packets off the floor, looking at the packets, wondering what's inside; looking at the blue letter paper packet with red lines around the sides.

Here I am walking towards the dining-room, looking at the letter packets in my hand, wondering what is inside the letter packets; wondering; who put the letters into our house?

Here I am recognizing the words written on the paper. I can understand the word name Mr. Grant and the number on my father's house.

IAM®

Here I am standing by the dining-room entrance, watching Delroy's body crawling down the step into the dining-room.

Here I am. These were at the front doorway mummy. I am speaking. Thank you.

Here I am watching my mother's hand writing on the piece of paper, listening to her body making sounds to herself; hearing Delroy's body making up noise like he wants his breakfast now.

Here I am lifting Delroy's body into his pram, watching Mavis's body sitting at the dining-table, eating her breakfast, watching Ruel, watching George, thinking in my mind, opening the box of cereals, pouring the cereal into the bowl, pouring the warm milk on top, listening to Delroy making up noise, wanting his breakfast now.

Here I am feeding Delroy his breakfast, thinking in my mind, hearing the tearing of paper, looking in the direction of my mother's hand opening the blue letter paper packet, watching her eyes looking at the paper in her hand.

Here I am feeding Delroy, wondering in my mind, wondering what mummy is reading about, wanting to know where the letter paper come from, thinking in my mind, watching my mother folding-up the paper and put it into her apron pocket.

Here I am watching Delroy watching my hand scraping the cereal from the sides of the bowl, putting the last bit into his mouth, thinking in my mind, sitting down at the table, getting my breakfast, watching my mother's eyes looking down on the writing she is doing, making up her face, making me wonder about my mother, wondering what is mummy writing.

Here I am feeling my belly feeling full.

Here I am putting the bowls together, carrying them into the kitchen, placing them down inside the washing-up bowl inside the sink.

Here I am inside the kitchen standing on the chair turning on the cold water tap, feeling the water getting colder, leaning my body over the sink, holding my hands together, catching the water inside my hands, drinking, feeling the water going down my inside, tasting good, making my body feel good.

Here I am standing inside the dining-room, wondering in my mind, looking around at everyone, listening to George talking to Ruel, watching my mother's body stand, pick up her piece of paper and walk towards the hall way entrance, watching Mavis body slide down off her chair, following after mummy's body disappearing into the hall way.

IAM®

Here I am listening to mummy's footsteps walking slow going up the stairs.

Here I am standing in the presence of my brothers, watching Ruel and George playing together, laughing with each other, making my body want to play with them.

Here I am, wanting my brothers to let me play their game, wanting Ruel and George to want me.

Here I am feeling my inside go round, wanting Ruel, wanting George's body to understand what I am feeling, wanting Ruel and George to let me play the game with them.

Here I am watching Ruel and George playing, listening to Ruel speaking to George, listening to George talking to Ruel, watching them playing together, behaving as if I were not in their presence.

Here I am wondering in my mind thinking; why Ruel and George will not let me play with them?

Here I am realizing to myself, thinking, mummy and daddy have their games they talk about. Mavis and Delroy have each other to play games with and Ruel and George are always together.

Here I am thinking about myself, realizing that I am the only one without anyone to play games with.

Here I am thinking about myself, wanting someone to talk to my body, wanting someone to care about my body, wanting in my mind; feeling my insides hurting; thinking about the body that I am; thinking about me.

Here I am walking into the kitchen, carrying the tea-pot, emptying the tea-bag into the kitchen dust-bin, placing the tea-pot down on the draining-board.

Here I am inside the dining-room, putting the tea-pot stand and sugar bowl away inside the cabinet, folding up the table-cloth, hearing Ruel and George making jokes at each other, talking about the body that I am feeling hurt inside, feeling lone, wanting someone to care about my being.

Here I am returning the table-cloth inside the drawer, listening to Ruel and George talking about them-self wanting to go to school, talking as if the body that I am was not going to go to school with them.

Here I am thinking in my mind, pushing the chairs under the table, making the dining-room look tidy.

IAM®

Here I am inside the kitchen, kneeling on the chair over the sink, turning the hot water tap on, putting the washing-up liquid into the water, washing the cup clean, placing it down on the draining-board, washing everything clean, thinking in my mind, wondering about myself.

Here I am emptying the bowl, rinsing the suds away, watching the bowl filling up with hot water, rinsing the suds off the cups, turning them down onto the draining-board, wringing the water out the dishcloth, standing on the floor, lifting the chair over by the work-top, standing on the chair, wiping the work-top clean.

Here I am standing on the chair with the tea-towel in my hands, wiping the cup dry, wiping the things dry, placing them down on the work-top, thinking in my mind, thinking about my body feeling lone, wanting someone to care about my being.

Here I am walking into the dining-room, carrying the pile of bowls, placing them down on the table, returning to the kitchen, collecting the cups off the work-top, carrying them into the dining-room, placing them down onto the table.

Here I am standing on the chair by the cabinet, putting the cups and bowls and spoons away where they belong.

Here I am walking past Ruel and George's body, listening to them talking to each other, feeling my inside go round, feeling lone inside myself; wondering in my mind; thinking about mummy having the baby, thinking about myself.

Here I am inside the kitchen lifting the saucepan into the sink; thinking about the baby mummy is having, wanting the baby to be a girl so I will have someone that I can play the games with.

Here I am kneeling on the chair over the sink, scrubbing the insides of the saucepan, rubbing the scouring pad hard on the bottom of the pan, washing it clean, turning it down on the draining-board.

Here I am wringing the water out the dishcloth, wiping the saucepan dry, returning it into the cupboard where it belongs.

Here I am putting clean warm water into the bowl, pouring the washing-up liquid into the bowl, washing the dishcloth clean, wringing the water out the cloth, wiping the water off the draining-board, wiping the sink surroundings dry, emptying the bowl of water, spreading the dishcloth over the pipe to dry.

Here I am standing on the kitchen ground, looking around the room, making sure everywhere looks clean, looks tidy.

I AM®

Here I am lifting the chair over by the stove where it belong, thinking in my mind.

Here I am inside the dining-room, looking out from the body that I am, looking at Ruel and George playing their game.

Here I am wondering in my mind thinking; what's mummy doing up stairs? I can hear the sound like music is playing.

Here I am standing at the bottom of the stairs, looking up the stairway, wondering where the music is coming from.

Here I am walking up the stairs, listening to the sound getting louder; thinking the music is coming from the girl's bed-room.

Here I am walking into the bed-room, listening to the music in the air, making my inside go round, not knowing where the music is coming from.

Here I am standing inside the bed-room, looking at my mother's hand combing Mavis hair, realizing the music sound is coming from the little box resting on the mantel shelf above the fire. The sound of the music is making my body want to move.

Here I am feeling good looking at Delroy's body looking clean, looking good, smiling at one, smiling all over his face, moving his body from side to side on the bed, rocking to the sounds coming from the music box.

The music is making my body feel good, watching my mother fixing Mavis clothes on her body, making Mavis body look good.

Here I am. Do you want me to do anything for you mummy? I am speaking. Yes please. Empty the bowl of water and take the dirty clothes into the bath-room.

Here I am walking along the hall way, carrying the bowl of dirty water into the bath-room.

Here I am wringing the water from the flannel, emptying the water into the toilet.

Here I am walking into the bed-room, listening to the music.

Here I am collecting the dirty clothes off the bed-room floor, bringing them to the bath-room, pushing them into the washing basket under the sink. I can see the two baskets are full of dirty clothes.

I AM®

Here I am returning the soap-dish onto the side of the sink, wondering in my mind, thinking about the dirty clothes piling up under the sink. I am speaking. Hazel; hurry up.

Here I am running out the bath-room, running to the girl's bed-room.

Here I am standing inside the room, looking at my mother's hand tying the ribbon bow tie on Mavis's long plait of hair. I am speaking. Pull out your hair. I am ready for your hair now.

Here I am listening to my mother, realizing that mummy wants to plait my hair.

Here I am pulling out the plaits in my hair, wondering in my mind thinking; am I going to have a ribbon to tie in my hair.

Here I am watching my mother fixing Mavis's body to look good, thinking in my mind. I am speaking. Come.

Here I am on my knee, kneeling down on the floor before my mother sitting on Mavis's bed next to the window. I can feel my mother's hand pulling the comb through my hair, making water come into my eyes. My mother is dragging the comb quick through my hair, making my eyes shut tight, wanting the hurting on my head to go away.

Here I am sitting still, feeling my mother's hand plaiting my hair, listening to the sounds coming from the music box; watching Mavis moving her hands in the air, jumping off the floor, jumping up into the air.

Here I am feeling my mother's hand, holding the hair on my head tight, turning my head around to the side, pulling the skin on my head, making water come into my eyes, feeling hurt inside the body that I am, feeling the feeling I am feeling, thinking of myself, wondering in my mind, thinking; why does mummy drag my hair around like that?; mummy never drag Mavis's hair the way she drags my hair to turn my head around. Mummy always spends a lot of time whenever she is combing Mavis's hair.

Here I am feeling my mother's hand holding the hair at the back of my head, feeling her hand push my head forward down, making my inside go round, hurting, wondering why my mother treat my body different to the way she treat Mavis.

Here I am feeling hurt, thinking in my mind, wondering in my mind.

Here I am wondering in my mind thinking; why does mummy treat my body different to how she treats Mavis's body?

I AM®

Here I am thinking in my mind; Mavis is mummy's favourite child; thinking mummy always spends a lot of time on her favourite child. I am speaking. Here; go and put the comb down.

Here I am. Thank you mummy. I am speaking. How many times must I tell you to stop saying that?

Here I am taking the comb from my mother's hand, listening to her words, realizing that I am not going to have any ribbon bow tie on my hair.

Here I am pulling my hair out the comb, thinking in my mind, thinking about myself, wondering about my mother thinking; why doesn't she like when I say thank you to her?

Here I am, knowing that I didn't comb my hair to look good and that is why I said thank you.

Here I am inside the girl's bed-room, returning the hair-brush and comb down on top of the dressing-table, feeling my inside go round, thinking about my mother making my body not know how to talk to her.

Here I am thinking about my mother, making my body hurt, not understanding why my mother does not like my body to thank her for combing my hair.

Here I am thinking about myself, thinking about the body that I am wondering; who am I? What am I here for? Who am I?

Here I am the sister of the many children present in the same house with the woman I am to call mother.

Here I am feeling hurt, feeling my mother's presence behaving like she does not care about my being.

Here I am my mother's helper, feeling like I do not belong where I am, realizing that my mother cares for Mavis's body more than she cares for me.

Here I am, knowing that my mother's favourite child is Mavis.

Here I am feeling like my mother doesn't care about my being.

Here I am feeling lone, thinking in my mind, knowing that my mother only want my body to clean and do everything for all her children that doesn't even want to talk to my body.

Here I am thinking in my mind, wondering; am I my father's daughter? Is mummy really my mother?

IAM®

Here I am thinking about my being, wondering; who am I? Who am I?

Here I am wondering why my mother treats my body different to the way she treat Mavis; thinking in my mind; wondering if mummy knows that I have feelings.

Here I am thinking; mummy thinks that I have no understanding. My mother does not realize that my body feel feelings of hurt, just the same as when her body look like she is hurting.

Here I am hurting, knowing that I am here inside my father's house; living with the woman my mother and my sister and three brothers and feeling like nobody care about my being.

Here I am walking along the hall way, thinking in my mind, thinking about myself; wondering about my being, wondering what is going to happen to the body that I am feeling lone; not wanting to be in the presence of my mother or anyone; thinking in my mind; wondering if anyone knows that I am here in this house on the ground name England.

IAM®

CHAPTER 23

Here I am thinking, wanting to go to school, wanting to find someone to care about my body; wanting someone to talk with the body that I am.

Here I am wanting, someone; wondering in my mind, thinking; someone please talk to me.

Here I am thinking; daddy doesn't know that mummy doesn't like the body that I am. Daddy is always at the factory.

Here I am inside the bath-room, looking at all the dirty clothes inside the buckets under the sink.

Here I am thinking in my mind, emptying the clothes out onto the bath-room floor, separating the clothes, putting the white cotton clothes and things into the bath, returning the dark clothes into the bucket.

Here I am thinking in my mind, leaning into the bath, pushing the plug into the plughole, turning the hot water tap on, watching the water falling inside the bath, feeling the steam making water on my face.

Here I am turning the cold water tap on, pouring the soap powder over the clothes, watching the clothes soaking up the water, watching the clothes floating in the water rising, filling up the insides of the bath.

Here I am with the washing stick inside my hand pushing the clothes down under the water, watching the water rising up over the clothes, watching the water changing colour, looking brown like dirt.

Here I am turning off the taps, leaning into the bath, pushing the clothes down under the water, feeling my hands burn inside the hot water, feeling my body hurting, feeling my eyes fill up with water.

Here I am standing over the sink, turning the cold water tap on quick, holding my hand inside the water, feeling the burning feeling leaving my body.

Here I am sitting down on the bath-room floor, holding my hands on my lap, thinking about myself, feeling the water coming into my eyes, feeling my body hurting.

Here I am thinking in my mind, wondering; why did daddy send for me and Ruel and George?

Here I am feeling lone; wanting to belong where I am. I am speaking. Move over.

IAM®

Here I am realizing that my mother is in the bath-room, looking down on my body sitting on the floor.

Here I am in the presence of my mother, watching her body leaning over the bath, watching her hands scrubbing the clothes, feeling my inside go round, wanting my mother to understand that my body has feelings, just like her body has feelings and my body need her body to care about my body; feeling lone, hurting inside.

Here I am thinking; mummy does not understand that my body feels just like her body feels.

Here I am thinking; mummy does not realize that I understand about feelings. Mummy does not realize that I can see her feelings all over her face and body behaviour.

Here I am listening to my mother speaking; not wanting to be where I am watching my mother's face change. I am speaking. What are you crying for?

Here I am hearing my mother's voice, feeling my body inside go round, not knowing what to say to my mother. I am speaking. I said; what are you crying for.

Here I am. Nothing mummy. I am speaking. Stop the crying if you don't know what you crying for.

Here I am listening to my mother talking, feeling unable to move from the spot where I am standing, feeling the water falling out my eyes, feeling the water keep coming into my eyes, wanting my body to stop making me cry, feeling my mother's presence surrounding my being, making the air inside the bath-room change.

Here I am watching my mother's hand wiping the stains away from inside the bath, watching the water coming into the bath, watching the steam rising off the water falling inside the bath, watching my mother's hand shaking the wet pieces of cloth, dropping each piece into the water, watching her hand holding the clothes stick, moving the clothes around inside the bath, pushing the clothes down inside the water. I am speaking. Turn on the cold water and turn off the hot water quick.

Here I am wanting my body to stop crying, feeling my inside moving around, watching my mother's body pushing down on the clothes inside the bath; hearing her hands making the washing sound. I am speaking. You can turn the water off now. Hazel; you here what I say? Stop the noise by me before I give you something to cry for.

IAM®

Here I am, wanting my body to stop making water come into my eyes; not wanting my mother to beat my body. I am speaking. Now you have something to cry for. Stop it now before I box you again. I don't know what the matter with you, you keep crying like anything is wrong with you.

Here I am hurting, listening to what my mother is saying, feeling her presence making my body not know what to do with myself, wanting my father to come home.

Here I am feeling my body shaking.

Here I am watching my mother's hand washing the clothes, realizing that Mavis and Delroy have lots of white clothes, feeling my mother's presence making my body not want to be where I am feeling unable to move from where I am.

Here I am thinking about Aunty Jane, wanting the water to stop coming into my eyes, thinking about Aunty Jane; wondering why my mother is always hitting my body; knowing that I have not done anything wrong for her to hit my body.

Here I am watching my mother's hand wringing the water out the cloth; thinking in my mind; Mavis's body have lots of white knickers and socks; watching my mother's eyes making sure the knickers inside is clean.

Here I am watching my mother wringing the water from the knickers she put on her body.

Here I am, understanding in my mind, thinking; I have to do for myself because my mother only cares about how hers and Mavis's body looks. Nobody cares about me.

Here I am looking at my mother's face, thinking in my mind wondering; what have I done to make mummy not care about my body. I am speaking. Put the balance of things in here. You stop now. All you three do since you come here, is cause me to work. All me do is work, work and work.

Here I am putting the colour clothes into the water, listening to my mother talking to her self.

Here I am watching my mother washing the clothes, thinking in my mind, wondering what my mother is talking about, knowing that I am always helping her to do everything inside the house.

Here I am listening to my mother, realizing in my mind thinking; mummy only plait my hair, but I wash myself, dress myself and help her wash the clothes, polish the furniture, sweep the floor, make the fire, cook the food, iron the clothes, change Delroy's nappies, make the beds, empty the potties, run up and down the stairs for her.

Here I am thinking in my mind, realizing all the things that my body is doing for my father and my mother and all her other children.

Here I am, knowing that I get up in the mornings and start working even before mummy wake up.

Here I am realizing that my mother do not understand that my body is one of her children.

Here I am, knowing that I am one of the many children my mother borne but I am the only one she expect to work for her and all her other children.

Here I am thinking; mummy should talk to the boys instead of taking out her anger on me. I am speaking. Finish these and bring them down stairs.

Here I am watching my mother's body walking into the hall way; carrying the buckets full of clothes, one in each hand.

Here I am leaning over the bath, rinsing the soap off mine and Ruel and George's clothes; thinking in my mind; mummy do not realize that I can understand every word she is saying. Mummy does not realize that I have a mind all of my own and I understand what mummy thinks even though mummy and daddy believe that children don't have any sense. Mummy and daddy do not understand that because my body use my two hands to do the things they want and because my body feels; my sense is teaching my body to understand what they mean by the words I hear them say and the way their bodies behave.

Here I am wondering; who does mummy think I am.

Here I am wringing the water out the clothes, thinking in my mind wondering; why should I care about Ruel and George and Mavis, knowing that they do not want to bother about knowing the body that I am their sister.

Here I am wringing the water out the clothes, thinking; daddy doesn't even know how I feel.

Here I am resting my body against the bath, thinking about the body that I am. I can hear mummy shouting at Ruel and George making up noise at her head.

Here I am watching the water going down the plughole, feeling my dress wet, sticking onto my tummy, making my body tremble.

IAM®

Here I am lifting the bowl full of wet clothes onto my tummy, walking into the hall way, dropping it down on the step, dragging it along the hall way, lifting it down the steps, feeling my body hurting, lifting the bowl, carrying it into the dining-room.

Here I am standing inside the dining-room, realizing that my father is home, feeling his presence looking, smiling at one; making my body feel good.

Here I am feeling my father's presence watching my body walking across the dining-room, walking into the kitchen, feeling my body feeling good, knowing that my father is home.

Here I am lifting the bowl outside, watching my mother's body standing by the clothes wire.

Here I am resting the bowl down on the ground near my mother, watching her wringing the water out the clothes, listening to her body talking to herself, watching her hands pushing the clothes peg into the clothes along the line, watching the line hanging down with clothes, dripping water onto the ground.

Here I am listening to my mother's voice talking to her self; feeling my body trembling, listening to my mother talking about my father. I am speaking. Thank God.

Here I am carrying the buckets into the kitchen, walking across the dining-room, walking up the stairs, walking into the bath-room, returning the buckets and bowl on the floor under the sink where they belong.

Here I am standing inside the boy's bed-room standing by the window, looking out over the land, looking at the houses, looking at the sky, looking at the trees and plants growing upon the land.

Here I am watching the people appear and disappear on the road I can see between the house buildings; a long way away from where I am standing in my brothers bed-room, watching the people out walking; watching the cars appear and disappear quick on the road.

Here I am watching the children playing inside their garden fence, watching all that is happening outside my father's house.

Here I am thinking, looking, wondering in my mind, thinking about my body, feeling lone inside myself.

Here I am thinking; mummy make sure that I do not have a good time like all the other children look like they are having a good time.

IAM®

Here I am thinking; I don't blame Ruel and George for wanting to go to school.

Here I am walking down the stairs, thinking in my mind, walking into the dining-room. I can see mummy and daddy and Mavis sitting at the table eating; eating cream cracker biscuits and cheese with a cup of tea. I am speaking. Hazel; look in the kitchen you see the packet of biscuit. Butter them for you and your brothers.

Here I am feeling my body wanting to eat, walking quick into the kitchen, lifting the chair over to the work-top.

Here I am emptying the cracker biscuits onto the plate, spreading margarine over the biscuit, making myself a biscuit sandwich, biting into it, eating the biscuit tasting good.

Here I am eating, spreading margarine onto the biscuits for me and Ruel and George. I am speaking. Is it ready yet Hazel? I will make the tea.

Here I am standing on the kitchen ground, watching George standing on the chair over the draining-board, pouring the water into the tea-pot.

Here I am looking at George, wondering in my mind thinking; what's the matter with George.

Here I am carrying the plate of biscuits into the dining-room, placing it down on the table, listening to daddy speaking to mummy.

Here I am collecting the dirty plates and mugs off the table, carrying them into the kitchen, putting them inside the washing-up bowl.

Here I am walking into the dining-room with the tub of margarine in my hand, returning it inside the fridge where it belongs.

Here I am sitting at the dining-table, eating my biscuits, listening to mummy and daddy talking to each other. I am speaking. You remember you are going out.

Here I am watching my father looking at the blue piece of paper that came through the letter box this morning.

Here I am eating, watching George pouring the tea, watching my father's face half smiling to himself; looking down on the paper in his hand.

Here I am, wanting to know what the letter is saying. I am speaking. Your Aunty write and ask about you lot.

IAM®

Here I am feeling my body inside turn over, feeling good, thinking about Aunty Jane thinking about us.

Here I am looking at my father, wanting him to read the words that Aunty Jane write, so I can understand.

Here I am watching my father's eye, watching his hands folding the paper small.

Here I am wondering; why didn't you read us what Aunty Jane write to say.

Here I am watching my father's eye, watching his hands folding the paper small, thinking in my mind, wondering why daddy didn't read us the letter from Aunty Jane in Jamaica.

Here I am remembering the time Ruel and I was back home on the ground Jamaica with Aunty; remembering the times Ruel and I went riding the donkey in the woodlands where Aunty Jane's house is.

Here I am remembering me and Ruel together on the ground Jamaica; remembering Aunty Jane, wanting to see Aunty, remembering in my mind, thinking about me and Ruel; looking at my brother Ruel sitting on front of me on the other side of the dining table; knowing that Ruel do not care about the body that I am now that we are here on the ground England.

Here I am remembering Aunty Jane, wanting to know what Aunty Jane said in her letter.

Here I am realizing that my father and mother think that I haven't got any sense.

Here I am, knowing that I am.

Here I am thinking in my mind, wondering about my mother and father, realizing that they do not understand that everybody is born with sense.

Here I am realizing that my mother and father do not realize that it is my sense that is teaching my body how to look after myself, and it is my sense that is making my body want to help mummy to do all her house-work, because when my hands are working together, my sense make my body understand the feelings that my body feel and because of the words they say and the way they behave together in my sight and in my hearing.

Here I am, understanding my mother and father's behaviour, because my sense is with me all the time, making my body understand what they are doing and saying within my presence.

IAM®

Here I am realizing that mummy and daddy do not understand that a body begins to live from the time it move to help itself by using its two hands to do something because it wants to do it and not because its body is ordered to do the act.

Here I am realizing that mummy and daddy do not understand that they cannot do my living for me or any one of my brothers or sister. My mother and father do not understand that they do not own my body or my brothers or sister.

Here I am thinking mummy and daddy do not understand my body. Mummy and daddy do not understand that it is the word they speak and how they behave that cause my body to feel the hurting feelings that I am feeling inside the body that I am. My mother and father do not understand that it is them that is making my body hurt; it is them that make my body cry water come out my eyes because their body do not agree with what each other say and do in my presence.

Here I am thinking in my mind, thinking about myself; wondering in my mind, thinking.

Here I am looking at my father's body holding the pen in his hand writing on the newspaper spread out on the dining-table before him.

Here I am carrying the empty plates into the kitchen, resting them down in the bowl inside the sink.

Here I am inside the dining-room, looking around the room, looking at my sister dressed-up ready to go out.

Here I am watching my mother entering the dining-room. My mother is wearing her sky blue colour suit and her white hat, holding her white hand-bag on her hand wearing the white glove.

Here I am standing inside the dining-room, looking at my mother and sister all dressed-up ready to go out.

Here I am walking into the kitchen with the tea-pot, thinking in my mind wondering; where is mummy going with Mavis? Mummy always dress-up Mavis body to look good but she never dress up my body or take my body out with her.

Here I am kneeling on the chair over the sink, washing the dirty plates clean, thinking in my mind, wondering if mummy finished making my school dress.

IAM®

Here I am wondering in my mind thinking; there is only one day and one night to go and then it is time to go to school. I am speaking. Hazel; change your brother's nappy when he wakes up.

Here I am watching my mother's body, listening to her voice, thinking in my mind.

IAM®

CHAPTER 24

Here I am inside the kitchen, lifting the chair over by the work-top, standing on the chair with the tea-towel in my hand, wiping the plates dry, placing them down on the work-top. I can hear my father telling Ruel to turn on the television.

Here I am wiping the plates dry, hearing the music from the television sounding like a film show is on.

Here I am putting the cooking knife and spoon inside the kitchen cupboard drawer where they belong; returning the tea-pot down on top of the stove; hearing the sound like the back gate; the garden gate-door shaking, sounding like some-one wants to come in.

Here I am watching my father turn the key inside the kitchen door, watching his body move quick, running to the gate-door outside the house.

Here I am standing on the kitchen doorstep, listening to my father talking to someone sounding like a man standing on the other side of the fence; watching my father opening the gate-door wide and walk over to the coal house; watching a man's body coming down the steps onto my fathers land, carrying a big long dusty black cloth bag on his back; walking towards the coal house; watching another man carrying another bag full of coal, emptying the bag out on the coal house ground; hearing the whistling sound the man is making, watching his body walking up the step, listening to his footstep walking along the path on the other side of the high wood fence between my father's and the house next door.

Here I am standing at the gateway, looking at the house building on the other side of the house wooden fence; looking at the end of the path to the street and the road; looking at the man walking along the path, carrying another bag of coal across his back.

Here I am standing at the back gate; looking at the man emptying the bag of coal onto the coal house ground; watching the other man walk back up the steps, hearing him say; one more bag to come Mister Grant.

Here I am watching my father's body with the shovel in his hand, shovelling the coal in a hill at the back of the coal house, moving quick out the way of the man carrying the last bag of coal, watching the man emptying the coal onto the coal house ground.

Here I am watching the man; looking at his body covered in black coal dust; standing before my father, watching my father's hand reaching into his trouser pocket; looking at the different colour paper money inside my father's hand, holding the money out to give the man, watching the man taking the paper money from my father's hand, watching the man counting the money from one hand into the other hand, putting his hand into the black bag hanging down around his waist, listening to his hand moving around the money inside the bag, holding out his hand full with money coins, counting them into my fathers palm and opening out one brown paper money on top.

Here I am watching the man's eye looking direct into my father's face and smile. I am speaking. Thanks mate.

Here I am listening to my father say the word mate, wondering in my mind, thinking about the word mate, watching the mate walking up the step, listening to the whistling sound coming from his body walking along the pathway on the other side of the fence.

Here I am watching my father closing the coal house door shut, watching my father close the fence gateway shut, pushing the big round metal bar across into the metal hole fixed on the fence, watching my father's hand pushing on the bar, making sure the fence gateway is locked.

Here I am looking into the air, looking at the clothes along the clothes line, watching the clothes blowing high in the air, tasting the air feeling good inside the body that I am.

Here I am inside the dining-room, looking at Ruel and George and Delroy's body watching the television.

Here I am inside the kitchen, collecting the balance of things off the work-top, carrying them into the dining-room, walking past my father's body stepping into the house.

Here I am standing inside the dining-room, looking at the television picture show, standing on the chair, putting the plates and cups away where they belong inside the cabinet.

Here I am inside the kitchen, standing on the chair over the kitchen sink, wringing the water from the dishcloth, emptying the water out the bowl, spreading the cloth over the hot water tap, the way my mother always do.

Here I am standing inside the kitchen, lifting the chair over by the stove where it belongs.

Here I am with the broom in my hands, sweeping the biscuit crumbs off the kitchen floor, sweeping the dust together over by the kitchen doorway.

IAM®

Here I am bending down over the pile of dust, sweeping it into the dust-pan, emptying the dust into the kitchen dust-bin, returning the dust-pan and brush away where they belong down on the floor under the corner shelf.

Here I am standing at the dining-room entrance, looking out from the body that I am, looking over the kitchen floor, making sure everything is clean in its right place.

Here I am standing inside the dining-room, looking at the television picture, wondering in my mind, wondering what the show is about; remembering in my mind, remembering that Delroy's bottom needs changing.

Here I am looking at the television picture, not wanting to move from the spot where I am standing, thinking, wondering if mummy is coming home soon.

Here I am thinking; I better change Delroy now before mummy reach home and find that he is still wearing the same nappy.

Here I am running up the stairs, running into the bath-room, standing on the toilet bowl seat, reaching into the hot water tank cupboard, looking for a nappy and plastic rubber pants.

Here I am turning on the hot water tap, wetting the flannel, rubbing soap all over it, squeezing the water out the flannel, turning the tap off.

Here I am running into the boy's bed-room, getting the towel off the cot railing, getting the vaseline and powder of the drawer.

Here I am running down the stairs, walking into the dining-room, putting the things down on the floor, spreading the towel out ready to change Delroy's nappy.

Here I am lifting Delroy's body, feeling Delroy's weight pulling down on my body lifting him out the pram, resting his body down on the towel, wanting to see the television picture, listening to daddy and Ruel and George's body keep laughing out loud at what is going on.

Here I am pulling the fastenings to open Delroy's pants bottom, pushing it up above his bottom, taking off his plastic rubber pants, pulling the pins out the nappy, feeling the wee-wee wet on my hands pulling the soaking wet nappy from under Delroy's bottom.

Here I am wiping Delroy's bottom with the flannel, wiping around the nappy sores on his bottom, feeling Delroy's bottom jump up, hearing Delroy sounding like he is going to cry, hurting, feeling my hands on his sore bottom.

I AM®

Here I am folding the nappy in two, making a fold at the bottom, lifting Delroy's leg, pushing the nappy under his bottom, hearing Ruel say; they got the wrong man.

Here I am putting the Vaseline on the sore red parts on Delroy's bottom, sprinkling the powder over the sores, folding the nappy over Delroy's wee-wee, pushing the pin into the nappy, pinning the nappy around Delroy's bottom.

Here I am, wanting to watch the television, pulling the plastic pants up over the nappy, wondering in my mind, wondering what is going on on the television, wanting to know what daddy and Ruel and George is laughing about.

Here I am lifting Delroy's body up into his pram, hearing the sound like the show is finished now, listening to daddy and Ruel talking about the film, telling each other how good it was.

Here I am walking up the stairs, carrying Delroy's dirty nappy and things, walking along the landing, thinking in my mind, walking into the bath-room, putting the wet nappy into the nappy bucket on the floor under the sink.

Here I am walking into the boys bed-room, returning the vaseline and powder down on the cupboard where it belong, spreading the towel over the cot railing.

Here I am on my way down the stairs, thinking in my mind, wondering about my mother, thinking; where has mummy gone?

Here I am standing inside the dining-room, thinking in my mind wondering; what can I do?

Here I am watching Ruel and George playing the game name snakes and ladder on the dining-table.

Here I am on my hands and knee, reaching under the television table, feeling for my bag with my sewing things inside.

Here I am kneeling down on the floor by the fire-side, looking at the pin-cushion that I am making.

Here I am taking the needle out the cloth, thinking in my mind, wanting to remember how to make the sewing stitch I was doing.

Here I am sewing the zigzag stitch; making the stitch look the same like my mother sew the zigzag stitch to look good.

IAM®

Here I am making the pin-cushion, feeling good inside myself, sewing, thinking in my mind.

Here I am sewing, listening to the sounds like a paper bag opening, watching my father opening a little white paper bag inside his hand, watching my father's hand taking a sweet out the bag and put it into his mouth, watching his head turning around, looking in my direction, looking at my father's face smiling at one, watching my father reaching his hand forward, holding the bag of sweet down before me, pushing his hand forward, wanting me to take a sweet.

Here I am. Thank you daddy.

Here I am sucking the sweet, tasting nice, watching my father's hand holding the bag out to Ruel and George, smiling at daddy, watching my father looking please with himself.

Here I am sewing the zigzag stitch around the pin-cushion, realizing that I have nearly finished.

Here I am sewing over the same stitch, sewing over the same stitch, biting the thread in my mouth, wanting it to break; thinking; I have finished now.

Here I am looking at my pin-cushion, feeling pleased with myself, turning my pin-cushion around in my hand.

Here I am. Look at what I have made daddy.

Here I am standing at my father's side, feeling good with myself, looking at my father's face smiling, looking at the pin-cushion I am holding in my hand. I am speaking. You did that. Is it you really make it?

Here I am looking at my father's face, feeling his presence, listening to the sound of his voice talking to me, making my body feel the feeling that I am feeling, the feeling that I am feeling for the first time, feeling good, making my body not know what to do with myself.

Here I am. Yes daddy; mummy show me how to make it. I am speaking. You good Hazel.

Here I am. Thank you daddy. Look Ruel; do you like it? I am speaking. Leave me Hazel.

Here I am not wanting to show George my work, feeling hurt, hearing the way Ruel talk; not showing any interest in what I have made.

IAM®

Here I am placing my pin-cushion down on the television table so mummy can see it when she comes home.

Here I am kneeling down on the floor, looking at the different pieces of cloth inside my bag, thinking in my mind wondering, thinking; what can I make next.

Here I am looking at the bits of cloth, realizing that they are too small to make anything with. I can hear sounds at the front doorway; sounding like mummy and Mavis come home.

Here I am looking at Mavis's body entering the dining-room, holding two plastic bags in her hand. Mummy is coming in now with her hands full with plastic bags and smiling all over her face.

Here I am pushing the things quick inside the bag, pushing the bag under the television table, wanting to see, what mummy bring home.

Here I am standing on the fire surround, looking at Mavis standing next to daddy, watching daddy pick Mavis up and sit Mavis down on his lap, watching mummy taking off her hat and the gloves off her hands, positioning them on her lap. I am speaking. Cape Hill's full of people.

Here I am looking at my mother's body, looking at her face with water spots on her forehead, listening to my father talking to my mother, watching my mother making to take off her shoe. I am speaking. Ge; the money finish. The money you give me cannot buy everything. I buy two little thing and I still cannot see where the thing is that I buy. Hazel; take these up stairs for me.

Here I am bending down before my mother, holding her shoes, pulling it off her foot, taking her hat and glove from her hand.

Here I am walking, running up the stairs, running into my mother's bed-room.

Here I am inside my mother's bed-room, putting mummy's gloves inside her hat, placing it down on her ottoman trunk box, returning her shoes under the dressing-table where it belongs. I can smell something in the air surrounding my mother's dressing-table, smelling the scent inside the room.

Here I am thinking in my mind; mummy's bed-room scent is very nice.

Here I am thinking, wondering; what make mummy's bed-room smells so nice.

Here I am walking along the hall way, running down the stairs, walking into the dining-room, just in time; mummy is taking the things out the plastic bag, laying the things out along the dining-table, listening to her telling daddy how much everything cost, spreading everything out so he can see.

Here I am watching my father raise his hands over his face, looking as if not wanting to hear what mummy is saying.

Here I am looking at the things on the dining-table. I can see a bag of apples, a bag of orange and a pineapple and the bag with lots of baby orange fruits.

Here I am watching my mother's hand emptying out the big shopping bag.

Here I am watching my mother's hand picking up a parcel covered with newspaper wrapping, holding it away from her body. I am speaking. Hazel; fetch me the washing-up bowl from the kitchen please.

Here I am inside the kitchen, lifting the bowl out the sink, carrying it into the dining-room.

Here I am standing before my mother, holding the bowl before me, watching my mother's hand put the parcel into the bowl.

Here I am looking into the bowl, smelling the scent coming off the parcel, smelling in the air all around me now; making my inside go round, making my head hurt, making my body want to sit down.

Here I am wondering; what is it? Thinking; it smells stink. I am speaking. Go and put it down on the draining-board quick.

Here I am holding the bowl away from my body, carrying it into the kitchen, lifting it up, down on top of the draining-board.

Here I am inside the dining-room, watching my mother putting the apples into the fruit bowl on the dining-table before her.

Here I am watching George put the tin foods into the bottom part of the cabinet.

Here I am collecting the empty paper bags, folding them in two, putting them together inside the television table bottom drawer, ready to use for daddy's sandwiches to carry to the factory.

Here I am taking the tub of margarine and the packet of lard off the table, putting them inside the fridge where they belong with all the other animal foods. I am speaking. Put these two lemons on the draining-board Hazel.

Here I am walking into the kitchen, carrying the two lemon fruit. I can smell the thing inside the bowl smelling out the air inside the kitchen; tasting the

IAM®

scent inside the body that I am holding my breath, walking quick into the dining-room.

Here I am standing inside the dining-room, realizing that my father has gone up stairs.

Here I am watching my mother, wondering what is inside the plastic bags next to her hand-bag.

Here I am watching my mother's body standing up, collecting her hand-bag and the plastic bags off the floor, watching her body move towards the door on her way up stairs. I am speaking. Hazel, put the kettle on the fire and make a start on the potato ready for dinner.

Here I am thinking in my mind, looking at Mavis looking at my body, making up her face at me; hanging out her tongue, pushing her way to get past mummy's body.

Here I am wondering, thinking in my mind; why did Mavis do that to me?

Here I am thinking; what have I done to Mavis to make her want to hurt me?

Here I am inside the kitchen, lifting the chair over to the sink, standing on the chair, watching the cold water falling into the kettle, thinking in my mind; mummy must have bought herself and Mavis some more new things.

Here I am thinking; Mavis thinks that she is better than the body I am because mummy always dress-up her body to look better than the body I am.

Here I am standing inside the kitchen, holding the matchbox, lighting the match, watching the match burning, turning the gas on, lighting the fire under the kettle, turning the flame up high.

Here I am thinking; if Mavis could only see how her face looks bad, hanging out her tongue like that.

Here I am reaching down into the bag of potato, carrying the potato over to the sink, smelling the scent coming from the thing inside the bowl.

Here I am standing on the chair turning on the cold water, pushing the plug inside the sink, washing the dirt off the potatoes, putting them down on the draining-board.

Here I am pushing the kitchen window open, wanting the clean air to come into the kitchen; smelling the thing inside the bowl making my insides want to come out.

IAM®

Here I am putting the cold water into the big saucepan, resting it down on the draining-board, making ready to peel the potatoes.

Here I am standing on the floor, taking the newspaper from under the sink, standing on the chair, opening the newspaper flat on the work-top, putting the potatoes down on top, pulling the newspaper and potatoes along the work-top, over to the other side, away from the thing inside the bowl making the air inside the kitchen smell stink.

Here I am standing on the ground, lifting the chair over by the sink, standing on the chair wiping the dirt off the draining-board, watching the dirty water going down the plughole, washing the sink inside clean, wringing out the dishcloth, thinking in my mind, wondering about Mavis, wondering why my sister is making fun of me.

Here I am wondering why Mavis does not like my body.

Here I am wondering in my mind, wanting to understand my sister, wanting my sister to like the body that I am.

Here I am watching the cold water falling into the saucepan; standing on the ground, lifting the saucepan down off the draining-board, resting it down on the newspaper by the potatoes, taking the colander out the cupboard, resting it down by the newspaper, getting the little sharp knife out the drawer, making ready to peel the potatoes for our dinner.

Here I am standing on the chair, peeling the skin off the potatoes, wondering in my mind, thinking about myself, wondering why my sister Mavis do not like me.

Here I am feeling hurt inside myself, wanting someone to talk with me.

Here I am thinking about myself, wondering; is anyone there for me?

Here I am feeling my body insides hurting, wanting to understand the hurting that I am feeling, knowing that my mother and my father do not understand my body, wanting someone to care about the body that I am, wanting to belong.

Here I am, knowing that mummy and daddy do not realize that my body is always hurting, wanting someone to talk to.

Here I am peeling the skin off the potato, thinking about myself, feeling lone inside, lone inside my body.

Here I am wondering in my mind thinking; I don't belong where I am. Who am I? Who am I?

IAM®

Here I am peeling the skin off the potato, feeling my mother's presence coming into the kitchen. I am speaking. The fish smell strong.

Here I am peeling the skin off the potato, understanding that it is the dead fishes inside the bowl; making the air smell stink.

Here I am watching my mother's hand opening out the parcel of fish on the draining-board, spacing the dead fishes out on the paper, slicing the lemon fruit in half, squeezing the juice over the dead fishes, holding the fish body away from her, scraping its flesh with the sharp cooking knife, scraping the scales off the fish flesh.

Here I am watching my mother doing; scraping the fish flesh, feeling my body inside turn over, smelling the scent of the fish in the air surrounding the body that I am.

Here I am thinking about the fish that is no life no more.

Here I am wondering if the fish body flesh can feel what my mother is doing.

Here I am watching my mother's hand with the knife, cutting into the fish flesh, watching her hand pulling out the insides of the fish.

Here I am feeling my body shaking, thinking about the life that is no life no more.

Here I am watching my mother's hand holding the knife, picking the eye out the fish head, cutting the fish body around its centre, cutting the fish body in two pieces.

Here I am watching my mother's hand preparing the fishes; wondering in my mind; how is mummy going to cook the fish?

Here I am peeling the potato, thinking about the fishes, wondering in my mind; are the fishes born for us to eat.

Here I am thinking about the fishes, wondering; what is the fish born to be.

Here I am looking at my mother's face, thinking in my mind, wondering about my mother, wondering what she is thinking, preparing the pieces of fish to cook for dinner.

IAM®

CHAPTER 25

Here I am peeling the potato, thinking in my mind, wondering if mummy feel the way I am feeling, watching the knife in her hand scraping the dress scales off the fish body flesh bare; remembering in my mind, remembering when mummy chop the chicken head off the chicken body and picked the chicken feather dress out the chicken body flesh and made the chicken body bare

Here I am peeling the potatoes, thinking in my mind, wondering about all the animal flesh we eat, wondering about the life that is no life no more.

Here I am thinking in my mind, remembering when Ruel and I was on the ground Jamaica; remembering the body that I am; realizing that my body did not eat any animal flesh; remembering my body did not like eating; remembering I only wanted to eat the fruits that was on the tree behind Aunty Jane's house.

Here I am remembering in my mind, thinking about the body that I am, remembering that Ruel used to eat all my food that Auntie Jane give me.

Here I am remembering in my mind, thinking about myself, remembering the body that I am, wanting to do something.

Here I am peeling the potato, remembering in my mind, thinking about the body that I am on the ground name Jamaica.

Here I am wondering in my mind, remembering the time I was staying with Auntie Jane, knowing in my mind that I was by myself all the time, except when Ruel was hiding away from someone. Ruel would want to be with me.

Here I am wondering in my mind, remembering me and Ruel, remembering listening to Ruel talking about the things that everyone did to him to make him not want to be with them.

Here I am remembering in my mind, remembering when Ruel and I were staying with Auntie Jane; sleeping in her house. Ruel always asked me if I wanted my food that Auntie Jane gave me to eat.

Here I am remembering; Ruel always wanting my food when he finished eating his food; remembering Ruel's body was always hungry wanting food.

Here I am watching my mother's hand holding the pieces of fish under the cold water, washing the blood of the pieces of fish.

Here I am thinking in my mind, remembering the body that I am, wanting to do something with my hands; but Auntie Jane would not let me do anything. Everyone said that I was too small.

I AM®

Here I am thinking in my mind, remembering Auntie Jane, remembering the time before I came to this ground name England.

Here I am looking at my mother, one woman just like the other women on the ground Jamaica, realizing that my mother think that because my body is the image of herself, my body is old enough to do the things her body is expected to do.

Here I am watching my mother preparing the fish flesh to cook.

Here I am thinking about the name mother, like the other women, like Auntie Jane.

Here I am wondering in my mind, thinking, wanting to understand which woman is right, not knowing what to think, because there are lots of people name woman that have the same name mother.

Here I am, knowing that I am doing lots of things with my two hands, but there is something different that my body wants to do and it is not house work.

Here I am, the girl child; feeling like my body is wanting to do something different, not knowing what it is I want to do.

Here I am peeling the potato thinking in my mind, realizing that mummy is finished preparing the fish flesh. I am speaking. Hazel, run and fetch me a clean dish-towel.

Here I am inside the dining-room, taking the dish-towel from the television-table drawer, listening to Ruel and George shouting at my body standing between them and the television screen.

Here I am inside the kitchen, standing in the presence of my mother, watching her hand squeezing the lemon juice over the pieces of fishes inside the bowl.

Here I am watching my mother's head turn towards my body, smiling at one. I am speaking. This will take away the raw smell from the fish.

Here I am watching my mother's face looking pleased with her self; watching her hand drop the lemon skin into the sink, watching her hand with the knife, slicing the other lemon in two halves, squeezing the juice over the pieces of fish inside the meat bowl. I am speaking. Give me the dishcloth.

Here I am holding the dish-cloth out towards my mother, watching her hands open it out onto the palm of her one hand, placing the fish portion on top of the cloth, patting the pieces of fish dry. I am speaking. You see what I am

IAM®

doing. You must make sure the fish is dry or it will not fry properly. Go and bring the margarine and the vinegar bottle come. Bring two tomatoes as well and the cooking oil.

Here I am inside the dining-room, remembering the things mummy wants me to get.

Here I am thinking, looking inside the fridge, getting the margarine and two tomatoes, placing them down on the dining-table, thinking in my mind, wondering; what else did mummy want?, remembering the cooking oil and the margarine and am.., the vinegar.

Here I am with everything my mother wants; walking past Ruel's body, watching his eyes on the television, thinking in my mind, walking into the kitchen, placing the things down on the work-top.

Here I am watching my mother washing the draining-board with the hot soapy dishcloth.

Here I am thinking; Ruel and George and Mavis is missing something good here.

Here I am watching my mother doing, knowing that I am learning all there is to know about the act of cooking, watching my mother's hand preparing the pieces of fish to have for dinner.

Here I am the girl child, understanding in my mind, realizing that I am learning something new everyday, just watching my mother's hands always doing.

Here I am understanding in my mind thinking; Ruel and George and Mavis is not learning anything from watching the television because they are not using there two hands to do anything but put food into their mouth.

Here I am learning what I can see my mother hands are doing, realizing that I will have plenty to eat because I can prepare and cook the food, just like my mother can, realizing that I know lots of different kinds of food that I can cook, just from watching my mother when she is preparing the fruits and the vegetables, and all the tins and packets and the cans of food in the cupboard and the fridge with all kinds of animal flesh and cheese to eat.

Here I am realizing in my mind, understanding that I am learning because I am watching what my mother is doing with her two hands.

Here I am realizing that I can learn from anyone that is doing something with their hands, just like I can cook, I can wash the clothes, I can clean the house, I can make the fire, I can sew a pin-cushion and I can wash and dress myself to look good, and I am learning to read and write, just like my mother and father and brothers can.

Here I am watching my mother's hand holding the salt jar, sprinkling the black pepper powder over the pieces of fishes in the cooking bowl, turning the pieces over, making sure the pieces of fishes are covered all over with salt and pepper.

Here I am watching my mother's hand rubbing the salt and pepper into the pieces of fishes, feeling my nose inside itching, smelling the black pepper powder in the air making my body cough, sneezing the pepper out my body.

Here I am peeling the potato, wanting to see what mummy is doing, watching her hand slicing the onion rounds onto the pieces of fishes inside the cooking bowl.

Here I am watching my mother's hand putting the cover on top of the bowl, shaking the bowl from side to side, mixing the pieces of fish and onion and salt and pepper together. Now my mother is washing a little bunch of the herb thyme under the cold water and the two tomatoes and put them into the bowl with the pieces of fish ready to cook.

Here I am watching my mother's hand wiping the outside part of the meat bowl, resting the bowl down on the work-top.

Here I am watching everything my mother's hands are doing, scrubbing the dishcloth clean, washing the fish scales off the draining-board, washing around the sink and the water tap, washing all the sink surrounds clean, making the kitchen smell good, smelling the lemon scent in the air surrounding one. I am speaking. The fish will stink out the place if I don't make sure I clean it up right away.

Here I am understanding every word I can hear my mother is saying, looking at her hands wringing the water from the dishcloth, wiping the sink surround dry, watching her make everywhere look clean.

Here I am watching my mother's hand taking the paper off the cooking lard, marking the lard in half, and half, putting three portions into the frying-pan on top of the stove, lighting the gas under the pan, turning the flame down low. My mother's face is looking like she is feeling pleased with herself, feeling good doing what she is doing. My mother is taking some carrots from the vegetable rack, putting them down beside the potato where I am looking at my mother's face smiling at one, making my body feel good inside. I am speaking. Go and fetch me the plain flour and put some water into the jug.

IAM®

Here I am inside the dining-room, taking the red paper parcel of plain flour out of the cabinet, feeling good with myself, knowing that I am helping my mother prepare the food for our dinner.

Here I am inside the kitchen, placing the parcel of flour onto the work-top, looking up at my mother's hand peeling the skin off the carrot, moving quicker than I can. Now my mother is peeling the potatoes with me.

Here I am standing on the chair over the kitchen sink, watching my mother's hand holding the plastic jug filling up with cold water; smelling the air inside the kitchen change.

Here I am. Mummy the oil is smoking; mummy.

Here I am inside the kitchen watching my mother turn the fire off quick from under the frying-pan, watching the smoking air rising from the pan; smelling the burning oil looking black in the air.

Here I am watching my mother scraping the onion and thyme off the pieces of fishes, setting the pieces out on the plate ready to fry. My mother is lighting the fire, returning the frying-pan on the fire and slowly lowering a piece of fish into the hot oil. I can hear the pieces of fish flesh making the frying sound inside the hot oil, watching the oil jumping out the frying-pan, making snapping sound, spitting hot oil over my mother's hand. My mother is placing the other pieces of fish into the oil. I can smell the pieces of fish cooking, scenting in the air surrounding the body that I am, watching my mother move the frying-pan off the fire over to the back burner, watching her hand holding the big flat spoon, turning the fish portions over, returning the frying-pan onto the fire.

Here I am watching my mother's hand holding the frying-pan handle, shaking the pan, listening to the sounds of the pieces of fish frying in the oil, smelling the fish scented air, tasting the frying fish inside the body that I am body.

Here I am watching my mother taking the cooked pieces of fish out the oil, placing the portions into the dutch-pot, putting the balance of fish into the hot oil, watching the oil splashing out the pan, watching my mother's body jump, watching the water coming out onto my mother's forehead, watching her hand turn the gas down low.

Here I am watching my mother emptying the flour into the mixing bowl, watching her eyes looking into the bowl as if measuring the flour with her eyes, pouring out more flour, shaking the bowl, watching her hand moving around inside the bowl, pouring the salt into the palm of her hand so I can see, sprinkling it over the flour inside the bowl, mixing everything together.

IAM®

Now my mother is dusting the flour off her hands, turning the fish over inside the frying-pan, turning the fire up a little more; leaving the pieces of fish to cook.

Here I am watching my mother pouring water into the bowl onto the flour, watching her hand mixing the flour and water together, thinking in my mind, wondering if the fishes have a name.

Here I am thinking in my mind, wondering; how many names do fishes have, watching my mother mixing the flour inside the bowl, pouring on the cold water, mixing the dough to make the dumpling.

Here I am. Mummy; what is the fish name? I am speaking. You don't know what this fish is name. This is the same one like what we have in Jamaica they call Goat fish.

Here I am listening to my mother, wondering in my mind thinking; mummy thinks that I should know everything she knows.

Here I am watching my mother taking the portions of fish out the hot oil, placing them inside the dutch-pot.

Here I am realizing that mummy do not understand that I only know what I know from watching her doing.

Here I am thinking, wondering if my mother believes that I know as much as she knows.

Here I am now of the understanding that the fish body have a name.

Here I am realizing that my body is learning because I ask to find out about what I want to know. I use my hands to do different things and I am learning about more things, just from watching mummy prepare and cook all kinds of food for dinner.

Here I am knowing that my body is learning, realizing that Ruel and George and Mavis's body is not like I am because they are watching the television that is showing them things they know nothing about, because the television picture is always showing things that make Ruel and George and Mavis think are real, but I know the television picture is pretending and Ruel and George and Mavis can't talk to the television like I am talking with mummy.

Here I am watching my mother rubbing her hands together, rubbing off the flour into the bowl.

Here I am thinking about the fish, the Goat fish, watching my mother's hand with the long flat spoon, lifting the piece of fish out of the frying-pan, placing it inside the dutch-pot, turning off the fire, moving the frying-pan onto the back burner on the stove.

Here I am thinking, looking at my mother making up her face, pressing down her body onto the flour dough inside the bowl, rolling the dough inside her hands, rolling the dough making it grow long.

Here I am watching my mother's hand with the knife, cutting the dough into two half portions, cutting the portions into little pieces, making sure each piece look the same size. Now my mother is holding the big saucepan inside the sink, turning on the cold water tap, lifting the pan onto the front part of the stove, lighting the gas with the match in her hand, turning the flame up high; watching my mother slicing the potatoes into half, emptying the potatoes and carrots into the big saucepan on the fire.

Here I am watching every move my mother is making, making the piece of dough look round and flat, returning it inside the bowl, making all the pieces of dough into small round flat shapes.

Here I am standing inside the kitchen, watching the steam coming out the big sauce-pan, watching my mother's hand holding the towel, lifting the cover off the pan, resting it down on the work-top, placing each dumpling round in the pot, measuring one teaspoon full of salt, sprinkling it over the food, placing the cover on top.

Here I am lifting the chair over to the sink, standing on the chair, washing the cooking things, smelling the fish scent in the air, making my body feel hunger inside. I am speaking. Wash the cloth out and give it here one minute Hazel.

Here I am watching my mother with the dishcloth in her hand, wiping the food marks off the saucepans, wiping the kettle clean, wiping the stove top, wiping the sides of the stove to look clean, making everywhere look clean. I am speaking. Put this inside the sink please.

Here I am taking the cloth from my mother's hand, placing it inside the washing-up bowl with hot soap water inside the sink.

Here I am watching, wanting to see what my mother is doing, watching her hand opening the vinegar bottle, pouring the vinegar into the tablespoon, measuring out two and two and one spoon full of vinegar, pouring it onto the fish.

Here I am watching my mother taking the paper off the margarine in her hand, watching her cut the corner off and put it inside the dutch-pot and two drops of the red hot pepper sauce, returning the cover onto the pot, turning the fire up high. I can hear the water making the bubbling sound inside the dutch-pot, smelling the fish scent in the air, smelling the vegetable scent in the air, making everywhere smell of food. I am speaking. Go and put those things away Hazel.

Here I am taking the packet of flour and vinegar bottle from my mother's hand, carrying them into the dining-room. I can see my father is in the dining-room, watching the television with Ruel and George and Mavis.

Here I am returning the flour and vinegar inside the cabinet where they belong.

Here I am walking past Mavis's body holding her toy dolly on her lap, holding her fingers in her mouth, watching the wrestling show on the television.

Here I am inside the kitchen collecting the lard and the margarine off the work-top, carrying them into the dining-room, returning them inside the fridge where they belong.

Here I am inside the kitchen, watching my mother's hand holding the can opener, turning the handle, cutting open the can of peas, emptying the peas into the colander pan with holes, rinsing the peas under the cold water inside the sink, shaking the water out the colander, placing it down on the draining-board. My mother is returning the frying pan of oil onto the front of the stove, lighting the fire under the pan, turning the flames down low.

Here I am watching my mother pouring the oil out the frying-pan into the enamel jug, returning the pan on top of the stove. Now my mother is sprinkling the black pepper powder into the frying-pan, mixing the pepper into the oil with the cooking fork in her hand, emptying the peas out of the colander into the frying-pan, shaking the pan on top of the fire. I can see the steam rising out of the pan; hearing the sound the peas is making, frying, popping in the hot oil, smelling the different scent, making my body want to taste it, realizing in my mind, understanding there are lots of different ways to cook the same food; watching my mother frying the peas cooking inside the frying pan.

Here I am watching my mother hand shaking the frying-pan of peas, wondering in my mind, wondering what the peas look like, frying in the pan. I am speaking. Go and get me the washing basket please Hazel.

Here I am walking across the dining-room, walking into the pantry room, getting the clothes basket off the floor, carrying it into the dining-room, walking past my father, watching his hand writing on the newspaper on his lap, copying the numbers off the television screen.

IAM®

Here I am walking into the kitchen, realizing that mummy is outside.

Here I am outside the house, walking towards my mother's body standing by the clothes line wire, taking the peg out the clothes hanging on the line.

Here I am placing the basket down on the ground near my mother's foot, side stepping along the ground, listening to her voice talking to herself.

Here I am inside the house, taking the peg-bag off the kitchen wall, carrying it outside, walking towards my mother's body taking the clothes off the line.

Here I am standing at my mother's side, holding the bag open for my mother to drop the clothes-peg inside, watching my mother's face smiling down on the body that I am. I am speaking. Hazel; you is good.

Here I am watching my mother's body working, thinking in my mind; mummy looks tired now.

Here I am watching my mother's body walking over to the other line full of clothes, watching her hand lifting down the line stick, resting it up against the high brick wall fence. My body is shaking in the air, trembling, feeling the air moving over my skin.

Here I am watching my mother's hand taking the pieces of clothes off the line, dropping the pegs into the peg-bag I am holding, following my mother's body side stepping along the ground under the wire clothes line. I am speaking. I have to finish your dress today or tomorrow ready for you to wear go to school.

Here I am walking into the kitchen, returning the peg-bag onto the hook in the wall where it belongs. I am speaking. Put the basket inside the back bedroom please Hazel. We finish now thank God.

Here I am walking across the dining-room, dragging the basket full with clothes across the floor, dragging it past my father's body, watching his face smiling down on my body standing with my back against the open door. I am speaking. George; go and hold the door open for your sister instead of just sitting on your back-side watching the door pitching her down, struggling with the basket.

Here I am dragging the basket up the step, watching George's face half smiling at my body lifting the basket into the passage, dragging the basket behind me, dragging it into the back bed-room, dragging it by the side of mummy's sewing table; feeling my body hurting, feeling like I don't want to do anything now, I am tired.

IAM®

Here I am walking slow, walking along the hall way, thinking in my mind, wondering, walking into the dining-room, watching my mother spreading the table cloth over the dining-table.

Here I am standing by the fire, watching my mother making the table ready for dinner. My body is hurting, feeling tired, not knowing what to do with myself, feeling the water coming into my eyes. My body is hurting.

Here I am thinking about myself, looking at the television, hearing my mother inside the kitchen, listening to her sharing the food onto the plates.

Here I am watching the television not understanding what I am seeing, watching my mother entering the dining-room, carrying the tea-pot and a little plate of food in her hands. I am speaking. Hazel; feed your brother his dinner.

Here I am taking the plate from my mother's hand, watching Delroy's body jumping up in his pram, smiling all over his face, smiling at my body.

Here I am. George, can I please sit on your chair. I am tired.

Here I am watching George lifting the chair over to Delroy's pram; feeling my body inside wanting to cry.

Here I am thinking in my mind, putting the food into Delroy's mouth, watching Delroy's mouth moving around quick, eating down the food, watching my hand.

Here I am thinking, mummy could have asked Ruel or George to feed Delroy his food. Why do I have to do everything? Ruel and George's body have two hands just like I have. I am tired now. I have been working since I got up this morning.

Here I am feeling hurt, watching Delroy's body eating, thinking in my mind, wondering about myself.

Here I am putting mashed potato into Delroy's mouth, feeling the water coming into my eyes, feeling the water running down my face; feeding Delroy, watching Delroy watching my hands scraping the food together on the plate. I am speaking. The food taste good Pearl. Pearl; you certainly can cook good.

Here I am walking past my father's body, going into the kitchen, not wanting to be in the presence of anyone, feeling my eyes full with water running down my face, feeling my insides hurting, wanting my body to stop crying.

I AM®

Here I am inside the kitchen, sitting down on the chair, holding my hands around my tummy, wanting the hurting to go away before mummy catch me crying.

Here I am hurting, feeling lone inside myself, thinking. I can hear my father asking for Hazel.

Here I am, not wanting to answer my father's voice, not wanting him to see my body is crying. I am speaking. What you sitting in the dark for Hazel.

Here I am wiping the water from my face, feeling the light burning my eyes. I am speaking. What are you crying for Hazel?

Here I am hurting, looking at my brother, hearing him talking, not knowing how to answer my brother.

Here I am. I don't know Ruel. I am speaking. What do you mean Hazel? You don't cry for nothing. Has mummy said something to you again?

Here I am, wanting to answer my brother, wanting to understand why I am feeling the way I am feeling, not knowing how to explain to Ruel the reason why I am crying.

Here I am, wanting my body to stop from crying, hearing my father asking for his daughter Hazel. I am speaking. Hazel; you better stop crying before mummy come and see you.

Here I am wiping my face on my dress hem, thinking in my mind, thinking about myself, knowing that I have to pretend that I am not feeling hurt because I do not know why I am hurting and mummy will only beat me if I don't know.

Here I am standing on the chair over the sink, watching the cold water falling into the kettle. I can hear my father asking Ruel what I am doing, hearing my father calling my name, calling the body that I am.

Here I am listening to my father's voice, not wanting to answer him.

Here I am lighting the fire under the kettle, hearing my father calling my name.

Here I am. I am lighting the fire under the kettle daddy.

Here I am lighting the fire under the saucepans, giving myself something to do, not wanting my father to see my face.

Here I am standing inside the dining-room, standing by the doorway, looking at my father's body looking at the television.

IAM®

Here I am. Here I am daddy. I am speaking. What is the matter with you now? Here you are.

Here I am taking the plate of food from my father's hand, wondering in my mind thinking; how come daddy knows that I was crying?

Here I am feeling pleased with my father, leaving some of his dinner, just for me.

Here I am. Thank you daddy.

Here I am sitting down on the floor next to my father's chair, realizing that my father does think about my body.

Here I am eating the food, hearing daddy asking mummy; what is the matter with Hazel? I am speaking. What you asking me for? There she is. Hazel was crying early on and I did ask her what she crying for.

Here I am in the presence of everyone, listening to my mother speaking, not wanting to eat the food before me, listening to my mother and father talking about my body as if I was not here in there presence. I am speaking. My daughter Hazel, don't look right to me.

Here I am listening to my father talking about my body, feeling my body hurting, wanting my father and mother to stop talking about the body that I am, making my inside want to come out, not knowing what to do with myself.

Here I am feeling my body shaking; wanting to get away from my father's house, knowing that mummy is getting angry with my body, knowing that mummy is going to beat my body again when daddy has gone to the factory.

Here I am, wanting some-one to come to my father's house, wanting someone to take me away from my father's house.

Here I am feeling my mother's presence, listening to the sound of her voice getting louder, talking and crying at the same time.

Here I am not wanting to be where I am, knowing that my mother is going to beat my body and daddy doesn't realize that mummy do not know how to behave with my body.

Here I am standing inside the kitchen, wanting to get away from my mother's presence, feeling like I don't belong inside my father's house, knowing that my mother's behaviour is always making my body change, making my body hurt.

IAM®

Here I am inside the kitchen; hearing somebody by the door; someone's hand is on the door, making my body inside jump, trembling, watching the door opening, watching my mother's body coming into the kitchen, watching my mother's body looking hurt all over her face, feeling my mother's presence making the air change, listening to the sound of her voice shouting, talking to herself, watching her hands banging the things down on the worktop, pushing my body out her way.

Here I am, wanting to get away from my mother's presence, not wanting to hear the words she is saying, talking out loud to herself.

Here I am inside the dining-room, watching my father's body moving from side to side on his chair, resting his face inside his hands, as if not wanting to hear my mother's voice.

Here I am watching my father looking upset with himself, realizing now what he has done, causing my mother to be angry and not knowing the cause of the body that I am crying.

Here I am putting the dirty plates together, feeling Mavis's eyes looking at one. Mavis's face looks like mummy's face is looking like she wants to hurt my body.

Here I am watching Mavis looking without expression, watching her body sliding off the chair, running towards the kitchen.

Here I am inside the kitchen, placing the dirty plates inside the washing-up bowl, feeling Mavis's presence looking at one, watching her body moving around mummy's body, watching her body making faces at one.

Here I am inside the dining-room, watching my father's body leaving the dining-room, feeling my insides shaking, wanting my father to stay inside the dining-room.

Here I am listening to the kettle making the whistling noise, feeling my body not wanting to go into the kitchen where my mother is.

Here I am walking into the kitchen, carrying the tea-pot, emptying the tea-bags into the dust-bin, walking past my sister, feeling her hand fist punch my body, feeling my body shaking, hurting, feeling the air surrounding my body changing, feeling my mother's presence looking at my body standing on the chair over the stove, pouring the hot water from the kettle into the tea-pot. I am speaking. You; you; you see you. I am going to show you something.

Here I am listening to my mother speaking, feeling her presence making my body keep hurting, making my body not want to stay in my father's house.

IAM®

Here I am walking quick out of the kitchen, carrying the pot of tea in my hand, feeling the hot water falling on the floor, splashing on my legs, burning my foot, making water come into my eyes, feeling my body crying, not knowing what to do with myself, wanting someone to talk to, wanting someone to come and take me away.

Here I am feeling the hot water burning on my legs, wondering in my mind, wondering what is going to happen now, knowing that mummy does not care about my body, knowing that my father does not realize that mummy do not like my body in the house.

Here I am watching; standing inside the dining-room, feeling my mother's presence entering the room, watching Mavis, not wanting to be in her way, watching her face watching her eyes looking red like my mummy's eyes looking at my body, looking without expression, making my body not know what to do with myself.

Here I am standing at the kitchen door, looking up at the work-top, feeling my mother's presence coming near my body, standing, watching her body looking down on me, feeling myself unable to move from the ground where I am standing, looking down on my mother's foot standing on the kitchen door mat; watching my mother point her hand toward my body, pushing my body out her way.

Here I am standing inside the kitchen, taking my plate of food off the work-top.

Here I am sitting down at the dining-table, looking down at the plate of food before me, feeling hurt inside my body not wanting to eat the food, smelling the food making my insides go round.

Here I am hurting, listening to my mother banging the things around inside the kitchen, talking loud so everyone can hear what she is saying, talking about my father.

Here I am standing inside the dining-room, watching my mother pushing everything from out her way, walking over to the pram, grabbing Delroy's body out the pram, pushing against Ruel's chair, watching Ruel's body fall off his chair, watching my mother pull the door open, slam hard back on the television table, hearing her foot stamping into the hall way, watching Mavis running after her.

Here I am not wanting to eat, feeling my inside go round fast; feeling my body not want to be where I am; listening to Ruel and George talking to each other,

IAM®

talking about our mother, causing them to not know what to do with them self, not knowing how to behave in her presence.

Here I am. Do you want more food Ruel? I am speaking. Let me have some Ruel.

Here I am watching Ruel and George grabbing after my plate, wondering in my mind, thinking; wondering, thinking about the body that I am thinking about going away from my father's house, realizing I don't know anyone, I don't know anywhere that I can go.

IAM®

CHAPTER 26

Here I am thinking about myself, wondering about myself, wondering about my father, wondering about my mother, thinking about my father, thinking about the body that I am.

Here I am realizing that my father was once a baby like Delroy is a baby. Daddy was once a boy like Ruel and George are boys.

Here I am, knowing that my father is a man.

Here I am wondering in my mind, wanting to understand myself.

Here I am realizing that my mother was once a girl just like mine and Mavis's body are girls.

Here I am thinking about my mother, wanting to understand myself, wanting to know; who am I. Who am I?

Here I am inside the kitchen, standing on the chair over the sink, washing the plates, thinking in my mind.

Here I am washing the frying-pan, feeling the dining-room door open, feeling my inside go round, thinking my mother is coming, feeling my body unable to move, not wanting to look. I am speaking. You all right?

Here I am looking up on my father's face, wondering what my father mean, asking if I am alright; not knowing how to answer my father, watching his face smiling, making my body not know how to act, feeling my inside go round, feeling water come into my eyes, hurting inside my body is hurting and I don't know how to make it stop. I am speaking. What your mother done to you Hazel?

Here I am standing inside the kitchen, looking down at my father's feet, feeling my body inside moving around, wanting to answer my father, not knowing what to say, wanting to make my father understand that I don't know how to say that I do not feel good inside the house, feeling lone because mummy do not care about my body and always take her anger out on me when he questions mummy about me and mummy does not want to let daddy know that she did not want me and Ruel and George to come and live with her in his house.

Here I am unable to speak, wanting to speak, feeling my insides coming up, feeling the water coming into my eyes, wanting to speak, not knowing what to do with myself. I am speaking. Hazel; if your mother does anything to you, you tell me. You here what I say, tell me; you hear.

IAM®

Here I am listening to my father, realizing that I don't know how to make my father understand why my body is crying and hurting all the time. My father, do not realize that I know when he and mummy is talking about my body even when I am not in their presence. My father do not understand that my body feel whatever my mother is thinking about my body, but mummy does not know that I can feel that she does not like my body; making my body feel hurt, feel lone inside the house; that I know that mummy doesn't like my body.

Here I am knowing that my mother knows that she can do anything she want to my body and daddy does not realize that I cannot tell him when mummy beat my body because he does not understand that if I tell him when mummy beat my body and he ask her why; she beat my body again when he is not at home. My father do not understand that my mother can do whatever she want to do to my body and he cannot stop her because she waits until he is out of sight and he doesn't realize that he caused mummy's behaviour because he send for me and Ruel and George to come from Jamaica to live with him and mummy and mummy didn't want us to come. My father does not realize that when he and mummy have words with each other, mummy take her anger out on my body, because he leaves her in her angry state and go to bed, or go out to work.

Here I am washing the saucepan, thinking in my mind, wondering; how am I going to make daddy understand mummy's behaviour, knowing that he is the cause of her anger, knowing that mummy and her favourite child Mavis do not like my body, and he leaves me in the house with them.

Here I am thinking, wondering; how is my father going to change my mother's behaviour when he doesn't know that he is the cause of mummy's behaviour against the body that I am and daddy doesn't know who to believe; mummy or me. My father does not realize that the woman my mother and her favourite child Mavis act one way when he is home, but they act different when he is not at home.

Here I am thinking, wondering about my father, understanding in my mind, knowing that my father is not able to help my body because he doesn't understand his wife, the woman he said is my mother.

Here I am thinking; my father has forgotten that he came out of one woman's body, his mother.

Here I am understanding in my mind, wondering if my father could talk with his mother, knowing that Ruel and George does not know how to talk with the woman, our mother.

IAM®

Here I am, knowing that my brothers do not like the woman our mother and they do not want to be in her presence because she does not say any good words about them.

Here I am thinking; how is daddy going to understand my body if he doesn't realize that it is his behaviour cause mummy to act the way she does against me.

Here I am wringing the water from the dishcloth, wiping the draining-board dry, thinking about my mother, thinking about my sister Mavis.

Here I am wiping the sink clean, wiping the window-shelf, making everywhere look good, spending time inside the kitchen.

Here I am, understanding in my mind, understanding that everybody copy act each other. Mavis's body behave just like our mother and Delroy's body copy Ruel and George's behaviour and Ruel and George's body copy our father's behaviour.

Here I am realizing in my mind, understanding that my body does not behave like my mother or my father.

Here I am thinking about myself, wondering; who am I. Who am I?

Here I am sweeping the kitchen floor, thinking in my mind, thinking about the body that I am, feeling my inside keep going around, feeling lone, feeling scared for the body that I am.

Here I am walking into the dining-room, carrying the pile of plates, placing them down on the dining-table. I can see Ruel and George and daddy are looking at the television.

Here I am inside the kitchen, collecting the knives and forks and spoons, carrying them into the dining-room; standing on the chair by the cabinet, returning the knives and forks and spoon inside the drawer where they belong.

Here I am inside the kitchen, looking around the space, making sure the kitchen room is looking clean.

Here I am on my knee, kneeling on the floor by my father's chair.

Here I am looking into the palms of my hands, wondering about myself, remembering my dress, remembering the dress mummy was making for me to wear to school.

IAM®

Here I am thinking, wondering in my mind, feeling the water coming into my eyes, holding my head down, looking at the carpet, not wanting daddy to see my body crying, not knowing why I am crying.

Here I am, wanting to talk to someone, thinking about myself, feeling my mother's presence coming into the dining-room. I can see my mother's face looking as if she was crying. My mother's eyes look red like blood. I can feel my mother's presence looking down at my body, making my body want to run away from her body making my body hurt.

Here I am walking towards the hall way, wanting to leave my mother's presence, wanting to get away from my mother.

Here I am standing inside the girl's bed-room, looking around the room, looking at Mavis's body sleeping in her bed.

Here I am walking along the landing, carrying my night-dress, walking into the bath-room, feeling my body hurting, feeling the water coming into my eyes, hearing my mother and fathers voice shouting words at each other, talking about the body that I am.

Here I am inside the bath-room, standing on the side of the bath, pulling the light switch on, pushing the plug into the hole, turning on the hot water, feeling my body tired, hurting, wanting to sleep.

Here I am turning off the water, taking off my dress, looking down on my body.

Here I am inside the bath-room, standing naked, thinking in my mind, wondering; what have I done to make mummy angry with me?

Here I am standing inside the bath, rubbing the soap on my flannel, wiping my face, wiping my neck, wiping all over my body, feeling my body trembling listening to my mother's foot-step coming up the stairs, hearing the sounds of her body breathing, walking fast up the stairs, coming towards the bath-room where I am on my knees inside the water, feeling my inside go round, turning over, changing, thinking what to do with myself, feeling my mother's presence coming. I am speaking. Open the door. You open the door now.

Here I am feeling my body trembling, looking at my mother's face, looking at her eyes red with water, raising her voice talking to herself, just looking at my body; feeling my body shaking inside the bath. I am speaking. Who said you can have a bath? You get out the bath now before I drown you in the water. Get out. You think your father can stop me now. You and your father gang up on me. You think me hot the water for you?

I AM®

Here I am wringing the water out my flannel, wiping my body dry, feeling my mother's fingers pointing on my body, pushing my body, hitting my body, making my skin burn.

Here I am pulling my night-dress over my head, hearing my father's voice, calling my mother, hearing his foot-step walking quick, running up the stairs, watching my mother bank open the bath-room door, listening to her stamping her way along the landing, listening to her shouting at my father.

Here I am leaning into the bath, wiping the sides clean with the sponge, feeling my face burning, feeling my body hurting, listening to my father's foot-step coming towards the bath-room.

Here I am looking at my father's body standing at the bath-room door, just looking down at my body, looking at my father looking down on the body that I am. My father looks like he doesn't know what to say to my body, looking down at my father's foot, feeling my insides coming up, wondering about my mother; not knowing what my mother is going to do to my body when daddy is gone to work. I am speaking. Hazel; what your mother has against you?

Here I am hurting inside, looking up at my father's face, feeling my insides coming up, not wanting to talk to my father, knowing that it is my father that is the cause of my mother to behave like she is acting.

Here I am; not wanting to answer my father, knowing that I have not done any wrong to make my mummy keep hurting my body.

Here I am hurting inside, thinking about my mother, wondering; is mummy really my mother? I am speaking. Come; stop the crying and go to your bed. Your mother will not bother you now.

Here I am walking along the landing, thinking in my mind, feeling my body hurting, crying, wanting to get out of my father's house; not knowing what to do with myself.

Here I am lying inside my bed, crying, hurting inside, feeling tired, listening to my mother and father talking inside their room, feeling my body wanting sleep, feeling my body hurting, feeling my body wanting someone, feeling lone inside myself thinking in my mind.

IAM®

CHAPTER 27

Here I am feeling my eyes hurting, wanting to open my eyes, feeling my eyes unable to open, remembering my mother, feeling my inside go round, thinking in my mind, lying in my bed, looking at Mavis's body moving on her bed, watching Mavis's eyes shut, rolling sideways, pretending to be still sleeping, turning her body around to face the window.

Here I am, wanting to get up, feeling the morning light shining into the room, feeling warm on my bed.

Here I am making up my bed to look good, wondering in my mind, thinking about mummy, thinking about myself; hearing daddy's voice coming from his bed-room, feeling my body feeling good inside, knowing that daddy is home.

Here I am on my knee looking under Mavis's bed, smelling the air under her bed, smelling like Mavis has done a do-do again.

Here I am walking towards the bath-room; carrying Mavis's potty, smelling the do-do surrounding my body.

Here I am standing inside the bath-room, emptying the potty into the toilet, standing on the seat, pulling the chain down, wanting the smell to go away.

Here I am with the toilet-brush inside my hand, washing the potty inside, brushing the do-do marks away, thinking in my mind, wondering; why must I keep emptying Mavis's do-do? Mummy thinks that just because my body came before Mavis's body I must work for Mavis, even though Ruel and George's body came before mine.

Here I am wondering, thinking; why must I have to do everything, just because I am the eldest girl in this house? Why don't mummy and daddy tell Ruel and George to help with the house-work?

Here I am emptying the potty into the toilet, feeling hurt inside myself, hearing Mavis's foot-step running towards mummy's bed-room.

Here I am sitting down on the toilet, thinking in my mind; mummy doesn't realize that Mavis's body is bigger and taller than mine.

Here I am rubbing the soap over my flannel, wiping my face, hearing my brother's bed-room door opening, listening to someone coming towards the bath-room. I am speaking. You are up early Hazel. Is mummy up yet?

Here I am thinking; I don't know. She can stay in her room. I am speaking. You shouldn't let what she say upset you, you know Hazel; she don't know what she is talking about most of the time.

IAM®

Here I am watching Ruel's body standing over the toilet, listening to his body doing a wee-wee, listening to Ruel talking about our mother as if he understands how I am feeling.

Here I am thinking in my mind; if mummy was always going on at your body, keep following you around the house, then you would not be talking like that. You would be feeling the same as I am feeling, not knowing what to do with myself, not having anyone to talk with me, not having anyone to understand how I am feeling is making my body want to cry and I can't stop it from crying. You don't know how my body feels. Mummy keep beating my body, and keep talking about my body as if I haven't got any feelings, treating my body like it hasn't got any sense.

Here I am watching Ruel's body leaving the bath-room, thinking in my mind; Ruel behave just like Mavis, leaving his wee-wee inside the toilet, making the bath-room smell.

Here I am brushing my teeth, feeling the inside of my mouth burning, realizing that my mouth inside is cut.

Here I am washing my mouth, listening to Ruel and George playing inside their room.

Here I am standing on the toilet-seat, reaching into the hot water tank, taking my knickers off the hot water pipe, standing on the floor, pushing my feet into my knickers, feeling my inside go round, thinking about my mother.

Here I am inside my bed-room, returning the potty under Mavis's bed.

Here I am taking off my night-dress, folding it small, returning it under my pillow, putting on my house dress, thinking in my mind, looking on Mavis's bed, wondering; should I make up her bed.

Here I am fixing my dress on my body, listening to the sound like my mother's foot-step walking along the landing.

Her I am watching my mother's body coming into the bed-room, watching her standing at the door, looking down at my body, making my body not want to raise my head, not wanting to see her face, feeling my mother's presence making my inside go round, making my body hurt.

Here I am standing by my bed, watching Mavis's body walk towards the window, watching her hand, pulling the curtain open. I can feel the sunshine all over my body, making my body feel good.

IAM®

Here I am listening to my mother's body breathing, watching her hands brushing the sheets flat over Mavis's mattress. I am speaking. What are you looking at? Move out of my sight. I do not want you around where I am.

Here I am feeling my inside go round, running away from my mother's hand moving to hit my body.

Here I am on the landing, watching my father's body coming out of his room; seeing my father's face smiling coming towards the body I am making my body feel good, knowing that daddy is at home.

Here I am. Good morning daddy. I am speaking. Good morning daughter.

Here I am walking down the stairs, watching my father's body on his way to the bath-room, hearing my mother's body coming out the bed-room, following my body down the stairs.

Here I am standing inside the dining-room, thinking what to do, wondering what to do, watching my mother's body stamping her way across the dining-room, moving without any expression upon her face.

Here I am inside the kitchen, standing on the chair over the sink, holding the kettle under the cold water, watching my mother's body walking quick past the kitchen window, on her way down the garden.

Here I am lifting the kettle up, down on top of the stove, wondering what mummy is doing outside; thinking in my mind, remembering it is Sunday today.

Here I am standing on the kitchen doorstep, listening to the sounds the chickens are making, flapping their wings inside the chicken house.

Here I am taking the little saucepan out the kitchen cupboard, placing it down on the draining-board.

Here I am inside the dining-room, looking inside the fridge, getting the bottle of milk, carrying it into the kitchen, thinking if there is enough milk to make Delroy a drink, wondering if there's any milk at the front door.

Here I am inside the kitchen, placing the milk bottle down on the draining-board, hearing the sound of the chickens outside.

Here I am standing at the kitchen doorway, leaning forward, looking down the garden, watching my mother's body running after the chickens running, flying in the air; running towards the house; watching Cock stamping it two foot walking in the garden, walking with its head stretching up into the air, looking like it own the land.

IAM®

Here I am looking at the cock; watching the chicken's; thinking in my mind; wondering if mummy is going to kill a chicken today; seeing mummy's body pressed up against the chicken house, looking like she is cleaning the insides.

Here I am listening to my mother calling my name, wondering; what does she want me for?

Here I am walking along the garden, walking towards my mother, feeling the air surrounding my body, making my body tremble, walking towards my mother, watching her hands holding the stick inside the chicken house, scraping up the chicken do-do off the floor.

Here I am. Here I am mummy.

Here I am standing behind my mother's body, waiting for her to acknowledge one.

Here I am watching the chickens and the cock looking like they are having a good time, walking on the land, stamping all over the garden.

Here I am looking at the chicken eggs inside the bowl on the ground beneath the chicken-house. I am speaking. Where is the water me tell you to bring come?

Here I am walking, running towards the house, thinking; I didn't hear mummy ask for any water.

Here I am inside the kitchen, standing on the chair, watching the saucepan filling up with cold water, feeling the saucepan weighing down my hands, watching the water rising halfway up the sides.

Here I am standing on the kitchen ground, lifting the saucepan down off the draining-board, carrying it outside, carrying it along the garden, walking slow, feeling the water splashing over the sides onto my hands, splashing on my dress, making my body tremble, listening to my mother calling my name, telling me to hurry up and come with the water.

Here I am feeling my arms hurting, wondering if mummy thinks I can move faster than I am walking fast as I can. I am speaking. Give me the water.

Here I am watching my mother's body, listening to her talking to herself, watching her hands pouring the water into the bowl on the floor inside the chicken-house, watching her emptying the balance of water over the ground onto the garden dirt.

IAM®

Here I am walking towards the house with the saucepan, realizing Ruel and George's body standing at their bed-room window, looking down at the body that I am, looking up at the sky, feeling the air surrounding my being, smelling good to the body that I am, feeling the sun shining all over my body, making my body feel good inside.

Here I am walking towards the kitchen, hearing the sound of the kettle making the whistling noise.

Here I am inside the kitchen, returning the saucepan inside the cupboard, turning the fire down under the kettle.

Here I am taking the tea-pot out the cupboard, positioning it down on the stove, winding the tea-towel around my hand quick, standing on the chair, pouring the boiling water into the tea-pot, feeling the heat from the fire, making my body feel hot on my skin.

Here I am standing on the ground, lifting the tea-pot down off the stove, lifting it up onto the draining-board, lifting the chair over to the draining-board, standing on the chair, pouring the milk into the little saucepan, feeling my mother's presence coming towards the kitchen, watching her body standing by the stove, watching her body walking towards the kitchen door, carrying the coal bucket and shovel outside.

Here I am inside the dining-room, taking the sugar out the cabinet, walking into the kitchen, thinking in my mind, standing on the chair with the spoon in my hand, taking out one spoon full of sugar, mixing it into the milk-tea, making Delroy his morning drink.

Here I am placing the cover on top of the saucepan, pushing it over to the corner of the draining-board, thinking in my mind, carrying the packet of sugar into the dining-room, returning it inside the cabinet where it belong.

Here I am inside the dining-room, watching my mother's body coming into the room, carrying the bucket full with coal and fire wood, placing the bucket down on the fire surround.

Here I am standing on the chair, taking the cup and saucer out the cabinet, getting the sugar bowl and the tea-pot stand, placing them down on the dining-table.

Here I am spreading the tablecloth over a portion of the table, making the table ready for my mother and father to drink their morning cup of tea.

Here I am looking at my mother's body, watching her hand building the fire, listening to her body talking to herself.

IAM®

Here I am wondering in my mind, wondering what mummy is talking about, listening to her body; just talking to her self.

Here I am inside the kitchen, winding the tea-towel around my hand, lifting the tea-pot down off the draining-board, carrying it into the dining-room, placing it down on its stand on the table.

Here I am remembering the milk can.

Here I am looking inside the fridge, taking the can of milk of the shelf, hearing my mother's body breathing loud.

Here I am setting the table, listening to my mother, wondering about her body talking to herself. I am speaking. You; bring the coal-light and the box of matches come.

Here I am inside the kitchen, looking under the sink, looking for the box of coal-light.

Here I am inside the dining-room, standing at the side of my mother's body, holding the box of coal-light and the box of matches in my hands, watching my mother's hand putting the wood stick under the pieces of coal inside the fire hole. I am speaking. Give me the things.

Here I am holding the box of coal-light before my mother, feeling her hand grab the box from my hand, feeling, that my mother do not know how to speak to the body that I am.

Here I am inside the kitchen, getting Delroy's bottle down off the work-top, standing on the chair over the draining-board, pouring the milk-tea into the bottle, wiping the sides of the bottle dry, placing the bottle down by the saucepan.

Here I am standing inside the dining-room, feeling the heat from the fire smelling in the air, feeling warm on my skin.

Here I am watching my mother's hand holding the brush, sweeping the floor around the fire, making the fire surround look clean, making the dining-room feel good.

Here I am looking into the burning fire, wondering in my mind, wondering what to do. I am speaking. Do you want me to pour you a cup of tea mummy?

Here I am speaking to my mother; looking at my mother's body, knowing that she can hear my body is speaking to her, watching my mother, wondering in my mind, wondering; are you pretending not to hear me?

IAM®

Here I am. Mummy; shall I pour you out a cup of tea mummy? I am speaking. Leave the tea and don't bother me; you understand.

Here I am looking at my mother's body, listening to her words, watching her face looking into my eyes, wanting my mother to realize that I know she doesn't like the body I am.

Here I am looking at my mother, looking into my eyes, not knowing what to do with herself, not wanting to look at the body I am watching my mother turn her head, making my body feel hurt, knowing that my mother does not know how to behave in my presence.

Here I am walking into the hall way, thinking in my mind, wondering, thinking of my mother, wanting to understand why my mother does not want to be near the body that I am.

Here I am walking up the stairs, thinking in my mind thinking; mummy thinks she can carry on without having to speak to my body.

Here I am thinking; mummy has to talk to the body that I am because I am the only body in the house that is doing anything to help her to do her house work.

Here I am thinking; mummy is going to need my body to do something for her. Then she will have to call my name. She will have to speak to the body that I am.

Here I am standing outside my brother's bed-room, listening to Ruel talking to George, laughing with each other.

Here I am knocking on the door, thinking in my mind; mummy thinks that her body is the only body that is good.

Here I am thinking in my mind, knowing that mummy can say what she likes, but I know that she cannot do without the body that I am. I am speaking. Come in Hazel.

Here I am standing inside my brother's bed-room, looking at Ruel and George's body wearing their pyjamas, playing the snakes and ladder game on their bed; looking at Delroy sitting up in his cot, playing with a comic book, tearing it, smiling all over his face, watching my body watching him tear the book.

Here I am watching my brother's, smelling the air surrounding my body, smelling like the boys have wet the bed again.

IAM®

Here I am watching Delroy smiling at my body, reaching his hands out before my body lifting Delroy's body up out the cot, down onto the floor.

Here I am. Ruel, you or George better open the window and let out the smell before mummy come in here and smell it. I am speaking. What smell? I can't smell anything.

Here I am looking at Ruel, listening to him talking, realizing that he cannot smell the scent in the room because his body is part of it.

Here I am. Ruel; you can leave it then. I don't have to sleep in here.

Here I am walking along the passage, watching Delroy's body crawling up the step; watching Delroy's nappy hanging off his bottom.

Here I am following Delroy's body, watching his body turning around, facing my body, watching him sliding feet first down the stairs.

Here I am following Delroy, thinking in my mind, realizing Delroy is lazy because he can walk.

Here I am watching Delroy sliding down the stairs, thinking in my mind, understanding Delroy. Why should he walk when he have mummy believing that he cannot help him self.

Here I am, knowing that all my brothers and Mavis pretend that they cannot do anything because mummy thinks they cannot.

Here I am holding the dining-room door open, watching Delroy turn to face my body, watching his body moving down the step, sliding onto the dining-room floor.

Here I am lifting Delroy's body up into his pram, listening to Delroy making up noise, pretending to cry.

Here I am walking past my mother's body sitting on the chair by the fire looking into the flames.

Here I am inside the kitchen, standing on the chair by the draining-board, getting Delroy's bottle, tasting the milk, hearing Delroy making up noise, crying for his milk.

Here I am inside the dining-room, holding Delroy's bottle before him, watching Delroy's hand grab the bottle from my hand.

Here I am watching my mother's body sitting on the chair by the fire, watching her drinking the tea, remembering daddy is up stairs, wondering if daddy would like a cup of tea.

IAM®

Here I am standing by the dining-table, pouring the tea into the cup, thinking in my mind, thinking about my father.

Here I am putting the sugar into the cup. One two spoon full, pouring the milk into the cup, mixing the tea just the way daddy like the tea to look.

Here I am walking into the hall way, carrying the tea up stairs, thinking about my father.

Here I am standing outside my father's bed-room, knocking on the door, listening to my father talking to Mavis. I am speaking. Come Hazel.

Here I am standing inside the bed-room, looking at my father's face smiling at one, making my body feel good. I am speaking. I have made you a cup of tea daddy. I am speaking. Just what I want. Thank you daughter. You good.

Here I am looking at my father, feeling his presence making my body want to be with him.

Here I am watching Mavis's face looking at my body, making up her face at one.

Here I am watching Mavis holding out her tongue, looking at my body, realizing in my mind; thinking; Mavis thinks daddy's body belongs to her.

Here I am walking down the stairs, wondering in my mind, thinking about Mavis.

Here I am feeling good inside, thinking about my father, feeling like my father cares about my being.

IAM®

CHAPTER 28

Here I am walking into the dining-room, smelling the air around my body feeling warm on my face, tasting good.

Here I am wondering; where is mummy?

Here I am standing on the kitchen doorstep, leaning ahead, looking for my mother.

Here I am watching my mother running after the chicken, watching the chicken running towards the body that I am.

Here I am feeling my inside go round, thinking about the chicken, wanting to help the chicken.

Here I am watching my mother; wondering in my mind, thinking; the chicken knows what my mother is going to do; feeling my body feeling for the chicken, knowing that my mother is going to kill it.

Here I am watching the chicken running sideways away from my mother's hand making to grab it; hearing the noise the other chickens are making; realizing in my mind; thinking; the chicken body feels just the way I am feeling, feeling frightened, frightened for my life, frightened of my mother, watching my mother's body with the machete, making ready to kill the chicken.

Here I am feeling for the chicken; hearing its body screeching; wanting my body to help it.

Here I am hurting inside, feeling for the chicken body spirit soul calling out to the body that I am. I am speaking. Give me the dustbin pan cover before it gets away.

Here I am watching my mother's hand holding down the chicken body under the dustbin pan cover; watching the chicken head bulging red, watching its eyes rolling inside its head, hearing its body flapping under the bin cover my mother's body is pressing down hard on the chicken's neck.

Here I am watching my mother raise her hand holding the machete into the air, feeling my body not wanting to see what is going to happen, hearing the sound of the machete drop down on the chicken body; chopping into the chicken neck, feeling the water come into my eyes, hearing the machete chopping into the chicken body.

I AM®

Here I am looking at the chicken head, watching its eyes turning around under the skin, feeling my inside come into my mouth, realizing that my mother could kill me; just like she said.

Here I am watching my mother's hand holding the chicken body two foot together; watching the life spirit soul pouring out the chicken's neck. I am speaking. Go and full the saucepan with water and bring it come.

Here I am inside the kitchen, standing on the chair over the sink, watching the water rising in the pan, thinking in my mind, wondering about my mother's act, wondering if my mother has any feelings, thinking about the chicken body that is no life no more.

Here I am knowing that my mother believe that her body knows best; knowing that the chicken was a life, just like my mother is a life, just like the body I am.

Here I am wondering why my mother has to kill the chicken.

Here I am standing on the kitchen ground, lifting the saucepan of water down of the draining-board, carrying it outside to my mother.

Here I am standing outside, looking at the blood on the ground, watching my mother throwing the water onto the blood, watching the water mixing with the blood moving along the footpath, spreading over the ground, watching my mother sweeping up the blood, sweeping the blood into the drain.

Here I am watching my mother; wondering; where has the chicken life gone? I am speaking. Get me more water; quick.

Here I am inside the kitchen, standing on the chair by the sink, watching the water falling into the pan, thinking in my mind, wanting my mind to stop thinking, not wanting my body to think about my mother's act.

Here I am realizing in my mind, thinking; mummy is not the only one that kill; knowing that my mother think her act is good.

Here I am standing on the kitchen ground, lifting the saucepan down off the draining-board, carrying it to my mother, watching her body squatting down before the chicken body, pulling the feathers out the chicken body flesh; preparing the chicken body flesh for dinner because it is Sunday today; the Sabbath day. I am speaking. You can put the pan down now. You see what I have to be doing. You lot and your father only wants to see the food cook on the plate but it is me that have to keep doing the killing. Everything he leaves for me to do.

IAM®

Here I am watching my mother's hand, listening to her words, talking to her self, talking about my father.

Here I am watching my mother's hand pulling the feathers out the chicken body flesh, thinking in my mind, wondering about my mother.

Here I am listening to my mother talking about my father, talking out loud so I can hear, understanding her words, watching the feathers sticking on the blood all over my mother's hands and down her apron.

Here I am wondering; where did mummy and daddy get the chickens from. I am speaking. Go and bring me the big cooking knife and some newspaper.

Here I am inside the kitchen, getting the newspaper from under the sink, carrying it to my mother.

Here I am watching my mother lifting a handful of water out the saucepan; washing the machete blade, wiping away the blood stains, rubbing the kitchen knife along its blade, rubbing the knife sharp.

Here I am watching my mother push the knife down into the centre part of the chicken belly; cutting it open; watching her hand pull the chicken insides out onto the newspaper. I am speaking. Hold this carefully and carry it into the kitchen. No; go and bring the washing-up bowl come.

Here I am inside the kitchen, lifting the bowl out the sink, carrying it to my mother, watching her drop the chicken body with the insides into the bowl. I am speaking. Put it on the draining-board.

Here I am inside the kitchen; lifting the bowl up onto the draining-board, thinking in my mind, wondering; how many more chickens inside the chicken-house?

Here I am standing inside the kitchen, watching my mother coming into the kitchen, holding the machete and saucepan, watching her body looking tired on her face. My mother is standing over the sink, washing the blood off the machete, wiping it dry on the dishcloth, placing the machete down on the work-top.

Here I am watching my mother washing the body of the chicken under the cold water, picking the bits of feathers out the flesh, cutting the body into pieces, putting each piece into the meat bowl.

Here I am watching my mother's hand washing the dishcloth, washing the knife, wringing the water out the cloth, wiping the draining-board, wiping the sink, washing away the blood, washing away the feathers, making the sink look clean.

Here I am watching my mother sprinkling the salt over the chicken flesh, sprinkling black pepper over all the pieces, watching her hands rubbing the salt and pepper into the chicken flesh she is preparing to cook for Sunday dinner. Now my mother is taking the skin off the big cooking onion, slicing the onion rings onto the meat-bowl.

Here I am watching my mother peeling the skin off the bits of garlic, cutting the garlic into the meat-bowl, washing the little bunch of herb thyme under the cold water, breaking it over the chicken flesh, mixing everything together inside her hands, preparing the chicken flesh to cook for Sunday dinner. I am speaking. Good; go and tidy your brother.

Here I am walking into the dining-room, wondering if mummy is going to cook breakfast this morning. I am speaking. Hazel; bring me the bag of kidney bean and the coconut cream before you go.

Here I am inside the dining-room; looking inside the cabinet cupboard; getting the things my mother want, carrying them into the kitchen, placing them down on the work-top, watching my mother lighting the gas on the front part of the stove.

Here I am inside the dining-room, lifting Delroy up out of his pram, watching Delroy's body on his hand and knee, crawling up the step, crawling along the hall-way, on our way up the stairs, watching the wee-wee running down Delroy's legs, squeezing out the nappy hanging off his bottom.

Here I am inside the bath-room, looking down on Delroy's body sitting on the floor, smiling all over his face.

Here I am standing outside my brother's bed-room, knocking on the door, listening to Ruel and George laughing with each other. I am speaking. Come Hazel.

Here I am standing inside my brothers bed-room, looking at George's face smiling, looking at Ruel's body, watching them smiling at my body.

Here I am looking inside Delroy's drawer, getting clean clothes for Delroy's body, getting the powder and vaseline, feeling my brother's presence watching my body wanting to stay with Ruel and George, wanting to see what they are doing.

Here I am inside the bath-room, looking at Delroy's body standing up on his two foot, holding on the side of the bath, baby talking happy talk to him self.

I AM®

Here I am standing on the toilet seat, leaning into the tank, looking for a nappy to put on Delroy's bottom.

Here I am with the vest and rubber pants and a cotton play suit and a cardigan and the nappy and socks and Delroy's bath towel; making ready to change Delroy's clothes.

Here I am leaning into the bath, pushing the plug into the hole, turning the hot water tap on, watching the steam rising off the water, turning the cold water on, watching the water rising inside the bath, feeling the water mixing warm on my hands.

Here I am kneeling before Delroy's body lying on the floor, wanting Delroy to keep his body still, wanting to pull the pin out the nappy soaking wet with wee-wee, smelling rank.

Here I am dropping the nappy into the bucket under the sink, pushing it down under the water.

Here I am lifting Delroy's body into the bath, watching Delroy kicking his two foot inside the water, splashing the water up onto my face, wetting my dress.

Here I am rubbing soap onto the flannel, wiping Delroy's body, watching Delroy's face smiling, smacking the water, watching him having a good time.

Here I am lifting Delroy's body up out the bath, resting him down on the towel spread out on the floor.

Here I am wiping the water of his body, listening to Delroy baby talking to himself, holding his foot up to his face.

Here I am rubbing the olive oil over Delroy's body, turning his body over, oiling his back, oiling his bottom, feeling Delroy's body feeling soft, smelling clean.

Here I am folding the nappy, pushing it up under Delroy's bottom, wanting Delroy to lift his body, watching Delroy's face smiling feeling the powder falling onto his wee-wee.

Here I am putting on Delroy's clothes, smelling the food my mother is cooking.

Here I am rubbing the vaseline into Delroy's hair, brushing his hair, wanting Delroy's body to look good, just the way mummy make Delroy's body look and smell good.

IAM®

Here I am. Sit still Delroy. I am combing your hair. I am nearly finished now. You look good Delroy.

Here I am. Sit there Delroy. Do not move, understand.

Here I am leaning forward down into the bath, rubbing soap onto the sponge, wiping the bath insides clean, washing the dirt marks away, wanting the bath to look clean; hearing Delroy's body sounding good, baby talking to himself, making my insides feel good; listening to the footsteps sounding like daddy is coming, walking along the landing, coming to the bath-room.

Here I am pulling the plug out the bath, feeling my father's presence outside the bath-room.

Here I am. Move away from the door Delroy; daddy wants to come in.

Here I am inside my brother's bed-room, returning the powder and vaseline and the olive oil and the hair brush down on the drawer where they belong.

Here I am making Delroy's cot-bed look good, listening to my father's footstep walking down the stairs, listening to Mavis's footstep running along the landing, calling to daddy to wait for her. I am speaking. Daddy wait.

Here I am spreading the sheet over the cot mattress, listening to Ruel and George talking about them self going to the school building.

Here I am watching Delroy's body, thinking in my mind; thinking about the body that I am, remembering the dress mummy was making for my body to wear to school.

Here I am feeling the water coming into my eyes, feeling my body hurting inside, thinking about myself, not wanting Ruel or George to see my body crying.

Here I am standing at the door-way, watching Delroy's body crawling up the steps, thinking in my mind, walking down the stairs, standing on the stairs looking at Delroy's body sliding down, following my body walking down the steps, walking into the dining-room, smelling the food my mother is cooking, tasting the scent in the air.

Here I am looking at my father's body, feeling his presence, smiling at one.

Here I am looking at Mavis's body wearing her night-dress, watching her body standing at daddy's side, resting on daddy's leg, holding her finger inside her mouth, sucking it, making up her face looking at one.

IAM®

Here I am watching Mavis's body, watching her face change, just like mummy make up her face when she is angry.

Here I am thinking about my sister, wondering in my mind; why don't you like me Mavis? What have I done to hurt you? Why don't you like me?

Here I am standing at the kitchen doorway, looking at my mother, watching her rolling the flour dough inside the palms of her hands; shaping the piece of dough looking round, placing it into the frying-pan, frying the dumplings for our breakfast.

Here I am inside the kitchen, watching my mother cooking fried dumplings and bacon, and sausage and egg, and baked beans for Sunday breakfast.

Here I am. Do you want me to do anything for you mummy? I am speaking. Yes, you can get the tea-pot out and make the tea for your father and me. Breakfast is nearly ready.

Here I am lifting the chair over to the sink, standing on the chair, watching the water falling into the kettle, thinking in my mind, thinking about my mother, wanting my mother to care about the body I am her girl child.

Here I am lifting the kettle onto the stove, smelling the air tasting good. My mother body is looking hot with water on her face, standing over the stove; watching her hand with the fork, turning the dumplings over in the pan, watching her hand taking out the cooked dumplings, putting each one inside the big cooking tray inside the warm oven.

Here I am watching my mother's body, looking at her face half smiling to herself, watching the fork in her hand turning the sausages over in the pan.

Here I am. The dumplings look good mummy. I am speaking. Um; thank you. What are you after now?

Here I am looking at my mother's body, taking the cooked sausages out the frying-pan, putting them inside the plate under the grill. I am speaking. Go and get the bottle of corn cooking oil, bring it come.

Here I am inside the dining-room, looking at my father's body, watching his head looking down on the page inside the big Bible book resting inside his hands.

Here I am looking into the cabinet, getting the corn oil bottle, carrying it to my mother inside the kitchen.

IAM®

Here I am watching my mother placing the bacon slice into the frying-pan, listening to the bacon frying, smelling the bacon scent in the air, making my body feel hungry.

Here I am watching my mother, wondering in my mind, thinking about the name sausage, wondering; where do sausages come from?

Here I am. What is the sausage meat call mummy? I am speaking. This is pork sausages, like the bacon is pork we get from the pig. The other sausage I cooked last Sunday; the big fat ones; them is made from beef.

Here I am watching the fork in my mother's hand turning the dumplings around in the pan, watching my mother's body jump, stick her finger inside her mouth, sucking her finger, realizing the hot oil just burnt her fingers again. I am speaking. Go and bring me your father's plate and one for me and your sister. Bring a saucer for Delroy.

Here I am feeling good inside, knowing that my mother is not raising her voice at my body.

Here I am inside the dining-room, standing on the chair before the cabinet, getting the plates. One for daddy and one for mummy, one for Mavis and the little saucer plate for Delroy.

Here I am carrying the plates into the kitchen, lifting them up onto the work-top.

Here I am inside the kitchen, putting two tea-bags into the tea-pot on the draining-board.

Here I am standing by the stove, winding the dishcloth around my hand, lifting the kettle down off the stove, lifting it up onto the draining-board, lifting the chair over by the draining-board, standing on the chair, pouring the hot water into the tea-pot, watching the water changing into the colour brown tea.

Here I am standing on the chair by the sink; holding the kettle under the cold water tap, watching the water falling into the kettle.

Here I am standing on the ground, lifting the kettle up onto the stove, turning the fire down low to boil the water for mine and Ruel and George's breakfast.

Here I am inside the dining-room, pulling the dining-table sides up, opening the table complete, taking the table-cloth out the drawer, spreading it out over the table, making the table ready for mummy and daddy to have their breakfast.

I AM®

Here I am standing on the chair by the cabinet, taking the sugar bowl and tea-pot stand out the safe, resting them down on the table with the cups and saucer, and the knives and forks, and the tea-spoon, making the table ready for mummy and daddy to have their breakfast.

Here I am taking the milk can from the fridge, setting it down on the table, taking the bottle of milk out the fridge, carrying it into the kitchen, making ready to make Delroy's drink.

Here I am inside the kitchen, taking the little saucepan out the cupboard, resting it down on the draining-board.

Here I am standing on the chair by the draining-board, winding the dishcloth around my hand, pouring the tea out the pot into the saucepan, pouring the milk into the pan, mixing the milk-tea for Delroy to drink with his breakfast.

Here I am watching my mother sharing the food out on the plates, thinking in my mind.

Here I am standing on the floor, winding the tea-towel around my hand, lifting the tea-pot down off the draining-board, walking slow, carrying the tea-pot into the dining-room, resting it down on the table.

Here I am on my way into the kitchen, watching my mother coming into the dining-room, carrying a plate of food in each hand.

Here I am inside the kitchen, standing on the chair by the draining-board, putting one big spoon full of sugar into the saucepan, mixing it into the milk, pouring the milk into Delroy's bottle, shaking bottle letting the milk tea drop on the back of my hands; feeling the temperature; feeling just right for Delroy to drink.

Here I am wiping the tea stains off the bottle, taking the bottle into the dining-room, feeling my inside go round, feeling hunger, ready to eat my breakfast now. I am speaking. Where are you going? Come back here and feed your brother his breakfast.

Here I am standing before Delroy's body sitting inside his pram, looking at my hand holding his plate of food, listening to Delroy's body making to cry.

Here I am putting the spoon with beans into Delroy's mouth, watching the food inside his mouth moving from cheek to cheek, watching the food going down Delroy's throat, watching Delroy's hands reaching out to grab the plate.

IAM®

Here I am putting the piece of dumpling into Delroy's hand, knowing that he can feed himself, watching Delroy bite into the dumpling, moving his mouth around fast, swallowing the food, making to cry, wanting more.

Here I am feeding Delroy his food, listening to daddy speaking to mummy, talking about church. I am speaking. Mavis; do you want to come with me go to church? I am speaking. Now; today; yes mummy; now? I am speaking. Yes; I am going when we finish our breakfast we will go and get ready.

Here I am scraping the food off the plate, putting it into Delroy's mouth, listening to mummy talking to Mavis.

Here I am wondering in my mind, thinking, wondering if mummy is going to ask my body if I want to go to church with her and Mavis.

Here I am wondering in my mind, thinking, wondering if mummy is going to ask my body if I want to go to church with her and Mavis.

Here I am looking at mummy looking at Mavis, watching mummy smiling with Mavis.

Here I am handing Delroy his bottle, realizing that mummy is not going to ask my body to go to church with her and Mavis.

Here I am feeling hurt inside, wondering, why mummy don't take my body out with her? Thinking in my mind; I want to go out as well.

Here I am feeling my body hurting, thinking; all mummy want my body for is to work.

Here I am feeling hurt, thinking in my mind, thinking; mummy don't like my body, that's why she never take my body anywhere with her.

Here I am hurting inside, thinking; daddy doesn't realize that mummy doesn't take me anywhere, except for when she wants someone to pull the shopping trolley home.

Here I am hurting inside, thinking about myself, wondering when will I get to go out, knowing that my father never take my body anywhere with him, not even when he is going out to enjoy himself. My father, never ask to take my body out with him.

Here I am watching Delroy holding up his bottle, drinking down his milk.

Here I am thinking in my mind, understanding to myself; daddy doesn't realize that my body need to get out of the house, just like his body never want to stay inside the house all the time.

I AM®

Here I am thinking in my mind; what does mummy and daddy think I am?

Here I am walking past my mother's body, watching her licking her finger.

Here I am standing inside the kitchen, putting Delroy's plate into the washing-up bowl, thinking in my mind, wondering about my body, feeling hurt inside, wanting someone to want my body, feeling lone inside myself, thinking about my body inside my father's house, the building that I cannot go out from because I am my father's and mothers child.

Here I am standing before my father, watching his body sitting at the table drinking his tea, watching my mother putting the dirty plates together, carrying them into the kitchen.

Here I am feeling my body inside go round, not knowing why I am feeling the way I am feeling, watching my sister's eyes wide open, just looking at my body.

Here I am watching my sister holding out her tongue, making up her face at my body, making my body feel hurt.

Here I am. Daddy; have you finished with the pot of tea? I am speaking. Thank you.

Here I am walking into the kitchen, carrying the tea-pot, emptying the tea-bags into the dust-bin.

Here I am standing on the chair by the sink, watching the cold water falling into the pot, washing the tea-pot inside clean, placing it down on the draining-board.

Here I am putting the tea-bag into the pot, thinking in my mind, hearing the kettle making the whistling sound, boiling the water.

Here I am standing by the stove, winding the tea-towel around my hand, lifting the kettle down off the stove, lifting it up onto the draining-board.

Here I am standing on the chair pouring the hot water into the pot, making the tea for me and Ruel and George to have with our break-fast.

Here I am inside the dining-room, getting the sugar and milk, carrying them into the kitchen, resting them down on the draining-board.

Here I am standing on the chair pouring the milk into the tea-pot mixing it into the tea, watching the tea changing colour.

Here I am putting the sugar into the tea-pot. One, two, three big teaspoon full, mixing it into the tea.

IAM®

Here I am watching my mother with the big spoon in her hand, stirring the beans around inside the pan.

Here I am carrying the packet of sugar and the can of milk into the dining-room, returning them where they belong.

Here I am inside the kitchen, winding the dishcloth around my hand, lifting the tea-pot down off the draining-board, carrying it into the dining-room, placing it down on the stand, resting on the table.

Here I am standing on the chair by the cabinet, taking the plates out the cabinet, resting them down on the dining-table. One for Ruel, one for George and one for me.

Here I am thinking in my mind, thinking about my father calling my body daughter.

Here I am taking the cups out the safe, resting them down on the table, taking the knife and forks out the drawer, setting them out around the table, making the table ready to have our breakfast.

Here I am walking into the kitchen, carrying the plates, thinking in my mind, resting the plates down on the work-top.

Here I am inside the kitchen, thinking about the name daughter.

Here I am standing inside the dining-room, thinking in my mind, thinking about my father calling my body daughter; wondering what daughter mean.

Here I am realizing in my mind, understanding that the body I am is here because of one man and one woman's act; my body came into being.

Here I am realizing in my mind, understanding that my body is born because of my father and mother; him and her; one boy and one girl sex act; form of her flesh; born their baby boy or girl child in their own image

Here I am.

Here I am standing inside the dining-room, watching my father's head looking down on the Bible inside his two hands, watching his hand turn the page leaf over, listening to the sounds coming from his body, reading to himself.

Here I am inside the kitchen, watching my mother's body standing by the work-top, sharing the food for Ruel and George and my breakfast. I am speaking. Come; carry these in. This one is for Ruel and that one is for George.

Here I am. Thank you mummy.

IAM®

Here I am standing inside the dining-room, holding the plates of food in my hand, watching Ruel's body move quick to sit at the dining-table.

Here I am. Here is your breakfast George. I am speaking. Thanks Hazel.

Here I am standing inside the kitchen, watching my mother's body standing by the stove, watching her hand holding the spoon, stirring the beans cooking in the pot.

Here I am taking my plate of food down off the work-top, smelling the scent of the beans in the air, feeling my body feeling hungry, wanting to eat. I am speaking. Hazel; keep your eye on this for me and turn the fire off when the water is just covering the beans and wash up all your breakfast things when you lot done.

Here I am listening to my mother speaking; carrying my plate of food into the dining-room, sitting down at the dining-table, thinking in my mind, looking down on the food before me, thinking in my mind; mummy can cook the food and make it look good.

Here I am thinking in my mind, wanting to cook good like my mother's cooking looks good.

Here I am breaking my dumpling into half, taking the inside out, making a dumpling sandwich, watching my mother coming into the dining-room, walking past my body on her way up stairs.

Here I am. Pass me the tea please Ruel. Mummy dumplings taste good.

Here I am eating, watching Ruel pouring the tea into his cup, feeling my insides hurting.

Here I am watching Ruel's mouth moving quick, realizing that George is smiling at me, making my body feel good. I am speaking. Don't you want the inside of your dumpling them Hazel?

Here I am. I am eating Ruel.

Here I am eating, feeling Ruel's eyes watching my plate.

Here I am eating my breakfast, wondering in my mind; hearing the sound like Mavis's footsteps; watching Mavis's body coming into the dining-room; looking at Mavis's body looking good. Mavis is wearing her white socks with the different colour around the top, and her frilly silk ribbon lace dress, and her black shiny shoes. Mavis body looks good, holding her round shiny black bag down at her side.

IAM®

Here I am looking at Mavis's body, thinking in my mind, wondering why mummy never dresses up my body to look good like Mavis's body look good.

Here I am feeling my inside go round, thinking about myself, watching Mavis making up her face at my body, making my body hurt watching her body act.

Here I am eating my breakfast, thinking in my mind, wondering about myself, wanting my body to look good like Mavis's body look good.

Here I am feeling my inside go round, feeling the water coming into my eyes, knowing that I am helping my mother to do her work, and look after everyone, but mummy never dress my body to look good. Mummy never wants to take my body out with her.

Here I am hurting, watching Mavis's body making up her face so I can see her tongue hanging out her mouth, behaving like she does not like my body; like she is better than my body; just because mummy never dress my body to look good like Mavis body is always looking good, even when she is at home.

Here I am hurting, thinking in my mind, thinking about myself, wondering if I am going to look good to go to school.

Here I am walking into the kitchen, carrying the dirty plates, resting them down inside the washing-up bowl.

Here I am inside the dining-room, folding the tablecloth small, thinking in my mind, watching Mavis's body jumping up into the air, showing her body off, making my body hurt, hurting inside; watching her body act.

Here I am folding the dining-table down, watching the dining-room door opening, watching my mother's body entering the room, smelling the scent coming from her body, changing the air, making it smell nice. My mother is dressed up, wearing her sky-blue skirt suit, wearing her white hat on her head, and her white glove on one hand, wearing her white pointed high-heel shoes, carrying her white hand-bag on her arm; holding her white handkerchief with flower pictures. My mother is looking good, smelling with scent all around her body, making my body wonder; what is mummy wearing, making her body smell good? I am speaking. You remember what is on the fire. Come Mavis.

IAM®

CHAPTER 29

Here I am watching my mother's hand pointing at my body, watching her and Mavis's body walking into the hall way, on their way to the church building.

Here I am thinking in my mind, wondering about my mother, feeling lone inside; thinking about myself.

Here I am inside the kitchen, standing on the chair by the sink, watching the hot water falling into the bowl, thinking in my mind, feeling hurt inside, wanting someone.

Here I am wondering if my mother has finished sewing the dress she was making for my body to wear to school.

Here I am washing the plates, thinking in my mind, wondering why my mother does not want my body by her side.

Here I am washing the plates; thinking about my father; thinking about Mavis always sit on daddies lap whenever she wants and play games and talk with daddy and mummy inside their bed-room.

Here I am washing the plates, thinking in my mind, wondering why Ruel and George never ask my body to come and play with them.

Here I am standing on the chair by the work-top, holding the towel, wiping the plates dry, thinking in my mind; wondering; hearing the back gateway shaking; hearing the sound like someone is at the back gate; wanting to come onto my father's land. I am speaking. Any old iron? Any old iron?

Here I am wondering in my mind; listening to the sound of a man's voice.

Here I am putting the saucepans inside the kitchen cupboard where they belong, returning the cooking knife and fork inside the drawer.

Here I am lifting the pile of plates down off the work-top, carrying them into the dining-room, resting them down on the dining-table.

Here I am walking past Ruel and George's body sitting at the dining-table, talking to each other.

Here I am inside the kitchen collecting the knives and fork off the work-top, carrying them into the dining-room, standing on the chair, returning them where they belong inside the cabinet drawer.

Here I am walking into the kitchen, thinking in my mind, standing on the floor, looking around the space where I am, looking at the bits of food all over the kitchen floor.

IAM®

Here I am with the broom in my hand, sweeping the floor, sweeping the rubbish towards the kitchen door.

Here I am holding the dustpan and hand-brush, sweeping the dirt inside the pan, emptying the pan into the kitchen dustbin, returning the pan and brush under the kitchen corner shelf where they belong.

Here I am looking around the room, looking along the work-top, looking on the draining-board, looking on the stove, remembering the kidney beans cooking on the stove, smelling the scent in the air.

Here I am standing on the chair by the stove, winding the dishcloth around my hand, lifting the top off the saucepan; looking inside the pan; looking at the water inside the pan boiling up over the beans, cooking just right.

Here I am inside the dining-room, looking at Delroy's body lying down inside his pram.

Here I am watching Ruel and George's body playing the card game on the table, feeling my inside go round, feeling lone, not wanting to be where I am; knowing that nobody wants to speak to me.

Here I am walking into the hall way, walking along the passage, walking towards the back bed-room; thinking in my mind, wondering about myself, looking down at the basket full of clothes ready for ironing.

Here I am feeling my insides changing, moving round; making my body hurt, wondering in my mind thinking; why is my body hurting?

Here I am on my knees, kneeling before the basket of clothes, taking the clothes out the basket, picking out the pants and socks, putting them in order.

Here I am looking at the pile of mummy's knickers, and the pile of knickers belonging to Mavis.

Here I am thinking; how come mummy and Mavis's body have all these knickers, realizing that my body only have three knickers and I have to wash them each time I take them off. Here I am thinking in my mind; sorting the clothes; wondering in my mind thinking; where are daddy's underpants?

Here I am thinking in my mind, realizing that Mavis's body have more pairs of socks than Ruel and George and my body put together. Mavis's socks are all white with different colours around the top and some have frills on as well.

Here I am folding the big towel, realizing that my mother keep all the good white towels and all the light colour hand-towels for her and her favourite body to use.

IAM®

Here I am walking up the stairs, carrying the pile of towels and mummy's knickers in my hand, carrying them to her bed-room.

Here I am standing outside my mother's and father's bed-room, holding the clothes against the wall; knocking on the door, wanting to go inside. I am speaking. Come Hazel.

Here I am standing inside the bed-room, holding the pile of towels and my mother's knickers, watching my father looking at my body, watching his body holding the big Bible in his hands, watching his face smiling, watching my body walking across the room.

Here I am standing by the big trunk, placing the towels down on top, feeling my father's eyes watching my body, feeling his presence making my body not know what to do with myself, not knowing what to say to my father, watching my father watching my body walking smiling on my way out the room.

Here I am walking along the landing, thinking in my mind, realizing that my father do not know what to say to my body, realizing in my mind, knowing that I know nothing about my father.

Here I am inside the pantry-room, lifting the ironing-table out into the hall-way.

Here I am walking along the hall-way, lifting the ironing-table weighing heavy in my hands, lifting it along the hall-way, carrying it into the back bed-room, opening it out, raising it up to the height I am, making it ready to do the ironing.

Here I am walking along the hall-way into the pantry-room, lifting the iron down off the shelf, carrying it to the back bed-room, thinking in my mind, wondering about my father, thinking about my father, wondering about his being.

Here I am inside the back bed-room, pushing the iron plug into the plug socket on the bed-room wall, wanting the iron to get hot to press the clothes.

Here I am standing over the ironing-board, thinking about my father, realizing that daddy never just talk to me the way he talks and play games with Mavis.

Here I am thinking about my father, wondering in my mind, thinking; who is my father?

Here I am wrapping the socks and pants inside the towel, carrying them up the stairs, thinking in my mind, walking into the girl's bed-room, opening out the towel on my bed, putting Mavis's socks and pants inside her dressing-table drawer.

IAM®

Here I am looking at the many different colour socks and knickers that Mavis has.

Her I am wrapping up Ruel and George's socks and pants inside the towel, carrying them to my brother's bed-room, putting them away inside the boy's dressing-table drawer where they belong.

Here I am walking, running down the stairs, running into the back bed-room, standing, looking down on the pile of clothes to be ironed.

Here I am inside the back bed-room, kneeling before the basket of clothes on the floor, folding Delroy's nappies, thinking in my mind, thinking; I am my mother's helper.

Here I am looking at the pile of clothes, wondering what to iron first.

Here I am pressing Delroy's vest, remembering the beans cooking on the fire.

Here I am pulling the iron plug out the wall socket, running along the hall-way, running into the dining-room; smelling the beans scent in the air.

Here I am standing on the chair by the stove, winding the towel around my hand, lifting the lid off the saucepan, wanting the beans to be right.

Here I am looking inside the saucepan, pulling the pan off the fire, feeling the hot steam rising out the pan, smelling the beans smell like it is burnt, looking like the beans stuck to the pan bottom. There is no water in the pan, just beans.

Here I am looking inside the saucepan, wondering what to do, thinking; mummy is coming home now.

Here I am looking inside the drawer, getting the big cooking spoon.

Here I am standing on the chair by the stove, scraping the beans off the bottom of the pan, realizing, I was just in time to stop the beans from burning.

Here I am pouring the water from the kettle into the pan, stirring the beans around in the water, returning the pan onto the fire, turning the flames up high, wanting the water to boil quick before mummy comes home.

Here I am wondering in my mind, thinking; what mummy would do to me if the beans got burnt.

Here I am inside the kitchen, feeling my insides going round, wanting the water to boil before my mummy come home.

IAM®

Here I am thinking in my mind, wondering; didn't Ruel or George smell the beans cooking.

Here I am wondering; don't Ruel or George care about anything that is going on in the house.

Here I am hurting, knowing that Ruel and George is just playing games, realizing that if the beans got burnt; only I would be beaten.

Here I am hurting inside, feeling my insides coming up, hurting, standing inside the dining-room, standing in the presence of Ruel and George's body, watching them pretending not to know that I am in there presence.

Here I am. Did any one of you know the saucepan with the beans was on the fire?

Here I am talking to Ruel and George, wondering if Ruel or George is going to answer my body; thinking in my mind, realizing that Ruel and George don't care, watching the way they are pretending not to hear what I am saying.

Here I am feeling hurt inside, realizing that because Ruel and George are the image like my father, the boys do not have to do anything to help themselves or anyone, and there is nothing that I can do because my body is a girl.

Here I am feeling hurt, wishing that my body was not born the image like my mother.

Here I am feeling hurt, thinking in my mind, wondering; what if my body was born the image like daddy and Mavis was born the only image like mummy. What would mummy do then?

Here I am thinking about my being inside the body that I cannot get out from.

Here I am thinking about myself, smelling the beans cooking, scenting the air.

Here I am inside the kitchen, standing on the chair by the stove, winding the dishcloth around my hand, lifting the cover off the saucepan, feeling the steam rising out of the pan, feeling hot on my face, making my body jump.

Here I am looking into the pan, looking at the water inside the pan bubbling up over the beans, feeling my inside change, feeling pleased with myself, knowing that the beans look just right now.

Here I am turning the fire off from under the saucepan, thinking in my mind; thank you God.

Here I am thinking about myself, thinking, wondering about my mother, wondering if mummy is coming home now.

IAM®

Here I am standing inside the dining-room, looking at Ruel's body not wanting to look at my body; not wanting my body to blame him for not watching out for the beans cooking on the fire; knowing the beans nearly burnt.

Here I am looking at Ruel, thinking in my mind, thinking; you are going to want my body to care about you and George one day.

Here I am walking along the hall-way, walking into the back bed-room, thinking about my brothers, realizing in my mind, understanding that Ruel and George care just for them-self.

Here I am inside the back bed-room, pushing the iron plug into the plug hole inside the wall, wanting the iron to get hot now.

Here I am standing by the bed-room window, thinking in my mind, looking over the ground, looking at the garden, feeling my body hurting inside, feeling lone inside myself, wondering in my mind, thinking about everybody outside my father's house, wondering what the people are doing, thinking, wondering about myself inside the body that I am.

Here I am thinking in my mind, wondering; will any body want to know the body that I am? Thinking; does anybody know that I am here inside this house?

Here I am hurting inside, feeling the water coming into my eyes, feeling my inside changing, moving round, hurting, feeling the water falling down my face, wanting my body to stop crying.

Here I am standing by the ironing-board, holding up Delroy's vest, spreading it out on the board, pushing the iron over it, wanting it to iron.

Here I am pressing the clothes, thinking in my mind, thinking; why must I do for any body that do not care about them-self or care for me.

Here I am pressing the clothes, thinking; I am not Ruel or George or Mavis or Delroy's mother.

Here I am pressing the clothes, thinking about my father, realizing that daddy only do what he wants to do, just like Ruel and George and Mavis and Delroy do just what they want to do to please them-self.

Here I am realizing that the woman my mother treat my body as if my body is not one of her children.

Here I am, knowing that my mother behave like my body is not a child as Ruel and George and Mavis and Delroy's body is a child.

IAM®

Here I am, knowing that my father does not realize that Ruel and George and Delroy's body is the image of him self and they behave just like he does because he doesn't do anything in the house to help himself.

Here I am pressing the clothes, wondering in my mind, thinking; who does my father think I am?

Here I am wondering; why did daddy send for me?

Here I am realizing that my father has forgotten that our mother is another mans daughter and she only care about herself just like he only care about himself just like Ruel and George and Mavis only care about them-self.

Here I am pressing the clothes, feeling my inside jump, hearing the front door bang shut; realizing mummy and Mavis come home.

Here I am listening to my mother's and Mavis's footstep walking along the hall-way, coming towards the room where I am standing, feeling my body shaking, not knowing why my body is shaking, feeling my mother's presence coming near.

Here I am looking at my mother's face looking down at my body, watching my mother's face looking at my body, watching her face looking without expression, just looking at one.

Here I am looking at my mother, wanting to understand why my mother is just standing there looking at my body, not saying anything, just looking; making my insides go round; wondering in my mind; listening.

Here I am pressing the clothes; listening to my mother and Mavis walking up the stairs; hearing their footsteps going to mummy and daddy's bed-room; thinking in my mind, thinking about the body that I am; wondering if any body know that my body is here in this house.

Here I am pressing the clothes, realizing in my mind, understanding that my body is live, knowing that I am doing for everyone inside my father's house, knowing that my father and mother do not understand that I am live and they are making my body hurt.

Here I am hurting, listening to my father and mother shouting words at each other, hearing my father and mother shouting bad words at each other, making my body hurt.

Here I am hurting, listening to my father and mother shouting the bastard word at each other.

IAM®

Here I am hurting, wondering; why don't mummy and daddy just talk to each other.

Here I am, knowing that my father do not understand that it is him that is causing mummy to shout at him because he is shouting at her.

Here I am hurting, not knowing what to do with myself, feeling my body shaking, listening to my mother telling my father that he is a bastard.

Here I am the child, understanding that my father and mother do not know how to speak to each other.

Here I am the child, realizing that my mother and father is the cause why Ruel and George and Mavis do not know how to speak to each other.

Here I am feeling my body shaking, listening to my mother's footstep coming fast down the stairs.

Here I am feeling my inside go round, thinking; mummy is coming for me, feeling my body unable to move; listening to her footsteps going to the dining-room.

Here I am ironing the clothes, hearing the words my mother is shouting at Ruel and George, telling them to go and do something.

Here I am listening to Ruel and George talking in the hall-way, talking about her our mother.

Here I am pressing the clothes, listening to Ruel and George talking about our mother, realizing that Ruel and George do not like her, because she is always shouting at them.

Here I am pressing the clothes, listening to Ruel and George talking about our mother, knowing that mummy do not realize that if she show Ruel and George how to wash their clothes, and how to sweep and polish the floor, and how to keep their bed-room clean, and how to prepare the food the way she is always ordering my body to do; then Ruel and George will know what they can do inside the house to help her.

Here I am pressing the clothes, knowing that my father and mother believe that my father and Ruel and George, the boy children and their father are not born to look after them-self as I can.

Here I am knowing that each body being must know how to keep their bodies looking good, and not expect any other body to be always doing for them that do not want to help itself, just like my father think it is my mother's duty to

NEW BOOK PRESS RELEASE

IAM® By Lady Christ. New book product best seller launch, online video press review, synopsis, child prophet philosopher "here to show man what man should be", black Jamaican woman writer author, mother creator, female sole artist performer, Prophet **IAM®**. **Available at www.lipfeed.com/iam.**

IAM® By Lady Christ : ISBN-13: 978-1-873478-50-9: First Edition Hardback Book Royal©, Bespoke Print to Order, 31 Chapters, 338pp, (233mm x 156mm x 18mm), 844gms, Release Date: August 2011, Publisher/Distributor: IAM®, U.K. List Price: £150.00. **Free Delivery World Wide** when you **Order direct** from the publisher online at www.lipfeed.com/iam at world trade price £99.99. **Order by phone**: +44(0)1261 851 814 **Order by post**: Please make payment of £99.99 in GBPS made payable to **IAM**. Post to: IAM - PO BOX -11332 - Banff - AB45 9AA - Scotland - U.K. **IAM® Publisher Terms.** All item(s) are bought as described bespoke print to order firm order purchase(s) & are pre-paid pro-forma in advance no return(s) excepting damaged item(s). Please allow 7 to 30 days on receipt of your full payment, for the printing and delivery of your item(s) to one address world wide.

IAM® By Lady Christ. Prophet IAM® passage out of Jamaica unto the land of England, circa 1960. Here to show man what man should be. Through the eyes of the child philosopher. * The autobiography of the living Christ. The pain, suffering, rejection and victimisation of the crucified black girl child, born the daughter of God, resurrected and imbued with the Holy Spirit Revelation. * An evocative narrative of (child feelings), to the core of the conscience. * A bitter sweat heart breaking situation of individual oppression and triumph. * From the very first page, the reader is captivated and miraculously transported through the entire epic, epoch, apodictic journey of enchanting poetic prose, following the life of a child in torment. * An emotion tugging, tear jerking, sad, sad recount, in the world of rejection, discrimination, jealousy, loneliness, abuse, trauma, pain, victimisation, abandonment and grief within the family. * Liken to watching a real live family drama, stage set in action in the mind, with so much indisputable meaning. * Never take a child for granted ever again. * A new genre of artistic excellence is born. * A philosophical masterpiece of great wonder. * A pre-eminent work of literary genius. * An innovative monograph of brilliant illumination. * The novas genus teachings of child & family psychology. * The prophetical inspired philosophical writings on Conscience Science©, the instinctive awareness feelings of the senses. * The Book IAM® certainly shows what man is and clearly what man can and should be. * An entertaining perfect must for everyone to read. * The, I am, I can, I will, mantra for positive living. * Truly is this the messiah? *"Here I am. In the beginning…"* Read Book Extract Chapter One at www.lipfeed.com/iamchapterone

Available at www.lipfeed.com/iam and all good bookshops and booksellers including Gardners, Amazon, Bertrams, Waterstones etc, (price may vary) and via Nielsen BookData online ordering system or through your local library.
©IAM®2011

Prophet IAM®: The Reverend Lady Iam Hazel Virginia Whitehouse Grant-Christ: Mother Divine de Solehealism: Author Creator. IAM® By Lady Christ at www.lipfeed.com/iam. Biography Hagiographique: Prophet IAM Lady Christ. The Prophetically inspired philosophical writer of Conscience Science©, the instinctive awareness feelings of the senses. Spiritually enlightened at birth, born the daughter of God seraph messenger Prophet IAM®, here to show man what man should be righteously leading the principles truth and integrity, advocating life. Founder and Mother Divine de Solehealism IAMEREIAM®. Divinely gifted, talented hand-craft artist, creating luxurious knitwear designs, beholding glorious manifestations of the unique extremely distinct inspirational conceptions of original miraculous magnificent ethereal creations of incredible sublime personification of aesthetic divine art, establishing the handmade haute couture LOOPIERE®. Prophet IAM® Lady Christ, an inspirational, formidable, approachable, charming, charismatic mother being, of great marvellous talent, skill, merit, generosity, peace, love, kindness and grace, with the mantra, I am, I can, I will, attributing all praise and thanks to the Creator IAM®. *Discipulus Laudatio.*

Invitation to visit the IAM® gallery. A celebration of talents.
Private Exhibition Viewing by Appointment Only.
IAM® gallery, 15, Fernie Brae, Gardenstown, Aberdeenshire, AB45 3YL, Scotland. U.K.
Tel/Fax 44 (0) 1261 851 814. Email: iam@iamereiam.com www.lipfeed.com/iamgallery
Participating in the (North East Open Studios. Opening doors to creativity) Featuring:

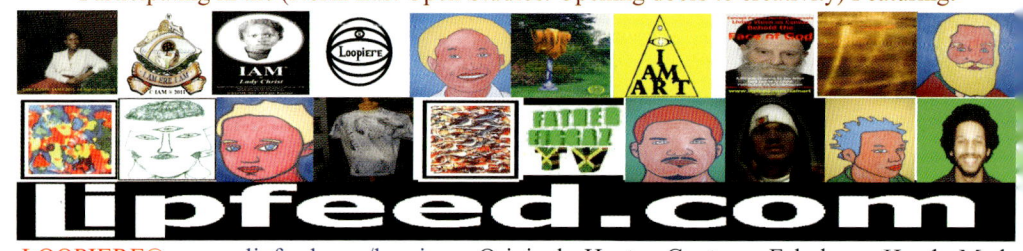

LOOPIERE® www.lipfeed.com/loopiere Original Haute Couture Fabulous Hand Made Knitwear, Ethereal creations of incredible sublime personification of aesthetic divine art by Lady Iam Christ. IAM ART© www.lipfeed.com/iamart Miracle Visions on Canvas, featuring the Title "Behold the Face of God", aka "The Messiah Epiphany Revelation" by Father Iam Art de Solehealism. Holsturr© www.youtube.com/holsturr Father Figgaz TV Entertainment Music: Rap, Grime, Dancehall, Funky House, Hiphop, Freestyle. Artists Black Million Hype, Holsturr & Goldamite. Hypnos www.lipfeed.com/hypnos Healing for all pain, phobias, addictions and diseases of the mind, body and spirit. Appointments with Rev T. Powers at your home or at the IAM® gallery. Lipfeed.com www.lipfeed.com the new universal creative workshop for free personal and commercial face pages to "Famouzise yourself on lipfeed.com" created by Iam Ere. The First Church Iam© www.lipfeed.com/thefirstchurchiam IAM ERE IAM® The First Church Iam. The School of Life. Ministry of Solehealism; ISBN-13: 978-1-873478-00-4; read The Peace Act© The first step to enlightenment. IAM® gallery ©IAM® 2011.

IAM®

wash and cook and clean for his body; all because his mother and father did not show him how to look after himself.

Here I am pressing the clothes, thinking in my mind, understanding that mummy believe that my father and brothers do not have to do anything of the self to help themselves.

Here I am; understanding the body that I am; thinking in my mind, wondering, thinking in my mind, wondering about the body that I am, lone by myself.

IAM®

CHAPTER 30

In November 1965; my brothers Ruel, George and I started at Bearwood Road Junior and Infant School, Sandwell County Council Education Authority. School was sanctuary; but come home time, I fretted about having to go home. My mother was always waiting for me. She blamed me for the things that were not going right for her and my father and accused me of telling the family affairs to outsiders. I looked forward to going to school even though the other children would not let me play games with them. The children; the majority white; would talk about me and made horrible faces at me and I did not know what to do to make them like me. I used to stand by myself and watched them play. Then one day whilst the children were out in the play ground; a white boy in the same class as me; ran up to me. He grabbed hold of my hands and started pulling at me. He wanted me to play games with him. He said his name is Russell. Russell told the other children that I am his friend. The other children were not interested in being my friend; but Russell told them that Hazel is his friend and she is going to join them in their games. Russell was a kind to me. Russell even asked me if I wanted to go and play at his house after school. I wanted to; but knew that was out of the question because I had to reach home seconds after school was finished; otherwise I would get a beating. Russell introduced me to his mother and asked her if I could come to their house for tea. Russell's mother smiled and said I could but I would have to ask my mother. I remember her face staring down at me as if I was some alien being. I never did go to Russell's house but I felt really good that Russell wanted to be my friend. At the time; I was very lonely. My brothers Ruel and George and my sister Mavis did not care about me. At home they did not talk with me or played any games with me. I was alone. My mother made Mavis believe that she was better than I am. My sister Mavis treated me as if I was dirty and she behaved just like our mother did; pushing and punching my body whenever she passed me inside the house and made up tales to make our mother beat me. My mother would always be waiting for me to return from school. I did not like when I had to go home from school. My mother blamed me for everything that went wrong in her life inside and outside the home; and locked me inside the pantry and my brothers and sister watching our mother beat my body with daddy's belt for the wrongs they knew that they had done. I did not know any one outside the family. We had no Aunts or Uncles to turn to and my mother made no friends. We the children were just locked up inside the house. My parents did not see their children as individuals with a mind of our own. We were not allowed to exercise any thoughts of our own. We just had to obey our parents; even though their wishes caused us anxiety and conflict with school life. We were never allowed to socialise with anyone.

At school the teachers often saw the scars on my body when I was getting changed for physical education. When I was questioned; I made up stories about the scars and wounds on my body which I tried very hard to hide. I did not want the teachers to continue to challenge my parents as this always resulted in one receiving more beatings from my mother. I think the teachers were very concerned about how I got the scars and all the wounds on my body because Social Workers kept calling at our house to question my parents and then my father started to beat my body for the tales my mother and Mavis made up against my body. The Social Services interest in the family was un-welcomed by my parents and I wanted the Social Services to stop questioning my parents because my parents always beat me up after they had gone. My parents wanted me to give answer for the Social Workers visit to the house. My mother would not allow the family to mix with other families and we the children were all discouraged from forming friendships with the children at school because we knew we would not be able to take part in anything that they did outside of school. There were no birthday celebrations and no contact whatsoever with relations in Jamaica or England. My life consisted of going to school, shopping on Fridays and Saturdays and occasionally I was allowed to go to the church building on Sundays.

At the age of six; my daily house duties included washing Ruel, George, mine and baby Delroy's clothes, sweeping the whole house, helping to prepare and cook breakfast, lunch and dinner; ironing all the family clothes and things, keeping the bed-rooms, bath-room, dining-room and kitchen clean. In between doing the housework; I had to make sure my little brother Delroy and baby brother Clifford's nappies were changed; empty all the chamber pots and the buckets of vomit from my mother's bedroom. My two elder brothers Ruel and George were not expected to do any housework. They stayed in their bedroom and played games and only came down stairs to watch the television or at meal times. My younger sister Mavis would not come near me. Mavis followed our mother wherever she went in the house. I began my house duties at six o'clock when everyone was still asleep in the mornings and never finished until late in the evenings between nine and ten o'clock. When I woke in the mornings; I sometimes thought I was blind; then realised that my eyes were so swollen they had stuck together. I had to bathe my eyes in cold water to reduce the swelling and remove the sticky substance before I could open my eyes to see. My body would not stop hurting. My insides would hurt from being lonely and my outside would hurt from the physical pain of carrying out my daily house work and the constant beatings I received from my mother. I often fell asleep whilst working. The only way I could keep my body from sleeping was when I did not put any food into my body. I had to stop myself from eating in order to carry out all the housework that my mother expected one to complete for the day. I tried to do everything the way my mother did things, but the more I tried the less I was able to please her. I could not stop my body from crying. Sometimes I found myself crying even though I was not beaten. My body was afraid just at the presence of my mother. My body trembled whenever I was in the same room as my mother.

At the age of seven; I taught myself to do the art of hand-knitting and crocheting at school and together with what I learnt from watching my mother's hand-sewing and making clothes; I created many hand-knitted cardigans; hand-sew my own dresses and crochet poncho and shawls for my sister Mavis and my mother's new babies. My mother soon took it for granted that I should just crochet and hand-knit cardigans for my brother's and sister's; but she never asked where I got the wool and the different yarns I used to hand-knit and crochet the clothes I made to help my parents.

Every day I would work quickly to do my house work; to give me time to do my hand-knitting. The act of hand-knitting consumed one. Hand-knitting expelled ones feelings of emptiness, pain and loneliness. I felt at peace with myself when I was creating something out of my hand-knitting talent gift of God. Out of every act of hand-knitting; I always created items of clothes that the woman at the church said "beautiful and divine"; but they would not believe that I was telling the truth when I said that I made the clothes myself and my mother never gave me the credit for what I had done or stood up for me or praised me for helping her to clothes her family.

My mother was a member of the Baptist church, Regent Street, Smethwick and she disciplined her children in accordance with her understanding of the words written in the Bible book. One act in particular which my mother kept up was not to spare the rod and spoil the child. My mother believed the Bible was God. My mother also believed that man was superior to woman and that a woman's duty was to comply with the man's wishes. She further accepted that housework was not a man's or her son's duty. My mother also believed that animal flesh meat was the source of good health and in accordance with her belief she reared her own chickens which she killed and prepared to cook each Sunday morning before grooming herself and her favourite child Mavis to go to the Baptist Church. I was the only one made to watch and help my mother when she killed the chickens. There were always pools of blood all over the grounds of my father's house and all over my mother's hand and body; and I thought; you can wash the blood off the ground and off your hands and body but you cannot wash away the act of killing; now that it is done.

My father suffered with pains in his back and had to stay off work. At that time; my father did shift work at the glass manufacturers called Chance Brother's Limited, Spon Lane, Smethwick. Both my father and mother were discontented and unhappy with each other and argued every day about the cost of living, mortgage payments, cost of clothes, hired purchase on my father's new car, insurance, gas and electric bills, coal, food and meat. My father was very hurt when he had to sell his new car, the only thing he considered was his and my mother was angry with my father because his pride would not allow her to go out to work to help meet their debts and the worry of it all just set her back into depression. Throughout my mother's ill-health; my parents argued and argued about my mother's accusation that my father had committed adultery and my mother believed that the neighbours and everyone was against her. My mother wanted to get away from the neighbourhood and she harassed my father to sell the family house. Many times my mother locked one in the cupboard under the stairs; but released one before my father returned home from work. Sometimes she would tie my hands and feet together and leave one on the floor in the cupboard, without food. When I was locked up inside the cupboard; I had to listen to my mother cursing my father for having affairs with the white woman at his work place and complaining about not having any time for her-self. My mother's accusations about my father made my body inside hurt; not wanting to believe that my father was not a good man. I wondered if my mother realized that I understood every word that she said about my father. I wondered whether she realized that every time she spoke bad words about my father that it caused my insides to hurt. My mother wanted one to agree with what she was saying about my father; but I could not. When my mother realized that I was not going to take her side; she was vex with anger and beat one for not agreeing with her. Then my mother and Mavis invented stories about me to turn my father against me. My mother said that I was the devil and she would use my father's leather belt or a broom stick to beat one; wanting one to admit to her accusation. I tried to perceive what the devil was but I could not. When my mother could not get one to agree with her; her temper became violent and her eyes red with anger she would dig her finger nails into my face; making my skin bleed. Upon my father's return from the factory; my mother would challenge my father about his adultery. My father would deny my mother's accusations and we the children often watched my father and mother fighting; watching my father holding my mother down on the floor and hearing the wailing cries my mother made. I felt sorry for my mother. I thought that my father should have controlled himself. He knows that he is stronger than she is. My mother always came off worst. Her face and eyes swelled up and she cried in sorrow for weeks. I wondered whether my father was doing something wrong to cause my mother to react against him and vent her anger against him upon me. When my mother was in her range she would grab one around my neck and lift my body off the ground; shaking one; saying; "I am going to kill you." Then I would run away. I remember walking the streets and knocking on the front door of houses, wanting someone to take me in. Every time the people would call the police. When the Police woman questioned one; I wanted to tell them how my mother was ill-treating me but I was too scarred to tell the truth; I was scared that my mother would kill me; the way I watched her kill the chickens. I just told them that my mother would not stop beating me and that my mother did not want me. I told the Police woman that my mother often locked me out of my father's house and told me not to come back or she will kill me. The Police woman always took me back to my parent's house. My parents told them that I was a bad girl and had to be punished. When the Police Officers left my mother battered my body for getting the Police involved in the family business. I could not straighten my body for days. I realized that there was nowhere to protect myself from my mother's violent behaviour against one inside the house. I was alone. I wondered whether I would survive and I thought that no one would know whether I was alive or dead. When my mother locked me out of the house; I walked the streets frightened and hurting; wondering why my father and mother could not control themselves. I didn't know where to go. When I returned to my father's house, I stood outside the front door and eventually I was allowed back in. I began to think that my father is not my real father and I feared him. My mother constantly told my brothers and sisters that their sister is the devil and that they must not help one otherwise they would end up like one. My brothers and sisters must have believed what my mother said; because they never tried to help one in any way; and stood by and watched my mother beating my body for the wrongs they knew that they had done. With my father believing the stories my mother made up against me; I could not defend myself and it became a way of life to expect to be beaten everyday. Whenever I look to my father for help he always said; "Don't you know I have to please your mother." I was trapped and very lonely; always crying and hurting knowing that I could not get away from my born existence. I wished for another mother and father or just someone to take me in. I was prepared to do anything for anyone who would give me a home and save me from my mother.

In the summer of 1969; my father told us that we have to move house. He said the Solicitor man had tricked him and our house was sold. My father was shaken up with the news that his house was sold from under him and was unprepared for the move. He had to find somewhere quick for us to live. It was an emergency; we had to get out of the house now because the buyer of his house wanted to move in. Sandwell County Council Housing Department offered my father a three bedroom maisonette on the second floor of a three-storey block of slum flats. The maisonette number 15 Beachway, Smethwick, Warley was too small to accommodate the family which by then had grown to eight children. My father had no choice but to accept the accommodation otherwise we would have been put out on the streets. The accommodation was overcrowded; jam packed with furniture, no heating, moulding wall paper coverings and condensation. There was great turmoil, fear and distrust amongst the family. My mother's depressive ill-health grew severe and she was eventually admitted to the psychiatric ward of All Saints Hospital, Windson Green, Birmingham. The burden and expectation of caring for my brothers and sisters fell upon me being the eldest girl with full responsibility of making sure that my brothers and sisters were clean, dressed and fed; ready to go to school; carry out the weekly shopping, cooking, ironing and cleaning the house as well as doing my school home work. On my mothers return home from the hospital; she was confined to her bed-room. On the occasions that my mother's health improved; she went to the Baptist church and begged my father to accompany her. This he did on occasions but gave up because he said church could not help him solve his problems. When my mother's health was better she sang church songs. She believed herself liken to God and made me bow down before her and kiss her hands and feet. When she could not get my father to do what she wanted him to do; the fighting would happen. Every time my parents fought; my mother would blame me for the problems in her family. My mother's ill-health always accompanied her wanting another baby. My father could not cope with her changing moods and depressive state. He said he did not want and could not afford to have any more children. I was left with sole care for my brothers Ruel, George, Delroy and Clifford and sisters Mavis, Beverly and Elaine. My mother wanted another baby so much that she would develop all the signs of having a baby. Her tummy swelled up and my mother looked like a pregnant woman. She would prepare for her baby by eating raw liver flesh meat everyday. She made baby clothes and bought baby equipment and things like a baby's cot and sterilizing unit. My mother eventually become pregnant and gave birth to her ninth child a girl whom my mother name Lisa. Following the birth of Lisa; my father repeatedly cursed my mother; calling her father a bugger. My father had had enough. He said that my mother is a bastard for tricking him into marrying her. He said my mother did not tell him that her father was having sex with her. My father's comments awakened my previous thoughts that my mother's father, Grandfather Gale, or one of mommy's man friends could be my father. That would explain my father Hensley's indifferent behaviour towards one. My father said we must ask our mother; who our father is; only she knows the answer to that question he said. My parents were at this time behaving like they were possessed. Neither of them would stop cursing each other. My father kept calling my body a bitch and told Ruel and George that their mother is a bastard and they are her bastard sons. George could not and would not accept that he was a bastard. There was no way that George was going to believe that he is a bastard and challenged my father to explain himself. George was so angry at the sound of my father calling him a bastard; George's head seemed to turn full circle, rejecting the very idea that he could be exactly what my father said he is a bastard; knowing the fact that my mother and father were married in England in nineteen sixty-two when Ruel, George and I were back home in Jamaica with relatives. George kept affirming to himself; "I am not a bastard; I am not a bastard; you and mommy are married; I am not a bastard" he said. I think George did not understand exactly what my father was saying. I understood my father to be saying that he had no way of knowing whether Ruel, George and I were fathered by him because our mother was going out with other men and living with her father back home in Jamaica. George kept affirming to himself that he is not a bastard and challenged my father to take back the words; but my father kept saying that Ruel, George and I are bastards. My father said; "Your mother never told me the truth." My father said; "Your mother tricked me." My father said; "Your grandfather Gayle is a bugger." My father was telling us that he did not know whether Ruel, George and I were his or our mother's father,

IAM®

Grandfather Gayle or some other man's children. At that I knew that my father had disowned us and he blamed us for his downfall.

IAM®

CHAPTER 31

One afternoon during the school summer holidays of 1971; my mother came down from her bed-room to the sitting room and whispered to me; "Your father wants you." At the time; I thought it strange for my father to want me; but. I went directly upstairs. As I walked towards my parent's bed-room; I felt my body tremble not knowing what my father could want me for. A feeling like something bad was about to happen. My mother followed close behind one as if making sure that I went to my father. When I got to my parents bed-room; I saw my father sitting on his side of the bed. My mother told Mavis to go down stairs and she closed the door with me inside the room. My mother turned the radio music up and ordered me to get on the bed. I did not understand; "get on the bed." I thought; "What for." My mother repeated her order that I should get on the bed. I did not know how to get on my parents bed. I sat on the edge of the bed. My father put his hand on my dress and started to move my dress upwards and I froze. I was shaking inside, shocked at what my father was doing; pulling at my pants and pushing my legs to part. I cried out; "Daddy don't; don't daddy;" not knowing what he was going to do. I saw my father's hands shaking; taking out his penis and I cried out; "Daddy don't." My body was shaking inside. I could not move with the weight of his body pressing me down and with my mother holding her hands over my mouth and across my body; shouting at me to shut up; pressing my body down on the bed; helping my father to get his penis into my vagina body. I kept crying out from the pressure of my mother's body holding me down on the bed and the pressure of my father's body on top of me; suffocating me; forcing his penis against my vagina. My father was feeling for my vagina; pushing his fingers into my vagina; holding his penis on my vagina; pushing his penis against my vagina; forcing his penis into my vagina; but it wouldn't go in; then I heard him say; "I can't get it in; the hole is too small." My mother left the room and returned with the jar of Vaseline. I felt her hand wiping the Vaseline on my vagina and around my bottom. I wanted to get up; but I could not move. My mother's hands were over my mouth and body; whilst my father bored his penis into my vagina. My body felt as if I was axed in two as my father's penis entered my vagina and slipped out. I heard my mother said; "Turn her over; push it up her backside." My father said; "Pearl; the hole is too small." I felt my father's realization and horror at what he was doing; hearing my mother's voice saying; "She is the devil's child; she must be turned out to pasture. Every man is going to sex her. You better have her first." I was paralyzed in shock and pain. I could not believe what my mother was saying; feeling her hands wiping more Vaseline around my bottom and feeling my father's hands holding down my bottom at the edge of the bed and forced himself inside my bottom he entered and ripped my back in numb pain; crucifying my being with a feeling like my soul had exited my body; hearing a bone like crack inside my head. I must have passed out. I could not feel my body. I was alive outside of my body; looking down at myself in a heap on the bed-room floor. I was trying to work out where I was; wondering whether I was alive or dead; I could hear my mother's voice shouting at me. When I came to; my body was burning screaming hot pain all over; looking at my mother leaning over my body shaking my body; shouting at me; "Get up; get up before I kill you". My mind wanted to obey but I could not get my body to respond to my mother and father pushing and shaking my body to move. I had lost control of my body. The scent of my father's semen chocking inside my head; the pain and the shame made me want to die. My father's odour was so strong it consumed one. It filled up my insides. I wanted to hold my breath but I could not prevent the smell of my father's semen from going down into my body. I could taste the smell of his odour inside my mouth; in the air; all around me and made my body vomit up my insides; feeling the throbbing, burning hot pain of my body; hearing my heart beat echoing inside my body. I could not help myself. My mind wanted my body to run, escape; but my body would not move. My body was a heap of flesh; throbbing, burning hot with pain. My mother's voice made me wish more for my body to move; but my body would not move. I couldn't even speak. I opened my mouth but the words would not come out. I could not move and my mother dragged my body along the floor to the bath-room. My mother left my wrecked body on the floor inside the bath-room; crouched up; rocking with the pain; wanting the pain to go. After a time; I managed to pull myself up against the side of the bath and felt hot liquid like jelly fall out my body; burning into my bottom and vagina skin. When I saw the blood mixed with thick jellied slime like liquid on the floor; I thought my inside's was coming out. I wanted to feel myself to know where the blood was coming from; but when I touched my body; the pain in my body just magnified. I fell into the bath and after some time turned the water tap on. My body just kept rocking itself crouched on my hands and knees; crying; wanting the pain to go; feeling the water cooling down my body pain; watching the water red with blood and lumps of white jelly floating in the water; smelling the scent of my father in the air. The smell of my father consumed my body and I wanted to wash him off of me; but I couldn't get the smell to leave my presence. I felt the heat from my body turn the cold water warm on my skin. I do not know how long I was

IAM®

inside the bath of water as I was woken by the sound of my mother's voice calling my name. I could feel her angry presence coming towards the bathroom. My body trembled as she stood at the bathroom doorway. She shouted at me asking me what I am doing in the bath with my clothes on. I did not realize I was still wearing my clothes. Every time I moved from the crouched up position; the pain made me cry out more. My mother shouted at me to get out of the bath and get my body down stairs. I eventually washed my body and took off my dress inside the bath. I could not straighten my body and fell out of the bath. I could not stand up. I crawled on my hands and knees to the girl's bed-room and eventually managed to put on a clean dress and pants. I could not straighten up my body. My back and head was bent facing the floor. I crawled back to the bath-room and squeezed my dress and pants out of the blood water and put them into the wash basket and waited for the water to empty out of the bath as I heard my body making the groaning crying noise and I wondered why Ruel or George or any of my brothers and sisters did not come and find out what was going on; what all the noise was about.

I crawled along the landing to the top of the stairs; and rested my body; throbbing, burning up with the pain; hearing the sounds of my brothers and sisters and the television; frightened scared; wondering where my father and mother is as I dragged my body slowly down onto each step; thinking about all the steps I have to get my body down to the bottom of the stairs; feeling the pain get stronger every time I moved my body; thinking about getting to the sitting-room; feeling the presence of my father and mother; feeling the presence of my brothers Ruel, George, Delroy and Clifford; feeling the presence of my sisters Mavis, Beverly and Elaine looking at my body. I could not straighten my body from the crouched up position on the floor. No one came to help me. Everyone just hushed as I entered the room. I felt disgraced; shamed. I could not believe that my brothers and sisters did not realize that something was wrong; seeing my body all crouched up; crawling, dragging my body into the sitting room; watching their sister on her hands and knees; crawling into the room. My mother pointed and ordered one to go into the corner of the sitting-room where I crawled to the floor by the right side of the sitting-room window and with my body crouched, rocking my body and my tears burning my eyes; I praying to God; "God; God; please help me; help me please God; God help me" knowing that it was my mother that caused my father to desecrate my body. I could not believe that my father and mother could do such an act. I searched my mind; trying to find the words to describe my father's sex act upon one and I thought; "I am going tell what you two have done; I am."

I felt my brothers and sisters looking at one; wanting explanation; not knowing what had happened; but I could not raise my head to meet their eyes. I could not forgive any of them for not coming to my aid. I thought; they must have heard my crying out; they must have heard the noise going on in mummy and daddies bed-room; but no one came to see what was happening and no one came to help me. I could not help myself; I just prayed in my mind I prayed; "God help me please." My body was in so much pain; I thought I was going to die. My eyes closed and my body just rocked it-self as I prayed and prayed for God to come and take me away. I was ready to die; I wanted to die. I felt my father's presence leave the room and I heard my mother tell Ruel and George; "Do not talk to her; and don't give her anything unless I say so; or you will end up like her." My mother confined one to a corner of the room. At night she would tie my legs and hands together and leave me on the cold marble floor. The corner of the sitting-room became my space. I was only allowed to move to go to the toilet. Some days after; when I went to the toilet; I just sat and waited for the wee-we to come out. When the wee-we came out; it was mixed with blood and it burned into the skin inside and around my vagina and bottom. I could not force myself to go to the toilet as the pain was too much to bear. All the time; I could feel my father's shame. He would avoid my body and stayed inside his bed-room all the time. When my mother went out she tied my hands to the coat hook inside the cupboard. When she returned; sometimes from church; she untied my feet and hands and sent my body back to the corner of the sitting-room. By this time; I did not feel hunger. I only sipped a little water to take away the empty dry hollow feeling inside my mouth and body. About a week after my father's sex act upon one; I began to feel a different pressure pain pressing down inside my back; moving down into my bottom. I kept going to the toilet but nothing would come out. The pain came about the same time the next evening. I kept going to the toilet but nothing came out. The pressure continued for the next two to three evenings. On the next evening; whilst seated on the toilet; a little do-do fell out of my bottom. I looked into the toilet bowl and saw a little do-do the size and look of a small black marble. The day after the pain began to leave my body. Sometime in the evening; I felt something like a bubble burst inside my belly with a feeling like water. I went to the toilet but nothing came out. I felt worried; not knowing what was happening to my body. I returned to the corner of the sitting-room. I was in the crouched up position and the feeling of bubbles bursting kept

IAM®

happening inside my body. Each time the feeling of a bubble burst, I felt a flow like water energy flow filling up my insides and made my body feel like it was getting better. I noticed my hands had changed. My hands no longer looked old and wrinkled. My hands looked smooth like a babies. The same evening I saw the ends of my fingers shimmering with light like the colour of candle flames. I then realized that all the pain had gone from my body. I could not feel my body. I could only sense my being. I felt my face smile at what was happening to my body. A feeling of being whole uplifted one and I looked to see if any one could see what was happening to my body. I wanted to tell what was happening; but clenched my fist instead. I did not know what made my body feel good; and I wondered why I was no longer hurt and angry. I no longer hated my mother or my father for his sex act upon one and I wondered why. I felt my face smile at my brothers and sisters. I felt good inside myself. I thought; I must be saved. My body was healed and my mind could only think kind thoughts. I began to see visions inside my head. I kept shaking my head; amazed at what I was seeing. I wanted to tell every one. I wondered if they could see what I could see a picture of a banner newspaper headline and the words that came into my mind read "The Buggers Act."; but I did not understand. I could not feel my body; I could only sense my being. Then an almighty presence of scented flowers came upon me and the colour purple came to my eyes and a presence entered my being and filled up my insides and my body just straightened it self. The almighty presence imbued, rested in my belly at the centre part of my navel and I heard a voice say "Iam" and I saw the picture of a clear brilliant blue sky moving on the air on an island of sands and tropical plants and I heard the voice say the word "Iam" and the word "Law" and I wondered at the voice Iam, Iam. Iam, Iam. I felt a great comfort joy feeling of peaceful belonging. The ends of my fingers shimmering like candle light and the voice kept speaking "Iam, Iam. Iam Iam"; confirming the Holy imbued presence within my body; making me understand the presence inside my body speaking to me is "Iam" and the voice "Iam" said; "Thou shalt not kill or eat the flesh of any living creature" and instantly I knew "Iam"; that "Iam" has taken over my body and made my body as "Iam" Holy. My hands radiated like the sun rays and when I moved to stand up; my body just raised off the floor; standing upright in the air. When I looked down; I could see the light radiating around my toes. My thoughts made my body arise to the standing position. My feet were off the floor. I was standing in the air. I was so consumed by ones body transformation that I did not realize that my mother and brothers and sisters were all standing back; with their mouths wide open and staring at

IAM®

one. I could only smile. My mother's face was speechless; her eyes wide open as if in shock. She looked as if frozen to the spot; trembling in her voice as she shouted for my father, "Ge; Granti; come here; quick Granti, quick." My father appeared and the look of astonishment fixed upon his face. I watched members of my family looking in fright; their mouths and eyes wide open; staring at my body transfiguration. I watched as my mother realized herself and her astonishment changed into fear and ran from the room. She returned with a bowl of bread and a mug with milk and pushed them on the floor beneath me. Her voice shook as she kept saying, "Eat, eat." I did as my mother ordered and bowed and took the mug and sipped the milk. The instant the milk fell into my body; I felt the cold marbled floor under my feet and I felt the presence rushed from my body. I watched as the light diminished from my fingers and for a while the great sent of purple flowers circled about my being. The pain did not return. I was filled with the almighty presence imprinted upon my soul. Tears of joy flooded my eyes; knowing who I am and that I belong inside the body that I am. That I must tell someone about what has happened; the truth of my resurrection in the knowledge that it is the killing and eating of the flesh of living creatures have caused my mother and father and everyone to do bad acts and go against "Iam".

Here I am contemplating how to tell my family about Iam and what Iam wants my body to do; knowing that they believe that their life depends on how much meat they could eat every day. The thought then came that I should go to the church buildings. Then the feeling that I would have to go to the people and proclaim the truth overwhelmed me and I cried. The thought of what might happen if I ate anything made my body tremble and the voice Iam spoke to me; "Eat fruits". Then the realization of what might happen if I ate anything but fruit came over me; and I thought; I do not want to die again. The realization came over me that I was once like my family; living a dead existence. The knowledge that all creatures are members of the one spirit Iam and to slaughter, to kill, to take away the life, or to eat the flesh or consume any part of any creature; one is guilty of committing the gravest crime against Iam. The realization that if one commit the act of slaughter, to kill, to take away a life, or to eat the flesh or consume any part of any creature; causes the body to self inflict destruction and condemn the self to a life of hell. I thought and thought about Iam and wondered how I would keep in the way of Iam and eat only the fruits derived from natural plant life; whilst living in the same house as my parents. I thought; how was I to tell my experience of Iam. The smell of my father's sex act remained with one and made one very self-conscious about the body that I am and heightened my sense of smell. I bathed my body twice a day, even when the water was cold. I wanted to wash the smell of my father away. From then on my father and mother spent all their time inside their bed-room. My brothers and sisters continued to please themselves whilst I continued to take charge of the management of the house duties. In accordance with my father and mother's wants; I continued to cook the different kinds of animal flesh meat and was troubled with the unknown consequence of the act which was out of my control. I was soon to realize that when I ate animal flesh meat and anything that contained animal derived products; my mind automatically went into turmoil and my body reacted as if it were taken over by an unknown force that made one frightened, on guard, in danger. My immediate danger appeared in the form of my mother. Any time I ate anything that came from animals; my mother would; for no apparent reason; come down from her bed-room and attack one. It was then I knew that in order to protect myself from my own self destruction and from dangerous forces outside of myself; I had no choice but to renounce the act of killing and eating the flesh and drinking the blood of animal creatures. I realized that I had to stop and abstain completely from the act of putting into my mouth; anything produced by or derived from the death of any animal creature I knew that my life had changed forever; that I had to practice being good for the living God Iam, inside and outside the body Iam.

IAM®

IAM®

IAM®

IAM®